ALSO BY ROBERT BUDERI

Engines of Tomorrow: How the World's Best Companies Are Using Their Research Labs to Win the Future

The Invention That Changed the World: How a Small Group of Radar Pioneers Won the Second World War and Launched a Technological Revolution

GUANXI

*Microsoft, China, and Bill Gates's
Plan to Win the Road Ahead*

Simon & Schuster Paperbacks

(The Art of Relationships)

Robert Buderi and
Gregory T. Huang

NEW YORK   LONDON   TORONTO   SYDNEY

SIMON & SCHUSTER PAPERBACKS
Rockefeller Center
1230 Avenue of the Americas
New York, NY 10020

First Simon & Schuster trade paperback edition May 2007

SIMON & SCHUSTER PAPERBACKS and colophon are registered trademarks of Simon & Schuster, Inc.

For information about special discounts for bulk purchases, please contact Simon & Schuster Special Sales at 1-800-456-6798 or business@simonandschuster.com.

DESIGNED BY PAUL DIPPOLITO

Manufactured in the United States of America

10   9   8   7   6   5   4   3   2   1

Photographs in the picture section have been provided as follows:
1, 4, 5, 6, 7, 8, 10, 11, 12, 13, 14, 15, 16, 19, 20, 21, courtesy Microsoft Corporation. 2, Conor Myhrvold. 3, 9, Xinhua News Agency. 17, Gregory T. Huang. 18, People's Publishing House.

Library of Congress Cataloging-in-Publication Data
Buderi, Robert.
  Guanxi (The art of relationships) / Robert Buderi and Gregory T. Huang.
     p.   cm.
  Includes bibliographical references and index.
  Contents: Beast from the East (November 8–11, 2004)—The Bell Labs of China (Fall 1997–November 1998)—From Beijing to Bill G. (November 1998–October 1999)—Microsoft's Chinese heart (November 1999–August 2000)—Ya-Qin Dynasty (August 2000–July 2001)—The Great Wall and other Microsoft creations (October 2001–January 2004)—Microsoft made in China (November 2002–November 2004)—The curious inventions of Jian Wang (September 1999–June 2005)—Search war (March 2003–March 2005)—The further adventures of one-handed Jordan and Mr. Magneto (March–May 2005)—Battle over Kai-Fu Lee (August 2000–September 2005)—How to make it in China (Summer and fall 2005).
  1. Microsoft Corporation—Management. 2. Computer software industry—United States—Management—Case studies. 3.United States—Commerce—China. China—Commerce—United States. I. Huang, Gregory T. II. Title

HD9696.63.A4-U(U.S.).x2+
338.8'8710040951—dc22   2006042253

ISBN-13: 978-0-7432-7322-0
ISBN-10:   0-7432-7322-2
ISBN-13: 978-0-7432-7323-7 (pbk)
ISBN-10:   0-7432-7323-0 (pbk)

*To Thomas and Margaret Huang,
parents who opened doors to a strange new
land, with love*

*To Aida, Andrew, and Adam Chan Buderi,
the best niece and nephews an uncle could wish
for, with pride*

*To the people of China and the United States
of America, with hope*

Contents

*Prologue: The Mysterious Journey to China of
the World's Richest Man, and Other Stories*   *1*

1 Beast from the East
(November 8–11, 2004)   *13*

2 The Bell Labs of China
(Fall 1997–November 1998)   *32*

3 From Beijing to Bill G.
(November 1998–October 1999)   *60*

4 Microsoft's Chinese Heart
(November 1999–August 2000)   *85*

5 Ya-Qin Dynasty
(August 2000–July 2001)   *111*

6 The Great Wall and Other Microsoft
Creations (October 2001–January 2004)   *130*

7 Microsoft Made in China
(November 2002–November 2004)   *147*

8 The Curious Inventions of Jian Wang
(September 1999–June 2005)   *168*

9 Search War
(March 2003–March 2005)   *187*

10 The Further Adventures of One-Handed
Jordan and Mr. Magneto (March–May 2005)   *209*

Contents

11 Battle Over Kai-Fu Lee
(August 2000–September 2005)   *233*

12 How to Make It in China
(Summer and Fall 2005)   *259*

Epilogue: "Congratulations, We Survived!"   *275*

A Note on Sources   *287*

Acknowledgments   *291*

Index   *295*

GUANXI

(The Art of Relationships)

Prologue

The Mysterious Journey to China of the World's Richest Man,* and Other Stories

Bill Gates's first visit to China, as described in Science Daily, *then the leading Chinese-language science and technology newspaper:*

". . . His first visit to China was very short. March 21, 1994, was his first visit to China, when he was 39, to sell Windows. He met [President] Jiang Zemin,† and the meeting was short. Jiang talked with Gates about Chinese civilization. Jiang said Gates should try to understand Chinese language and culture in order to be able to collaborate more."

Bill Gates's first visit to China, as described today by members of his company's Beijing research lab, Microsoft Research Asia:

The head of the Microsoft China business office, Jia-Bin Duh, went to the airport to pick up Gates. He was expecting a man in a suit, but Bill arrived in jeans and tennis shoes. He expected Bill to stay a week, but Bill only had a backpack: no luggage. He had a computer in the pack, and he looked just like a student, a computer-science student. When asked if that was all he had, Bill said, "Yeah, let's go."

---

* Our Prologue's title is taken from a Chinese newspaper article about Gates's second trip to China.

† Throughout this book, we use Western naming conventions—given name followed by family name—except for Chinese individuals, such as Jiang Zemin, who are already well-known in the U.S. by the Chinese convention of putting the family name first.

The next day, Bill went to meet the president, Jiang Zemin. He wore jeans again. It was a short visit. Jiang's spokesperson later told the press the Chinese leader had mentioned that Bill should learn more about Chinese culture. That was a polite way of saying the president was insulted.

The story that Gates had worn jeans to meet Jiang proved apocryphal, but since all the eyewitnesses were no longer with the company, it had spread as folklore. In fact, says Duh, the Microsoft founder wore a suit. Nor had Jiang been insulted. Still, his words were a pointed message that Microsoft had much to learn about the give and take of doing business in China, where both sides must benefit from the relationship. Says Duh, "After the first meeting Bill Gates [had] with President Jiang, we very clearly understood that the Chinese government wanted Microsoft to participate more in China and also learn how to better help the Chinese software industry."

Bill Gates's second trip to China, from Science Daily:

"For this trip, Bill Gates chose to go to China and didn't tell any media. Ten people accompanied him, including his wife, his father, and Warren Buffett. The reason he made this trip is because his first visit to China was very short. On the most recent trip, when Gates was forty, he arrived in Beijing on Monday, September 18, 1995 . . . On September 20 at 9 A.M., Jiang Zemin invited Gates to a resort. Jiang asked Gates where he would visit this time. Gates said the western part of China, including Xi'an, the Terra Cotta warriors and horses, the Three Gorges, and the Yangtze River. He also said he wanted to try all different kinds of transportation: Chinese airlines, trains, boat, bicycle, and camel!

"Jiang said, 'Three Gorges is a good idea.' He then recited several famous traditional poems about the gorges. Jiang talked with Gates as if he was Gates's father, giving him fatherly advice. Jiang said, 'You're doing well. If you keep working hard, you'll succeed even more.'"

Prologue

*Bill Gates's return to China in February 2003, as described by Kai-
Fu Lee, founding director of Microsoft Research Asia:*

"I went with him on the entire trip. I went with Bill to visit Jiang
Zemin. Jiang's first question was, Microsoft Research is a huge success;
Bell Labs used to be a huge success; what makes you different? Bill
answered that Bell Labs had great researchers, but our researchers
really care about customers, technology, and products. So we have
the same freedom but a higher, self-imposed desire for relevance.

"They talked for forty-five minutes longer than time permitted.
They had a great chat about children and so forth, truly like friends.
Bill did his duty to report the progress we've made in software, local
partnerships, research. But that was ten minutes. Then they got into
this great conversation. There were two translators; the person who
speaks must bring his own translator. This way, no misinterpreta-
tions can be blamed on the other party. Also, Jiang loved showing
off his English; he was mixing English and Chinese, maybe half and
half.

"The funniest part was when Jiang asked about the stock market:
how does the stock market work? Bill explained earnings per share.
Jiang said, 'I understand that, but why is Microsoft worth almost a
trillion dollars?' Bill explained projected earnings, how you do it for
thirty years, and how you do net present value. Jiang was really smart
and following all that . . ."

The conversation between Gates and President Jiang then proceeded:

"Okay, that makes sense, but a trillion dollars seems too much."

"Yeah, it was too much. It was inflated. Now Microsoft is more rea-
sonably valued; the whole stock market was in a bubble."

"Well, stock was in a bubble, so why didn't you sell all the Microsoft shares?"

"Well, I have certain responsibilities to my shareholders."

"Why didn't the company sell all its shares?"

"The company didn't have that many shares, plus that would be
viewed as not having confidence in the company."

"I guess I understand. This whole thing is not very rational."

"You know, Mr. Jiang, you are a real capitalist!"

A more recent Bill Gates visit to China, in June and July 2004:

On June 30, 2004, Bill Gates returned to Beijing. In his first few forays to the Middle Kingdom, the world's richest man had been accompanied to meetings by the head of Microsoft's China business office. Now, he traveled as well with the new head of Microsoft Research Asia, Heung-Yeung "Harry" Shum. Recalls Shum, "Every time he met with Chinese government officials, he said the best investment we have done in China is Microsoft Research."

The two met with Prime Minister Wen Jiabao, who next to the president and general secretary was the most powerful figure in China. Gates continued his efforts to build relations with the government, updating the prime minister on Microsoft's previous pledge of $750 million for helping foster local industry and training software engineers.

He also explained some of the Bill & Melinda Gates Foundation's work to improve health in rural parts of the country and asked for Wen's continued support. For his part, Wen warmly thanked the Microsoft chairman for his contributions to "humankind," to which he said the nation was also committed, and told him: "Mr. Gates, your name is a household name in China. No one in China doesn't know you. I studied you and your company. I read your books."

The next day, July 1, marked the eighty-third birthday of the Chinese Communist Party. It wasn't a national holiday, but celebrations had been planned throughout the country. Gates started early that morning, with a visit to an experimental middle school program in central Beijing—inaugurating a computer classroom that was part of a Microsoft-funded initiative to help improve computer literacy around China. Next up was an appointment with state councilor Zhili Chen, the former minister of education and one of the most powerful women in the Chinese government, with a rank equivalent to vice premier.

The Chen meeting was a bit tricky. It had been sandwiched in at 9 A.M., between the middle school visit and Gates's scheduled 10 A.M. keynote to software developers at the Olympic Sports Center—home to China's largest developer conference. The appointment with Chen had been set for a half hour: that left only thirty minutes to get from the downtown ministry offices to the sports center, part of the Asian Games Village in north Beijing. Worried that wouldn't be enough time, Shum had double-checked the route and hired a police escort to lead the way when the meeting with Chen was over. "Unfortunately," jokes Shum, "the state councilor really liked Bill." She asked question after question, each one engaging but making the research director agonize as the schedule grew more and more in doubt. Notes Shum, "She kept saying, 'My next question is . . .' or 'I have another question.' And I was thinking, 'Ahhh!'" Finally, Chen said, "I have so many other questions, but now the last one . . ."

A sweating Shum about came out of his shoes in relief.

They were already twenty minutes behind schedule. As he and Gates headed out of the meeting, Shum said, "We have to run."

Gates nodded. "Okay."

Shum swallowed hard. "I mean we really have to run."

Laughs Shum today, "So we walked out of the room, and we started running—and I said to the police car, 'Go, go, go!'"

Police siren blaring, Gates's limousine following its escort, they barreled through the streets of Beijing. And when a smiling and relaxed-looking Bill Gates finally took the stage, four thousand patient developers from a communist nation greeted the world's most famous capitalist with warm applause.

This is the story of Microsoft's adventures (and a few misadventures) in China since Bill Gates's first visit. In particular, it's the saga of the Beijing research laboratory—part of the organization that President Jiang asked the Microsoft founder about back in 2003—and how it has become the centerpiece of a unique partnership between the world's most powerful software company and the world's largest communist nation. It's a partnership, we think, that showcases what it takes to innovate in the age of global competition.

One caveat: this is the lab's story—and not the story of Microsoft's business operations in China. The book is not about outsourcing manufacturing or software-testing jobs. We have not delved deeply into the company's sales or market projections, or its efforts to fight off rampant digital piracy and beat back the Linux "open source" operating system that the Chinese government supports in tandem with Windows. To the extent we cover such issues, it is within the context of Microsoft's Beijing research arm and its relationship with its host country. Every major company these days has business operations in China, but none have anything like Microsoft Research Asia—at least, not yet.

And what a story the lab makes. The one-of-a-kind enterprise provides a compelling case study of Microsoft's long-term strategy of innovation, as well as the trials and tribulations of doing business in China. What emerges above all is the importance of finding better ways to innovate in the face of relentless and often cutthroat competition—and the larger imperative of looking at emerging nations not just as potential markets, but as sources of talent that make future innovation more likely. Because the rules of business and innovation differ across the globe, it is critical to adapt to those different cultures, so emerging economies like China's can be lifted up at the same time they are being tapped. In short, our story is about discovering and cultivating ways for everyone to win.

Guanxi (pronounced "gwan-shee") is the Chinese word for the mutually beneficial relationships critical to success in the Middle Kingdom. In China, there's no such thing as a purely business relationship. Instead, to be successful in business, you must blend formal relationships with personal ones. *Guanxi* refers to the delicate art of building and nurturing such ties. In China's old school of doing business, it can carry a negative connotation—of favoritism and cronyism. But the same word also conveys the deep and lasting relationships that can only be built over time—and it's that "good *guanxi*" we refer to here. Its four basic principles can be roughly translated as **trust** (respect and knowledge of others), **favor** (loyalty and obligation), **dependence** (harmony and reciprocity, mutual benefit), and **adaptation** (patience and cultivation).

Forging good relationships in the Middle Kingdom has not been easy for Microsoft. Gates's seemingly casual air at the first meeting with Jiang reflects his company's carelessness as it entered the world's largest market. The company first established a Beijing business arm, Microsoft China, in 1992. But a series of tactical blunders and minor scandals, ranging from unsuccessful product introductions to a book published in Chinese and Japanese by an influential former business manager who blasted the company and its tactics, made for a less-than-stellar initial foray into the country. And all along Microsoft has been dogged by charges of heavy-handed marketing and of pricing its software beyond the means of even many professionals.

But in the midst of its shaky and uncertain business relationships came Microsoft Research Asia. Originally envisioned in 1991 by former chief technology officer Nathan Myhrvold, the Beijing lab held its seventh anniversary in November 2005. Over its brief lifetime, it has proven to be an extremely effective means of mending broken fences and building *guanxi*. Through its outreach programs, new relationships have been formed with industry, academe, and government—giving Microsoft a leg up on introducing new products into the rapidly developing Chinese and broader Asian markets. Putting the lab's story with what's going on in the company's Redmond, Washington, headquarters gives us a new perspective on Microsoft's ambition: to vanquish its image as a bully devoid of innovation and to lead the world in making computers interactive, entertaining, and ultimately more useful. Indeed, with nearly 500 researchers and engineers (more than double its size just a year earlier), 300 student interns, and well over $100 million that has been invested by the company since its opening, Microsoft Research Asia has become an international powerhouse of infotech R&D. It is now an integral part of Microsoft's vision of doing pioneering research to ensure its global future in everything from its mainstay operating systems to Internet search to video games and wireless computing. Even as we watched, the sense of urgency in the enterprise rose dramatically. A stream of technologies coming out of Beijing turned into a torrent bound for virtually every Microsoft business: text-to-speech tools for word processing, software interfaces for mobile-phone cameras, lifelike graphics simulations for Xbox games, more effective Web searches for its MSN Internet portal, and a host of features bound for Vista, the company's long-awaited new Windows operating system due out sometime in 2006.

"It's interesting how much of the research directed at the Asian marketplace turns out to be generally applicable," says Rick Rashid, senior vice president of Microsoft Research, which besides its main facility in Redmond, also runs labs in San Francisco; Mountain View, California; Cambridge, England; and Bangalore, India. "They'll often attack a problem differently from what would happen in Europe or the U.S., because they come from a different perspective. They often find solutions that are different—and in some cases different turns out to be better."

Although this book spans some seven years, it was chiefly reported in Beijing and Redmond over one year, beginning with a critical week in November 2004 when the lab took center stage in Microsoft's efforts to battle competitors Nokia, Sony, and especially Google. The story then unfolds through the experiences of those who were central to the action. Almost all were born in China or Taiwan, native Chinese speakers who have spent much of their lives in the United States and then returned to the Middle Kingdom out of a strong sense of duty and a drive to improve conditions in their ancestral land. A curious blend of traditional Chinese and upstart American—they follow the Pittsburgh Steelers, the Seattle Mariners, and the Houston Rockets, where Chinese superstar Yao Ming plays—they are exactly the kind of hybrid souls who will drive the future of technology as the sources of innovation spread throughout the world.

Over the past year, we have conducted scores of interviews with these individuals and witnessed dozens of technology demos—far more than we could ever incorporate into a book. We journeyed to company events to observe the staff in action, met with Chinese officials at the foot of the Great Wall, played basketball with students and lab staffers at Tsinghua University in Beijing, and sat in the Microsoft box drinking beers and eating nachos with lab members to watch Yao Ming battle the Seattle Supersonics. All this provided myriad insights and personal anecdotes (for instance, what was behind the decision to locate the lab in Beijing instead of more high-tech and business-savvy Shanghai) that reveal the messy and more colorful side of innovation—and the real-life experiences and connections that make it possible. Yet it is important to stress that despite our proximity to Microsoft people and events, we made no promises about what we would include, and Microsoft had absolutely no say in what we wrote. We hold no stock in Microsoft, and outside of a few meals (which we typically reciprocated) and the basketball tickets, we paid our own way.

It's a vast understatement to say a lot has changed in China since Gates first visited. Just the conversation with President Jiang, in which the Microsoft founder good-naturedly called him a capitalist, would have been unthinkable a dozen years ago. It might have been just as unthinkable up until a few years back that a Chinese premier would read *The Road Ahead*. All told, Gates has made seven or eight visits to China, watching carefully as the nation has exploded economically. In 2003, China became the world's leading recipient of direct foreign investment, ending a multidecade U.S. reign—and holding the title for two years until being supplanted by the United States again. China is now the number one user of cell phones and the number two buyer of new PCs (behind the U.S.). It also is spawning a thriving homegrown Internet industry. The financial weekly *Barron's* rated Shanda Interactive Entertainment, an Internet gaming startup in Shanghai, the top tech IPO of 2004. Then, on August 5, 2005, in a stock market debut reminiscent of the U.S. dot-com explosion, the country's leading Internet search engine, Baidu, surged almost fivefold in value, reaching nearly $120 a share.

But there's a much deeper transformation than just the financial story, for Gates and company saw relatively early in China what many others had missed—it's not about the market as much as the people.

In 1949, only 107 students earned postgraduate degrees in China. In 2004, the number hit 160,000. China is now home to more engineers than anywhere else on the planet. Its 19 million college undergraduates dwarf the 14 million in the United States. Some of the best computer scientists in the world can be found in China, and more are on the way at an unforgiving pace. Finding new ways to attract that kind of talent is Microsoft's secret for future success. After being welcomed halfheartedly at initial recruiting visits on Chinese university campuses, the lab now receives some 10,000 résumés during its annual six-week recruiting drive, and thousands more arrive throughout the year. Its Computing in the 21st Century conference, held in conjunction with the National Natural Science Foundation of China, fills gymnasiums and auditoriums around the country, as busloads of students hang on the distinguished speakers' every word and even post on Web sites about their dreams of working at the Beijing lab.

In nearly all these areas—from its vast investment in research to bringing Chinese researchers into executive ranks (both the lab's first two managing directors were promoted back to Redmond as corporate vice presidents)—Gates and Microsoft are either going against the grain of conventional wisdom or finding ways to succeed where others have stumbled. In the midst of American outrage over the outsourcing of jobs to countries like China and India, they are "insourcing" incredible talent—creating powerful products that create *more* jobs at home and abroad, ultimately making Microsoft more competitive.

So this story is about China, yes, but it's more broadly—and importantly—about the global future of technology and what it takes to be a truly multinational company in this age of change. And the stakes rose dramatically before our eyes. As we prepared to wrap up our story, Kai-Fu Lee, the Beijing lab's charismatic founder and one of our main characters, was snatched away by Google in a $10 million bidding war that devolved into a bitter courtroom fight, settled, on still-undisclosed terms, just before this book went to press. Google wanted Lee to start a research and development center in China—in essence to do for Larry Page and Sergey Brin what he had already done for Bill Gates. Microsoft countered, opening its own search center in China and unifying its R&D centers there under its own charismatic leader, former child prodigy Ya-Qin Zhang (another main figure in this story). The move signaled China's emergence as a new epicenter of the search war—and perhaps the most important corporate battleground of this still-young century.

From markets to talent to the future of innovation, Gates was not exaggerating when he once advised us: "People should pay attention to China. It is a phenomenon in every respect."

1

Beast from the East

November 8–11, 2004

This is a new kind of manufacturing in China. Not just shoes, socks, baby strollers. Now we manufacture MIT students, papers, and software.

—HARRY SHUM, MANAGING DIRECTOR OF
MICROSOFT RESEARCH ASIA

Half a world away from the calm beauty of Puget Sound, there's a lab where Bill Gates's software dreams come true. At Microsoft Research Asia, the drive to succeed is as intense as the traffic that roars by its front door in unbridled fury. If the software megagiant's other facilities around the globe seem idyllic, this one, in Beijing, is pure street. Microsoft's mantra here: work hard to get in the door; work harder to survive; then work even harder because the real work—that of creating the global future of computing—is just beginning.

If you find it hard to root for Microsoft, you've probably never met Harry Shum. The Beijing lab's managing director is hearty, engaging, and quick to make jokes. In his late thirties, he's also surprisingly young. "This is a new kind of manufacturing in China," he smiles, waiting outside his office. "Not just shoes, socks, baby strollers. Now we manufacture MIT students, papers, and software." His longtime colleague, HongJiang Zhang, walks by and concurs. Cultivating talent, he says, "is another level of 'Made in China.'"

Zhang, who's a little older than Shum and initially comes across as more reserved, heads the Advanced Technology Center. An offshoot of the research lab housed in the same building, this first-of-a-kind division was created to accelerate the movement of the lab's technologies into Microsoft's product pipeline—for China and the entire world.

Together, Shum and Zhang lead a nearly 500-strong organization that looks like a typical corporate lab but *feels* like a hungry start-up. Come in at almost any hour and you'll find scores of students—in addition to their staffs, the two groups support some 300 interns at any time, most from Chinese universities—tooling away on projects jointly supervised by their professors and Microsoft researchers. It's a place where 10,000 résumés arrive in a month and interns spend some nights on cots next to their cubicles. Add the buzz of Mandarin conversations, the window views of Beijing's sprawl, and the hint of cigarette smoke, and you are constantly reminded: this isn't corporate U.S.A. anymore.

Every week is busy here—but one particular week in early November 2004 was special. The events packed into that whirlwind week spoke to every level of the company's strategy in the Middle Kingdom—and to the all-out, breakneck pace of global innovation today. To celebrate the sixth anniversary of the Beijing lab's inception, Shum and Zhang entertained a host of distinguished visitors from around the world. The dignitaries included their superiors from Microsoft Research headquarters in Redmond, Washington: Dan Ling, vice president of research, and his supervisor, senior vice president Rick Rashid, one of a handful of Microsoft executives who report directly to Gates. Also on hand were notables from the lab's technical advisory board, which encompassed some of the biggest names in computer science, among them Chuck Thacker, winner of the 2004 Draper Prize, a $500,000 award considered by many to be engineering's top honor; Jitendra Malik, chair of the department of electrical engineering and computer science at the University of California, Berkeley; and Victor Zue, co-director of the Computer Science and Artificial Intelligence Laboratory at the Massachusetts Institute of

Technology. In addition to a series of advisory board meetings, the frenetic week would include a Faculty Summit of 207 professors from throughout Asia, many of whom collaborated with the lab, and the Computing in the 21st Century conference that was co-sponsored by Microsoft and the National Natural Science Foundation of China.

On an overcast Wednesday in the midst of this hectic week, two large meeting rooms down the hall from Shum's office overflowed with animated conversations and dozens of research demos. Jet-lagged vice presidents, technical advisors, professors, and other studious-looking visitors milled around perusing the demos while eating personal pan pizzas catered by a nearby Pizza Hut. Microsoft demos are legendary: mastering the art takes technical know-how, showmanship, and a clear understanding of why a project is important to the company. A good demo can erase months of frustration and get you noticed. That's why the Beijing researchers had been living and breathing this stuff for months. Eager to impress, some were nervous and struggled with their English, while others pulled it off without a hitch.

To Microsoft, what was in these rooms portended the future of computing—and which competitors the software superpower was lining up in its sights. Target number one, which would loom ever larger in the crosshairs over the coming year: Google. An entire wall of demos highlighted smarter Internet search tools designed to take users right to where they need to go for answers instead of giving them a bewildering list of links, and to provide more highly targeted Web advertisements based on the exact nature of a person's search query. These efforts aimed to derail the Mountain View, California–based search company, whose faddish popularity once led Gates to quip, "There's companies that are just so cool that you just can't even deal with it."

Almost as urgent a competitor: Sony. The Beijing lab played a growing role in Microsoft's push for new kinds of graphics and interfaces to help it win the digital entertainment space over the consumer electronics giant. One of the more curious-looking demos employed a camera to track human faces, a key part of the next-generation interactive video games Microsoft envisioned. "PlayStation 2 already has something like this for motion, but not faces. We need something in Xbox," said researcher Dongmei Zhang, referring to Microsoft's video-game platform, which was slated for a major new release called Xbox 360 in late 2005.

The third company in Microsoft's sights: cell-phone maker Nokia. Software for mobile devices was still a relatively small business for Microsoft. At the time of the meeting, the company's Windows Mobile operating system had just surpassed Palm's in conventional PDA market share, but still trailed Nokia's system significantly when it came to cell phones and mobile e-mail devices. To this end, another set of Beijing demos showcased software that enables wireless video-conferencing and "seamless roaming"—so that any cell phone or handheld organizer can provide voice, video, or data communication anywhere in the world, anytime, on any network.

Increasingly, the Beijing lab was where the action was in all these battles—and the technical advisory board seemed impressed by the show. "They're doing really first-class research," said MIT's Zue, an advisor to the lab since its inception. After an hour of seeing demos and asking questions—some superficial, but many complex and detailed—the board retreated to a large room on the sixth floor for a private, closed-door meeting. Inside, the air was thick with anticipation. Researchers guzzled tea and coffee as they exchanged pleasantries. As technical assistants scrambled to get audiovisual systems up and running, Microsoft's top research brass, Rashid and Ling, took seats front-row center, flanked by other high-ranking staff and the advisory board. The room could seat seventy, but only half the chairs were filled. About 25 researchers sat in, some from Microsoft's main lab in Redmond, most from the Beijing lab. It was like a wedding, where the guests of the bride and groom occupy pews on different sides of the church: for the most part, Redmond and the States sat on the left side of the room, Beijing and China on the right.

The board had gathered, together with the lab's leaders, to discuss competitors and give more detailed feedback and criticism on key lab projects than was possible in the demo rooms. Harry Shum, a people person, kicked off the meeting by introducing all the visitors by name. He then called attention to a couple of new faces brought in from the States as assistant managing directors of the lab: speech expert Hsiao-Wuen Hon, who had done both research and product development for Microsoft in Redmond, and graphics guru Kurt Akeley, a co-founder of Silicon Graphics, who had recently finished his long-delayed Ph.D. at Stanford (he had taken a leave of absence in 1982). Both were heavyweight hires whose presence bolstered the lab's standing in China and also spoke to its status as a haven for top talent, not just from China, but from anywhere.

Shum then served up a few stats to demonstrate the lab's growing prowess on the global stage. In 2004 it was responsible for 7 papers out of 58 accepted for SIGIR, the world's largest and most prestigious conference on information retrieval (a key component of search), and 5 papers out of 80 presented at SIGGRAPH, the top graphics conference, where the next generation of gaming and entertainment wizardry is often unveiled. No other lab or department came close to these numbers, even those many times larger than the Beijing center. And it wasn't esoteric research, Shum reminded his visitors. To date, close to 100 technologies had been transferred to Microsoft products—tops among the company's research arms outside of Redmond—and the figure was growing fast.

After Shum's presentation came technical talks by key researchers on user interfaces, wireless networks, multimedia, graphics, and search—the lab's five main areas of focus. The talks were all informative and spoke to Microsoft's competitive battles, but one stood out in particular—and it came back to Google, Microsoft's archnemesis. Wei-Ying Ma, the smooth-talking, cherub-faced manager of the Web search and mining group, spoke with a light Mandarin accent, but his intensity and desire to help Microsoft compete came through. He explained how his team had solved a key problem in the search business. Today's search engines make much of their money by selling Web ads that pop up next to search results, but they typically rely on human workers to evaluate how relevant the ads are to any particular search query (a domain called "relevance verification"). This manual labor takes a lot of time and effort. Ma's team had found a way to equal human results automatically—potentially saving many millions of dollars.

This automation, Ma said pointedly to the closed-door crowd, provided a key advantage over Google. A longer-term approach that could help Microsoft win the search war outright, he explained in expanding on some of the demos the group had seen earlier, centered on "mining" the expanse of data on the Internet for deeper patterns in the links between Web sites. Understanding those patterns could eventually yield much more accurate search results—for instance, by allowing results to be grouped in easy-to-recognize categories so that users don't need to scroll far down the page to find the returns they are looking for. His team members, recruited for their expertise in the fundamentals of pattern recognition and information processing that underlie search algorithms, were in the process of honing the technology on thousands of users of Microsoft's MSN Web portal, which they had usurped as the company's personal testbed in the search war—not just with Google, but also Yahoo and other competitors.

The presentations, which took up much of the day, painted a picture of an all-out assault on the state of the art in computer science. By the time it was Hong Jiang Zhang's turn to speak, the stage was set to drive home what this all meant for Microsoft's businesses. As the director of the Advanced Technology Center, the fastest-growing part of the Beijing outpost, Zhang was charged with accelerating lab research into products and spurring the company's innovation worldwide. In his talk, Zhang was all business himself. He detailed projects in the works for virtually all of Microsoft's business divisions. In fact, research was moving out of the lab so quickly that Zhang announced that the 100-strong technology center, itself only a year old, would double by the middle of 2005, surpassing its research-lab sister in size.

After his overview, Zhang turned the floor over to two of his top lieutenants, Baogang Yao, a lead developer of new Web-advertising technology for MSN, and Wei-Ying Ma, who again brought it home to Google and the search war. Ma spelled out the numbers behind one of the company's major growth markets, one where Google had totally cleaned its clock—the paid ads tied to search. As of the third quarter of 2004, he noted, online advertising as a whole constituted an $800 million market—double what it had been just a year earlier. "This is a new business, a new market to Microsoft," he summed up. A major goal of his group's work, Ma stressed, was "to make MSN stronger, to win in this online advertising space."

After the presentations there were some detailed questions from advisory board members. Rick Rashid, Dan Ling, and the rest of the visitors sounded enthusiastic and upbeat. They asked a few more general questions about resources and technical approaches. Then they sat back in their chairs and seemed to soak up the power of the Beijing atmosphere. Rashid was especially pleased by the first-year progress of the Advanced Technology Center. "There are just things [here] they can't even do in Redmond, they're just not capable of staffing," he enthused. "The whole point is really to do things that wouldn't have otherwise gotten done."

The seven-story building where more and more of Microsoft's global battles are fought sits a few blocks off Zhongguancun Road in Haidian, Beijing's high-tech district. The Sigma building, as it is called, has a large glass-front lobby with plenty of shiny metallic trim. A Microsoft Windows sign runs along the side of the roof and is easily visible from the street. In the mid-1990s, the Zhongguancun area was dubbed the "Silicon Valley of China." Today it is home to more than a thousand technology companies and is situated within a few miles of a dozen top universities and academic institutes, including two of the most prestigious schools in the country, Peking University and Tsinghua University.

To get to Zhongguancun, hop in a taxicab or hire a car and driver and head to the northwest part of town. Beijing doesn't blow you away at first—the surrounding brown farmlands make the outskirts look more like rural Indiana than the capital of the world's next economic superpower—but the city is relentless in getting your attention. From ubiquitous billboards to endless construction projects, the city exudes a gritty, raw energy as it gears up to host the 2008 Summer Olympics. In the residential areas, block after block of drab beige apartment buildings are crammed together. Crowds of elementary school kids hone their basketball skills on outdoor courts. Closer to the Microsoft lab, high-rises compete with smokestacks for skyline supremacy. Run-down buildings squeeze in next to bustling consumer electronics markets and the Beijing Satellite Manufacturing Factory, where China conducts its spaceflight research.

Everyone knows China is a waking giant. Its booming population of 1.3 billion represents the largest potential market in the world. It is already the undisputed world leader in everything from low-cost manufacturing to mobile-phone usage (400 million subscribers by the end of 2005). With more than 100 million people on the Web as of 2005 and 19 million PCs projected to be sold that year, it has roared past Japan to become the second-leading user of the Internet and second-leading purchaser of new personal computers in the world (after the United States in each case). And the penetration of wireless and mobile applications is well ahead of the rest of the globe. Computer gaming, text messaging, and social networking on mobile devices are exploding as a way of life. On Chinese New Year, typically more than a billion instant messages are exchanged nationwide.

To succeed here—to tap into both this immense market and the incredible talent from the world's largest university system—multinational companies like Microsoft have learned, often the hard way, that they must find a way for both themselves and their host to gain. China is a land of striking contradictions that must be navigated deftly and carefully. On the one hand, its leaders are outspoken about wanting the nation to become a technological powerhouse. On the other, its Internet censorship is among the most severe in the world and its intellectual property laws are weak and unenforced; piracy runs rampant. While China preaches education for its students, it restricts the very information available to help them learn. And although China is a communist nation, its level of entrepreneurship has never been higher: in spots you find a 24/7 drive for financial success that is unrivaled even in places like Silicon Valley.

For Microsoft, the Beijing lab has become pivotal to navigating this minefield of competing interests. For foreign companies, a big part of giving back to China—what its leaders want to see—involves training students and workers in cutting-edge research and management techniques. In China, government leaders control almost every aspect of their citizens' education and training, not to mention the mainstream media and consumer markets. Academia and government are intimately tied together, much more so than in the States. That's why establishing strong relationships—the art of *guanxi*—with education officials and academe is so important. And that's why making research and teaching connections with Chinese universities is such a top priority.

This is what the busy week in November 2004 was all about. It began rather pointedly, on the Monday, with Microsoft hosting an international Faculty Summit less than a mile away from the lab. The gala took place at Beijing's aptly named Friendship Hotel. It's an older hotel with traditional Chinese décor—lots of red paint and drapery, gold trim, pillars, wall murals, and sparkling chandeliers. In a spacious hall on the second floor, the 207 computer science and engineering faculty members the company had brought in from across the Asia-Pacific region gathered behind long rows of tables to hear the latest from Microsoft Research and some of its collaborators. Two-thirds of the professors hailed from Chinese universities; the rest came from Japan, Korea, Singapore, Malaysia, Thailand, and Australia.

At nine in the morning, Harry Shum took the stage to the beat of rock music blaring over the PA system. He made opening remarks under a small spotlight. "This meeting is about partnership with academia in Asia," he stated. "The important thing to the lab is quality of people." He proceeded to tout the lab's pride and joy—the 1,500 student interns who had come through its doors over the past six years, most from top computer-science programs across China. "In fifteen years, I'm just saying, suppose Bill [Gates] runs out of money. We can still keep the lab running from our alumni donations," he joked. In closing, Shum mentioned that Microsoft Research Asia had recently been dubbed "the world's hottest computer lab" by an influential U.S.

technology magazine: "I finally figured out why. It's because we don't have enough money to run air conditioning in the summer."

China's director general of higher education, Yaoxue Zhang, followed Shum at the podium. You couldn't ask for a better view of what China was looking for in its relationships with Western companies than Zhang. His remarks, in Mandarin, were translated in real time into halting English relayed through headphones connected to a wireless receiver. "We're faced with a very exciting, changing world due to the globalization of technology and the worldwide flow of talent," said Zhang. "Our students need the ability to compete internationally." Continuing on this theme, he cited the importance of foreign companies like Microsoft in bringing Chinese computer science up to speed. "Our science and technology level needs to be raised . . . We hope to attract more corporate investment in this area and, through international collaboration, improve our quality of education."

An elaborate buffet lunch of noodles, dumplings, meat dishes, and seafood followed the rest of the morning talks, which were focused and technical: posters and demo booths were set up around the food tables, so diners could continue to bask in the air of Microsoft and its collaborations. Above the din of conversation, the reactions from visiting faculty members were overwhelmingly positive. "Microsoft's academic outreach is focused on long term, which is really smart," said Helen Meng, an MIT-educated professor of systems engineering and engineering management at the Chinese University of Hong Kong. "Most other companies ask for turnkey solutions, but that's not what we're good at." Later that day, Roland Chin, vice president of research and development at Hong Kong University of Science and Technology, remarked, "Microsoft raises the standard in technology, and that will help Chinese students—they want to work for multinational companies." All of this reflected a coming shift in the center of gravity of technology development, said Berkeley's Jitendra Malik: "The world in twenty years will be different. In terms of the U.S., instead of looking to Europe, it will mean a greater percentage of the action is in Asia. That's obvious."

It was a productive luncheon, full of ideas; lots of business cards were exchanged. But the man in charge of Microsoft's outreach didn't have time to eat. While most guests were still savoring the last of their dumplings, Shum was off to continue his academic campaign. He headed downtown in the backseat of a private car to the ultra-modern Grand Hyatt Beijing hotel, whose lobby boasts impressively tall windows that look out over an elaborate fountain. That afternoon, Microsoft Research Asia would sign a historic agreement with China's Ministry of Education to create collaborative computer-science labs at four of the country's top academic institutions: Hong Kong University of Science and Technology, Zhejiang University, Harbin Institute of Technology, and Tsinghua University. Microsoft saw this as a way of showing that its commitment to Chinese education and training was serious, and that the company was investing in China for the long haul.

On Tuesday, the day after the Faculty Summit, Microsoft's *guanxi*-building kicked into even higher gear. It was a cold and rainy Beijing morning, but the sprawling campus of Tsinghua University teemed with life. Packs of undergraduate students navigated the wide, tree-lined paths that run along rows of old buildings. Some chatted noisily with their friends; others walked quickly with heads down. Many students and professors hurried to class on rusty old bicycles, weaving to and fro to avoid the pedestrians and the large puddles forming in the streets.

Tsinghua University is widely regarded as the top engineering school in China. Established in 1911, it is the alma mater of the country's current top three leaders, one-quarter of the members of the Chinese Academy of Sciences, and one-fifth of the members of the Chinese Academy of Engineering. It's no coincidence, then, that Microsoft Research Asia picked the campus as its home base for academic collaboration and recruiting. The lab drew more students from Tsinghua and supported more collaborations here than at any other school in China—and it was a centerpiece of the Ministry of Education agreement that Shum had signed the day before. So its importance made the school a natural choice to serve as the first leg of the annual conference on Computing in the 21st Century. Each year this conference and "tour" had opened in Beijing and, beginning in 2000, had then moved to a different second city—providing a showcase of top experts and the latest advances in computer science that had wowed and inspired thousands of Chinese students.

On the east side of the Tsinghua campus, attendees were greeted by a strange sight that you would probably never see on an American campus. Seven-foot-tall placards with the faces of Rick Rashid, Dan Ling, Harry Shum, Chuck Thacker, and other notable speakers lined the steps leading up to the university's sports stadium. Rashid's poster smile beckoned as if to say, "Enter here, top students, and we will educate you." In the distance, framed by the placards, an enormous smokestack belched clouds of white steam into the sky. It was a vivid snapshot of today's China, as it steps forward into the information economy of the future with one foot mired in its industrial past.

Inside the gymnasium, the Microsoft tour received a celebrity's welcome from 3,400 Tsinghua students, faculty, and assorted dignitaries. A stately brass melody played over the speakers as Shum once again took the stage to introduce the day's events. Spotlights careened around the stadium's interior, beaming Microsoft's logo to the upper decks. Flashing streams of digital bits were projected onto the sides of midlevel balconies. Many students and guests wore headphones to hear translations in English or Chinese. The president of Tsinghua University, Binglin Gu, followed Shum to provide the official welcome. "This is a great opportunity to learn from Microsoft's cutting-edge computing techniques," he remarked. "It is very inspirational for us. I hope in the future we will have more world-class scientists born out of the students here today."

Rick Rashid, the next to take the podium, echoed the sentiment, saying to the audience, "The next ten years will be the time for you to create new applications" in information technology. He appeared to be doing well for having stepped into a 16-hour time difference two nights before. The students in the stands and on the gym floor seemed to hang on his every word, many eschewing the Chinese translation available on their headphones. On the left side of the stage, his slides were projected in English; on the right side, a Chinese version appeared. Rashid pushed for the "democratizing of information"—to put raw materials out there so that people can eventually be connected to everyone and everything in the world using a wide array of intelligent devices.

It was an ambitious and long-term vision of global technology that might make some in China uncomfortable. But the growth of Chinese information technology and the country's hunger for knowledge and training in computer science was already insatiable. In a backstage VIP room, Ya-Qin Zhang, a soft-spoken, China-born Microsoft vice president who had been the managing director of the Beijing lab for nearly four years before Shum, relaxed with a cup of coffee. Zhang, a major figure in Microsoft's China story, would also speak on the tour. He said he felt proud to see that his company was continuing to attract and nurture computer-science talent in his native land. "This is truly, truly a phenomenon," he gushed.

Maybe the last two days had gone too smoothly. After the main presentations, Microsoft put on a press conference for about twenty Chinese journalists. Severe-looking guards in green uniforms manned the doors to the room, locking hands with each other to block outsiders from entering. Up at the interview table were most of the day's keynote speakers, including Shum, Rashid, Ling, Thacker, and Tsinghua professor Chen Ning Yang, a Nobel laureate in physics who had taught in the United States for decades and probably ranks as China's most famous scientist. Yang had spoken on the history of physics and computing—and had stolen the show. Almost all the questions from the local journalists were directed to him: When will Chinese universities be considered world class? (Research-wise, within ten years, he said; but at the undergraduate level, his students at Tsinghua already exceeded their counterparts at Harvard University.) Should the government spend more on high-energy physics research? (No, was his surprising answer.) At one point, Microsoft's media representative, Sheila Shang, reminded the reporters that this was a Microsoft event and that questions should be directed to all the speakers. But that did little to change the nature of the queries, which kept going to Yang. The unintended message to Microsoft—it's not always about you—was a sign that the company still had a lot of work to do in China.

The press conference was a glitch, but Shang would still count scores of articles touting Microsoft and its vision of computing. The next day, Wednesday, brought the technical advisory board meeting—a midweek interlude of private discussions, and a bit of a respite from the public hustle and bustle of the rest of the week. But as that day came to a close, a private bus waited outside the lab and the pace picked up again. The second leg of Microsoft's conference tour was about to begin. Next stop: Chengdu, a rising high-tech metropolis in the southwestern province of Sichuan, a two-and-a-half-hour flight from Beijing. There, on the following day, many of the "21st Century" speakers would repeat the same demos and speeches, as if they were on a concert tour, playing the same sets in different cities.

On the ride to the Beijing airport, Rashid, Ling, Shum, Ya-Qin Zhang, Hsiao-Wuen Hon, and a handful of others gathered their thoughts and reflected on the week's events to that point. It was dinnertime and already pitch-dark outside. As the bus hit the highway, the Microsoft team wolfed down a distinctly un-Chinese meal of hamburgers and french fries delivered to the lab from a nearby McDonald's restaurant.

The air buzzed with excitement as they talked—much of the conversation centering on the wonder of China. Rashid noted that cellphone reception to call his Seattle-area home was better in Beijing than it was in his own office in Redmond. None of this came as a surprise to Zhang, who had long appreciated the exploding mobile market in China and had launched the Beijing lab's research focus on wireless networking. Back in Redmond, Zhang ran the engineering side of Microsoft's mobile-device software division, which aimed to provide the dominant platform for handheld devices—in other words, to do for cell phones and PDAs what Windows had done for PCs.

The mood was light, and the Microsoft team was starting to

loosen up amid a stressful week. Rashid was in a particularly good mood, waxing eloquent as the talk turned to competition with Finland-based Nokia in the wireless arena. "When Ya-Qin crushes Nokia, he'll get the Nobel Prize," the senior vice president proclaimed. The others burst out laughing while Rashid continued in fine form with his tongue-in-cheek cultural analysis. "I'm serious. See, the Swedes hate the Finns. If Ya-Qin puts Nokia out of business, the Swedes will give him a Nobel Prize."

Rashid *was* joking. But as the executives headed west to the next stop on their tour, it was just another reminder that Microsoft was here in China for one reason: to win.

If Beijing is the hard-driving East Coast, then Chengdu is the Wild West. The frontier city of 9 million is rawer and hazier than Beijing. It's darker at night, the air is smokier, the airport more desolate. But Chengdu is also known for its pleasant teahouses, restaurants, gardens, and relatively relaxed pace of life. It has a rich 2,000-year history and was the capital of several ancient kingdoms. By most accounts, it was the birthplace of printed paper money and a pioneer in manufacturing silk brocades. These days, it is the closest big city to Tibet, which lies 250 miles to the west—making it a popular gateway for travelers to the land of the Dalai Lama.

None of this, of course, was what brought the Microsoft team here for what would be a short, focused visit. Late at night, as they touched down at Shuangliu Airport and walked briskly through the terminal, flashbulbs popped all around the visitors; unknown photographers, presumably from local newspapers or government organizations, snapped pictures without asking any questions. The group was treated like an entourage of celebrities. A private bus awaited to whisk them to their hotel, the relatively posh Sheraton Lido near the center of Chengdu, about thirty minutes away.

The bus came equipped with its own tour guide, a cheerful young woman who sat at the front facing the passengers and doubled as a standup comic. She seemed to delight in practicing her English but was extremely nervous—she mentioned this several times and apologized, citing what an honor it was to entertain this group. Sichuan, the birthplace of the country's reform leader Deng Xiaoping, was the fourth-largest province in China, she pointed out. It was home to 85 million people and well known for its spicy cuisine, Yangtze River cruises, and giant pandas—its dense bamboo forests harbored 80 percent of the world's panda population. The jittery guide proceeded to tell a series of awkward jokes about pandas—how it's impossible for them to appear in color photographs (only black and white), how they look like they never take their sunglasses off, and so forth. (Something was lost in translation, perhaps.)

The Microsoft group was a fairly tough crowd, but they let her continue, reveling in the corniness of jokes that were so bad they were good. People from Sichuan, she went on, are known for being easygoing, hardworking, and having a good sense of humor. At the mention of these traits, the Beijing crew immediately poked fun at Baining Guo, the manager of the lab's graphics group who was along to run the demos during various presentations. Guo was originally from a small town about an hour's drive from Chengdu. When the guide said Sichuanese people are hardworking, the others mocked him: "Hardworking, or heartbreaking?" they laughed. Guo took the good-natured ribbing in stride, as if he'd heard it all before.

In the center of town, the Chengdu version of Boston's "Big Dig" construction project was under way to build a huge underground traffic tunnel. Overlooking the scene, an eerie statue of Chairman Mao stood in a large square with one arm extended, dimly lit by nearby streetlights. According to the tour guide, the statue stood 12.26 meters high, to commemorate Mao's birthday (December 26), and 7.1 meters wide, to mark the anniversary of the founding of the Communist Party in China (July 1, 1921). "Very thoughtful design," muttered one China-born member of the Beijing crew.

Along the nearby Tai Sheng East Road, storefronts were packed tightly into each block, seemingly braced for the crowds that would appear at morning's light. During the day, these sprawling street markets full of computers, cell phones, and other electronic gadgets sold whatever you needed—much of it secondhand or counterfeit, especially in the back alleys off the main avenues. That brought to mind Microsoft's long-awaited next version of its Windows PC operating-system software, Vista, which at the time was codenamed "Longhorn" and slated for release in mid-2006. "They probably already have Longhorn here," quipped Ya-Qin Zhang, as he gazed down one of the streets.

The next morning, Thursday, it was time to meet with the mayor of Chengdu, Honglin Ge, and then kick off the "21st Century" conference at the nearby University of Electronic Science and Technology. Founded in 1956, the school is considered one of the cradles of the Chinese electronics industry. The scene outside the main auditorium on campus was similar to that at Tsinghua University two days earlier, with placards of the distinguished speakers, rows of buses running down the street, and students lined up to get in. Here, where Microsoft Research had never been before, the conference was an even hotter draw, and there were rumors of a black market for tickets. Just outside the doors, a young woman, apparently an undergraduate, approached one of the authors and asked if he was Rick Rashid—and could he let her into the proceedings, because she didn't have a ticket.

Inside the auditorium, classic rock music from the Eagles ("Heartache Tonight") blared through the speakers. Most students were in their seats thirty minutes before the start of the event. The smell of cigarette smoke in the hallways was much stronger than at Tsinghua University, but that wasn't the worst of it. In the back "VIP" room, the bathroom had only a foul-smelling squat toilet—basically a hole in the tiled floor—and no ventilation. Even distinguished speakers had to come through to use it. (This probably wasn't what Chuck Thacker had in mind when he said he was "astonished by the progress that's been made" in the eight years since he last visited China.)

The lights went down. The president of the university and the mayor of Chengdu started the show with opening remarks praising the conference and Microsoft's role in bringing world-class computer-science researchers to campus. Then it was time for the keynote lectures from Shum, Rashid, Zhang, and Thacker. (Nobel Laureate Yang didn't make the trip, so no one worried he would steal the show this time.) After the talks, the keynote speakers took part in a panel discussion. The best question came from a student who approached the microphone and spoke forceful if broken English: "Good afternoon, super scientist stars! What is Microsoft doing on privacy and security, with increase in personal information on network?" It seemed that Chinese students everywhere were well aware of the hurdles to Microsoft's vision of democratizing information flow in China.

Perhaps the most telling scene, though, came after the event finished. On their way out, students lined up in droves to pick up a free gift being handed out by conference volunteers: blue and yellow bags bearing the Microsoft logo that contained fleece sweaters embroidered with "Microsoft Research Asia." As they carried the shiny gifts back to buses waiting to take them to their dorms and living quarters, the party favors seemed well worth their cost to the company of three U.S. dollars each.

That night, in a grand finale to the nonstop week, the Microsoft team indulged in a lavish 21-course banquet in a downtown Chengdu restaurant. With all the events and meetings finished, they could finally relax and let their hair down. They filed into a large private room decorated in the style of ancient Sichuan and sat down around three circular tables with pristine white tablecloths. At the main table, Shum, Zhang, and Hon sat to either side of the ranking executives Rashid and Ling. Chuck Thacker and his wife joined them, as did Ling's mother, who had flown in from Shanghai. The exquisite meal featured such regional delicacies as mushroom soup, chicken feet, Sichuan-style spicy beef, noodle soup, cured tofu, and custard. As they ate, the group rehashed the week's events and what they meant for the company—and took time out to poke fun at one another whenever possible.

Dinner was accompanied by professional performances of traditional Chinese music, comedy skits, and Sichuanese opera. The latter came complete with mysterious *bian lian,* or "face changing" performers wearing elaborate, colorful masks and costumes. Face changing originated as an entertainment form in the 1700s during the Qing Dynasty, supposedly in a performance about a prisoner who startled his captors by changing his appearance—allowing him to escape. As a performer dances and flutters his arms around in the air (women are not face changers, traditionally), a mask is removed faster than the eye can follow. The technique, kept secret for generations like a prized magic trick, allows one actor to play up to four or five different roles at a time.

After dinner, the face changers danced and mingled around the Microsoft tables, shaking hands with the patrons and magically changing their masks in front of the startled and amused diners. That led Rashid to point out that face changing would be a useful skill to have in certain sporting situations, as when a hitter in baseball squares off against a pitcher in a tense showdown. At the end of the night, Shum did his imitation of face changing as he shook hands with people—turning away and suddenly turning back with a funny, contorted expression.

The whole scene symbolized an issue crucial to Microsoft's future in China and the rest of the world. In the coming year, as it had begun to do in the past decade, Microsoft (or any other multinational concern) needed to keep up with the changing face of innovation. To do that, the company would need to evolve its own practices, improve its own relationships, and change its own face around the globe. Over the past six years, the rise of Microsoft's Beijing research lab had proved a major coup in the struggle to improve the company's image in the Middle Kingdom. But what was truly at stake was not image, but the company's very lifeline to innovation and, ultimately, survival: recruiting top foreign talent and creating the novel products that propel future growth.

That, as Chairman Bill might say, was the way to win the road ahead.

2
The Bell Labs of China

Fall 1997–November 1998

*The key thing is we wanted to have a place where we could
successfully recruit great Chinese.*

—NATHAN MYHRVOLD

N athan Myhrvold is a gregarious soul with a neatly cropped,
curly beard and an infectious laugh who doesn't take himself too seriously. That's a good trait, because he could. He
retired as chief technology officer of Microsoft in 1999 with a personal fortune worth an estimated $500 million, bought himself a
Gulf Stream V jet, and began touring the world, devoting himself to
photography, digging dinosaur fossils, Formula 1 race car driving,
and cooking. He is a renowned chef who has "guested" at Rover's, an
acclaimed Seattle French restaurant, and once won the world barbecue championship. Although for Myhrvold the game is far from
over—at age forty-six, he's well on to his next big thing, trying to
unite brilliant inventors around the world into a massive invention
machine—by most yardsticks he's already won.

Myhrvold is also the architect of Microsoft Research—the reason
his former colleagues are in China to begin with. MSR, as it is known
around Redmond, is one of the few world-class corporate research
organizations formed in almost a half-century. In the world of infor-

mation technology, MSR is rivaled only by IBM Research. Big Blue's research division is much larger than MSR—some 3,000 workers in eight labs worldwide. But IBM dives into a much wider array of topics—mainframe computers, storage, semiconductors, nanotechnology. When it comes to software research, a case can be made that Microsoft is the biggest, and the best.

It wouldn't have happened if not for Myhrvold. A modern-day polymath, Myhrvold earned separate master's degrees in mathematics and geology from UCLA at age nineteen. He went on to get his doctorate in mathematical and theoretical physics from Princeton, then won a postdoctoral fellowship to study quantum field theory under Stephen Hawking at Cambridge University. When his own software start-up, based in Berkeley, was purchased by Microsoft in 1986, Myhrvold stayed on. He quickly rose to stardom inside the firm as a visionary and strategist, taking just a few years to be named senior vice president and chief technology officer, reporting directly to Gates.

Myhrvold's greatest gift may be to think big—and then convey his thoughts in easy-to-follow arguments. In mid-1991, Myhrvold proposed that Microsoft allocate $10 million a year to support a research center designed to help the company control its destiny. For three decades, his vision statement argued, the technical agenda for computing had been set by academic computer-science departments and big hardware makers who chiefly developed applications for mainframes—and then concentrated on creating ways to help those advances work on smaller computers. They weren't focused on the things Microsoft's customers wanted, such as ways to make computers friendlier. "The only way to get access to strategic technologies," wrote Myhrvold, "is to do it yourself." He noted that Microsoft took just fifteen years to reach a stock market value of $200 billion. That growth showcases "the power of technology. Technology in the future could make us redouble that or it could drive us to zero. And so it would be crazy for us not to be involved."

Gates and the Microsoft board of directors concurred, and the lab was formed that same year. The original plan was to grow to 100 researchers over five years. By 1997, just past the five-year mark, MSR had eclipsed that mark and opened a satellite branch in San Francisco, and Myhrvold was thinking about how to grow the organization further: a new mandate would target 600 researchers by 2000. In his 1991 memo arguing for a research lab, he had noted that eventually Microsoft would want to have branch facilities in Europe and Asia—probably China. But by the time the idea for a China lab really caught fire six years later, he relates, "I had actually forgotten it was in the original memo."

Relaxing in his present-day digs in a modern office park in Bellevue, barely ten miles from his old Microsoft haunts, Myhrvold explains his reasoning. "The key raw material in research is smart people, smart trained people. If you don't have that, nothing else works. And the fact is you're never going to get all the smart people to come to any one place. So what can you do? Well, if you can't get them all to come to Redmond, you have to go to them."

The two big swaths of the globe outside the United States to find talented computer scientists had long been Europe and Asia—that's why he had named them in his original vision statement. In 1997, Microsoft had cracked the European end, establishing a research lab in Cambridge, England, on the campus of Cambridge University. Moving into Europe was easier than Asia. The European culture was more similar to that of the United States, travel was easy and visa-free, and, in the case of England, no language barrier existed. But in the long run, Myhrvold felt, Asia might be more important. Says he, "If you look forward ten years, no place in the world is going to have growth in the number of computer-science Ph.D.s, for example, anything like the growth that's going on in Asia."

Several countries sounded promising: Singapore, Malaysia, Japan. A case could be made for each, and a few American firms, from IBM to Hewlett-Packard, had established labs in Japan. But as he considered the variables, "China seemed like the thing to do." For one thing, the country was virgin territory for U.S. research labs. A handful of American companies had opened what they called labs, among them IBM and Nortel. But, says Myhrvold, they were far closer to the "D" of development than the "R" of true research. "They weren't really doing research. They were doing [other] stuff to make it look like the company was investing in China. I don't think at the time anybody had a real research center in China."

Myhrvold had some different thoughts about China on a couple of other matters as well. Most Western companies seemed interested in it as a huge emerging market and a source of cheap labor—witness the outsourcing of manufacturing and, more recently, rote software production jobs. "Well," says Myhrvold, "we didn't care about either one of those. We were interested in China not as a place to dump our products and not as a place to hire people for peanuts. We were interested in China as a place to do computer-science research." He notes that in terms of sheer numbers, no country could rival China's computer-science undergraduate population. "We were hoping that if we could establish ourselves as a player in doing great research in China and give Chinese computer scientists, young ones, because that's mostly what they have, great research opportunities, we'd create an institution that over time would become revered as one of the great research institutions in China—like the Bell Labs of China."

Besides, he figured, opening a research lab might be the best way to tap the Chinese market in the long run. A lot of the features likely to make for successful software applications in China—speech input and new interfaces to help type the complex written characters into computers—were probably best done by the Chinese, Myhrvold felt. And what better way to sell well in China than to offer products created in China?

A jumble of problems came with opening a lab so far away, across a huge time difference and linguistic and cultural boundaries that made communication difficult. But Myhrvold had an answer for those as well. In software development, when long strings of code, different for each feature, are rigorously tested and melded together into commercial products, you have to coordinate like crazy—and so having parts of the operation far away from the main base is very problematic. But in research, he argued, communication links don't have to be as tight. "Fundamentally, you're telling people, 'Look, I'm not going to manage you 100 percent. You're going to go follow a dream.'"

In short, China worked. "If you look at where is the big growth rate for new Ph.D.s in computer science, it will come in places like China," reiterates Myhrvold. "So if you want to keep your finger on the pulse of what is happening . . . having a great tradition in China where you're out there recruiting great Chinese people and getting them to work on your product is a great thing to have in the long run."

At the time, the full furor over outsourcing and worries about China catching up with the U.S. in computer science had yet to materialize. But even today, Myhrvold has no compunctions about his views. Says he, "Every nation has to worry about competitiveness, but the way you should worry about your competitiveness is to say am I investing enough? Worrying about somebody else is a mistake."

Myhrvold worried about Microsoft. Sometime late in 1997, he made the China pitch to Gates and the Microsoft board of directors. "Bill was quite in favor of it," he remembers. "That was the wonderful thing about what I did at Microsoft—Bill was very supportive and understood the value of making long-term investments. And so that's what we set out to do."

The top priority, even as Myhrvold and his lieutenants debated where to put the new lab, was hiring a director. Much of the research organization's early success had been based on hiring absolutely top talent. Myhrvold had originally teamed up with Gordon Bell, a Microsoft consultant famous as the so-called father of the minicomputer from his days at Digital Equipment Corporation. Together they had selected the first director for the lab: Rick Rashid, a highly respected Carnegie Mellon University computer scientist who had led the university's advanced Mach operating system project, which later became a basis for Apple's Macintosh OS X system, among many other influences. Rashid, in turn, had joined Myhrvold in recruiting the best of the best to lead the lab's core efforts.

Among MSR's early recruits were Bell himself and a suite of former stars from Xerox's famous Palo Alto Research Center, including Draper Prize winner Chuck Thacker, co-inventor of Ethernet; laser printer pioneer Gary Starkweather; Charles Simonyi, inventor of the WYSIWYG ("what you see is what you get") word-processing program; and Butler Lampson, winner of the Turing Award, computer science's equivalent of a Nobel Prize. Also signing on in those early days were Apple multimedia megastar Linda Stone; Jim Gray, a database guru who had also won the Turing prize; and graphics legend Alvy Ray Smith, a founder of Pixar animation studios, which had blazed to fame with the movie *Toy Story*. Another core component came from raiding IBM's famous research organization, including a trio of its vaunted speech and natural language processing experts and Dan Ling, a young research manager who had led IBM efforts in everything from data visualization to workstation architecture and had co-invented video random-access memory. Ling had been Rashid's undergraduate roommate at Stanford University, and soon became Microsoft's research director when Rashid was promoted to vice president of research.

The philosophy behind the research organization was that such top-level stars would make up about one-third of the lab. Another third would be talented midlevel researchers, with the last segment filled by rising stars straight out of university. Myhrvold, Rashid, and Ling wanted nothing less for the new China lab—and the first, critical step was finding the right director. For starters, they envisioned a native Chinese speaker who understood the local culture and could forge ties with government and academia, the source of all that talent Microsoft wanted to tap. But that was just step one. "We wanted somebody who was up to the challenge of starting a brand-new lab, understood how research was done, had a perspective that was based on a successful research institution here, and who wanted to go live in China for a while," says Myhrvold. That last part was problematic. Living in China, especially then, "Well, it is an adventure is the best way to put it," he says.

Sometime in the first few months of 1998, Kai-Fu Lee's name came up. Myhrvold can't remember exactly who suggested Lee. But that hardly mattered. As soon as Lee's name was uttered, everyone perked up. "We had known of him for a long time," says Myhrvold. "He sort of fit every single bill."

•   •   •

Kai-Fu Lee was already a minor Silicon Valley legend when Myhrvold and Rick Rashid homed in on him as the best choice to start the China lab. Slim and babyfaced—he had been married when he was twenty-one and joked that he looked twelve in his wedding picture—Lee had made his name at Carnegie Mellon University, where Rashid hailed from, with a pioneering approach to speech recognition. He had gone on to work at Apple Computer, where he helped then-CEO John Sculley move the company into speech recognition software—and from there had joined Silicon Graphics. SGI, as it was known, had been a Valley high-flyer, but Lee arrived not long before the end of the glory days. In early 1998, Lee had helped find a buyer for the part of the company he ran—and he wasn't planning on staying on with the new owners. Although his own reputation was unsullied, Lee worried that he had failed, and, at age thirty-seven, he burned for another opportunity to prove himself. That was the very time Myhrvold and Rashid came knocking.

In talking to Lee, it quickly becomes clear that he carries a burden of proof that goes back far earlier than Silicon Graphics. He was born in Taiwan in 1961—the Year of the Ox—and was sent to the U.S. for schooling when he was eleven, joining an older brother who worked as a research scientist at the Oak Ridge National Laboratory in Oak Ridge, Tennessee. "I don't have a Tennessee accent because half the city is from outside," he jokes. But none of this personal background comes up right away. The first thing Lee talks about when you ask him about background is his parents—and their story. His sense of familial duty and respect for his mother and father are inescapable.

Both Lee's parents came from mainland China. His father, Tien-Min Li* was a legislator in the governing Kuomintang, or National Party, administration when Mao came to power during the commu-

---

* The Pinyin, or English alphabetic representation of the tones and syllables of Chinese words, was the standard of people from mainland China, and hence the father's name is spelled differently. One of Kai-Fu's brothers chose to spell the family name as Lee because Westerners often mispronounced Li as "lie"—and the rest of the family eventually followed suit.

nist revolution of 1949. At the time, members of the old government were given two tickets to escape to Taiwan; those who didn't go would be executed. "They all got two tickets," Lee relates. "Most took their wife or son, and families were separated." Lee's parents already had five children. "My father knew that if he left his family, they would have a hard time, but if he left his executive assistant, he [the assistant] would be executed. So he left my mother and five children in China, a courageous and unusual thing to do. My mother in equal courage managed to take the children and escape to Hong Kong and then Taiwan. So my father has one of the very few families of people in the government who managed to stay whole." It took another year for Lee's mother, Yah-Ching, to work her way out. The couple eventually had two more kids. The last one was Kai-Fu.

The story for other family members is not as happy. Lee's father was one of three sons. His mother, a widow, sent them all to college. "That was extremely rare in those days," Lee says. "She sold her land to educate them; that was unthinkable in Chinese culture." All had done well. His father had gone into politics. An older brother also enjoyed close ties to the National Party government. Unlike Lee's father, though, he did not get a ticket out and was executed by Mao's forces. The third brother had not joined the nationalists and thrived; he passed away a well-to-do man in 1998. "It's a very sad part of Chinese history," Lee says. "Three brothers forced to take sides, not on the same side."

Under Taiwanese law, Lee's father retained his legislator title for life, along with a modest salary. But he took only a minimal role in government, concentrating on his work researching and writing about political science issues. At age fifty-three, he took up English and studied for nearly a year in the United States at Stanford and Harvard universities. After returning to Taiwan, he spent the rest of his career writing books and papers, and teaching political science at National Chengchi University, hoping for Chinese unification. Lee's oldest brother, Kai-Lin, was already fourteen when the rest of the family made it to Taiwan. He eventually went to the U.S. for graduate school and then joined the Oak Ridge lab as a biochemist. When Lee was ten, Kai-Lin visited Taiwan. "He was appalled at how horrible the education was, memorizing ancient literature, math formulas," Lee relates. "He offered to my mother, if his younger brother—me—moved to the U.S., he'd take care of me. He was twenty-five years older than me. My mother took him up on the offer. After I finished elementary school, I went to stay with my brother and his family. My mother spent about half of every year living with me."

Lee knew no English when he came to the United States. Still, despite struggling with grammar and related issues, he placed ninth out of some 500 students in high school, and entered Columbia University in 1979. He planned to study political science, like his father. After a year, though, Lee fell in love with computers, changed majors, and then devoured everything about the field he could get his hands on. It was still the Fortran days, but Pascal, another computer language, was also being taught. He mastered both, and Carnegie Mellon accepted him for graduate school. In Pittsburgh, Lee felt instantly at home. "I was surprised everything was so high-tech, and so many more people like me there," he recalls. The Coke machine was connected to a local area computer network: students could ping the machine to see if there were enough Cokes before wasting a trip to the cafeteria.

At CMU, Lee was perceived as a bit of a prude, because he often wore a suit. His advisor was Raj Reddy, himself a legend in speech recognition and robotics. One day, Reddy asked Lee to take a particular approach to building a speech recognition system that would form the basis of his doctoral thesis. Lee studied it, came back, and said he wanted to take a different approach based on statistics and machine learning. What Reddy said amounted to, "I disagree with you, but I'll support you in what you want to do." He lived up to his words, and Lee took home an important lesson: when managing people, it often paid dividends to give them their heads.

The thesis made Lee's name in speech recognition. "If you read my thesis, there's not that much new grand theory," Lee relates. "It's more like saying, the things people have tried on statistics you can apply to speech." His approach helped make possible speaker-independent continuous speech, meaning the recognition engines did not have to be specially trained for each individual user and that they could handle input at normal speaking speeds. This methodology forms the foundation for almost all of today's leading speech recognition engines, although only a small core of Lee's work remains in use.

Reddy surprised Lee by asking him to stay at CMU as an assistant professor. Lee leaped at the offer, expecting to spend his career in academe. But after two years, he grew frustrated with the demands of university life—raising money, finding graduate students, serving on committees—which left little time for research. One day in late 1989, two charismatic people from Apple called. One was David Nagel, later CEO of PalmSource, which makes the operating system behind many personal digital assistants, including Palm Pilots. The other was Hugh Martin, who has enjoyed a long track record as a Silicon Valley executive, most recently as CEO of Nanofluidics, a Menlo Park, California, gene sequencing start-up. They explained how Apple was going to incorporate speech recognition into its computers—would Lee want to lead the effort? "Hugh gave me the sugar-water speech Steve Jobs gave John Sculley," Lee relates. That pitch had become a famous Silicon Valley tale. Sculley was CEO of PepsiCola when Steve Jobs recruited him as the new chief executive of Apple in the late 1980s. Jobs, known for his charisma and persuasive powers, flew to New York to see Sculley and reportedly sealed the deal by asking him: "Do you want to sell sugar water the rest of your life, or do you want to come to Apple and change the world?" Lee got the variation that said, "Do you want to spend your life cloistered in academia, fighting for funding—or change the way people interact with computers by making speech recognition a reality?" He bought it.

It was fun at Apple. In 1992, Lee made a notable appearance on *Good Morning America,* pushed by John Sculley and Apple's public relations team into showing off the early speech recognition software his team had spent the last two years developing. The demo included ordering a computer to schedule a meeting and make sure the VCR recorded a particular TV show. If there was ambiguity, such as which

"John" you wanted the meeting with, or how long the meeting should last, the computer would talk back, asking for more details. Sculley, Lee, and show co-host Joan London all tried it out. Lee says London felt certain the demo was faked—that someone was sitting behind the scenes manipulating things. But the demo was real. Word spread that Apple had cracked speech recognition and that day the company's stock rose $2 a share.

Still, speech recognition wasn't ready for prime time, and Lee knew it. "John wasn't hyping it, but seeing the demo, one could extrapolate and think it was worth more than it was," he says. In the end, Apple shipped a speech recognition product—but it was never widely adopted.

Lee inherited another product that did better—QuickTime, a multimedia software architecture that underpinned many successful applications and products, including, more than a decade later, the Apple iPod. But Apple, which had watched its market share in computers erode dramatically, was struggling. Hundreds of workers were laid off: Lee had to let many of his own people go. Steve Jobs had already left in disgust—forced out, by some accounts—selling all but one share of his founder's stock. Sculley himself, once the darling of Silicon Valley, was also shown the door.

That was it for Lee. "When John left, his successors weren't people I had equal fondness for," he admits. "So I left and went to SGI." Lee managed two businesses for Silicon Graphics: a Web server unit aiming to take advantage of the Internet's rising popularity, and an effort to pioneer 3-D graphics software for the Internet under the auspices of the company's Cosmo subsidiary. Recalls Lee, "The former, we did a great job; we grew the business from $100 million to $200 million. The latter, we did a lousy job. We were too mesmerized by the cool technology. We didn't think enough about usefulness." That was another lesson he never forgot. Years later, for MIT's Distinguished Lecture series, he was asked to leave a sentence with the students that they could put on a plaque for posterity. "The first thing that came to mind was, 'What really matters is not innovation, but useful innovation.'"

It wasn't long before Cosmo was put up for sale—and Lee was handed the task of selling it. In early 1998, Lee brokered a deal with Platinum Software and was looking for a new job when the Microsoft call came. (Platinum was later bought by Computer Associates, which closed the Cosmo operation.) At the time, he was being heavily recruited by Intel, which also wanted to open a research lab in China. Lee had gotten as far as speaking with CEO Craig Barrett and senior vice president Albert Yu, one of the company founders.

"I really liked Intel, but thought it was cultural mismatch," he says. "Apple and SGI were young, empowered, go out there and do anything. Intel was more traditional, larger, mature management. But still I would have said yes if I didn't have such a great alternative: my friends at Microsoft."

It was a call from Hsiao-Wuen Hon that turned things around. Hon had arrived at CMU for doctoral study as Lee was finishing his Ph.D., in time to help build the speech recognizer for Lee's thesis. He had later followed Lee to Apple but then had jumped to Microsoft not long before Lee moved to Silicon Graphics. *Star Wars* was Hon's favorite movie, and he had felt kind of like Darth Vader, going to the Dark Side by joining Microsoft—but had made his peace with the move. He and Lee had stayed good friends, and so had their wives. They were chatting, and Hon asked what his friend was planning to do in the future.

"Well, I'm looking at an Intel opportunity—something as crazy as going to China."

Hon knew about Microsoft's plans to open a Beijing lab, but couldn't reveal that at the time. Instead, he said, "Oh no. Maybe you should talk to us first. There may be something interesting—let me check."

The next call came from Xuedong Huang. "X. D.," as everyone called him, was Hon's supervisor in the speech platforms group that was introducing speech recognition into Microsoft products. He had worked with Lee as a visiting scientist at Carnegie Mellon, joining the faculty after Lee had left for Apple.

"I'm thinking of a job at Intel," Lee told Huang.

"No, no, come here, talk to Dan Ling, Rick Rashid, and Nathan, see what we're doing," his friend countered. "We're starting a research lab in China."

That was enough for Lee. "So I came up," he relates.

It was the spring of 1998. Lee was amazed. "I found the perfect intersection of the bright thinkers of a university and practical doers in industry. I didn't think such a group of people existed . . . All these smart people, all these resources, support."

And they were keen on having him. "If you can come, we could make the research lab in China bigger and better," Rashid pitched Lee.

"How big? And how good?" Lee asked bluntly. The original Microsoft plan Rashid had detailed involved starting in China with just 10 people. But Lee stressed that he was interested in magnifying the lab's potential impact: he knew that if he told people in China there would only be 10 staffers, the operation would be ignored.

Rashid took a leap of faith. "Same as Cambridge," he responded. The Cambridge, England, lab had been set up the previous year and Microsoft had committed to investing $80 million over the next five years—growing the lab to 100 researchers in the process.

"But what are the deliverables?" Lee asked.

"Hire great people, do great stuff."

"In what areas?"

"Whatever the great people want to do, as long as it's relevant to Microsoft in five to seven years."

"How much money do you want to save, compared to Redmond?"

"We're not there to save money. Pay the great people what you need to hire them."

"It was too good to be true," Lee relates. But it was true.

In his heart, Lee felt a bit like he had failed at both Apple and Silicon Graphics. However, he relates, "the key disappointment at Apple and SGI was that the hard work didn't see the light of day—it just got killed when the company got in trouble." He couldn't resist going to work for Bill Gates, whom he deeply respected as a technological and business genius with the patience and perseverance to see good ideas through bad times.

But that was only part of the reason he formally accepted Microsoft's offer in June 1998. There was another nagging consideration: his father. "My father, his heart was always in China," Lee says, emotion filling his voice. In fact, when Tien-Min Li died in 1995 he was working on a book about unification he had titled *The Hope of China*. "My father always felt China had not realized its potential," explains his son. "He always wanted to do something. His incredible passion in this area, [which] I wanted to have a try at understanding, was one of the main reasons I took the job."

At the time Kai-Fu Lee joined Microsoft, a debate was under way at MSR over where to locate the China lab. There were two camps—two logical choices—Beijing and Shanghai. Beijing was close to the center of government, Shanghai the faster-moving, younger, more reform-oriented center of business and commerce. In Europe, Microsoft had decided to locate its lab close to Cambridge University. Which universities did Microsoft want to be closest to in China? As Nathan Myhrvold describes it, "There's as many rivalries inside China as there are in the United States. It's like deciding between Silicon Valley or Route 128 near Boston, and am I friendly with MIT or Stanford or Harvard or what?" The various consultants specializing in doing business in China didn't help much, either. "The kind of things that people would tell us were all over the map," says Myhrvold. "There's this whole cadre of experts, consultants of every possible variety, who exist in order to try to help you understand China. And it's not clear to me that any of them understand it."

Lee settled the argument. If you visited Microsoft Research Asia years later and wondered why the lab was in Beijing and not Shanghai, people would laugh and say: "Ask Kai-Fu. He has a good story to tell." Lee feigns innocence, then relents. "Okay, if you insist. It's a joke. My mother has lived in Beijing and Shanghai. I told my mom I was going to accept a job, either in Beijing or Shanghai. She said, 'Oh, Shanghai is the most beautiful place. I grew up there, the food's wonderful, weather's nice. Beijing is a god-awful place, cold, sandstorms, so serious and government-like. If you go to Shanghai, I'm going to move and live with you; if you go to Beijing, I'll stay here in Taipei.' I told my wife, and my wife joked, 'Let's definitely move to Beijing!'"

"It's only a joke, a good joke, so I told it," Lee says. "What really mattered was I visited Beijing and Shanghai. I visited universities in both places, gave a couple talks." From these visits, and especially questions from the students, he notes, "My conclusion was Beijing students were more interested in the future of research. In Shanghai, they were more interested in when will this technology make money, and how to get a job."

And there were more top schools in Beijing as well, notably Tsinghua University and Peking University, arguably the two leading science and technology institutions in the country. This was vital to the lab's future—both for recruiting and successful collaborations. Several key institutes of the Chinese Academy of Sciences were also there in Beijing—important connections might be made through them. "People say if you don't want the attention of government, go do it in an unknown area. If you want to get attention, do it in Beijing," says Lee. "I was sure we were going to do great work they'd be proud of, and that would be good visibility for Microsoft. So I decided to go with Beijing. I told Rick. He said, 'No problem, it's done.'"

Back in California not long after accepting the Microsoft job, Lee arrived at his Saratoga home to receive a bit of a shock. His wife, Shen-Ling, greeted him by saying someone was on the phone for him. His wife had told the caller Kai-Fu was out, but the man was persistent, asking questions about when Lee would be back and where he was working. Finally, she told him that her husband had joined Microsoft in China. "Why would he go to China?" the caller asked. "And why would he join Microsoft?" Was she going to go to China as well, or staying behind? She had been troubled by the familiarity and personal questions.

"Well, what is his name?" Kai-Fu asked.

"It is a Steve something," Shen-Ling replied.

"Steve who?" There were a million Steves—it could be anyone.

"Steve Jobs," she thought it was.

"Steve Jobs!? Not the guy who just went back to Apple?"

"I don't think so—you don't know him."

But it was the Apple co-founder, who had only recently returned to the company, trying to rescue it from the brink of disaster. The two had never met, but it turned out that Jobs knew a lot about Lee. He got right to the point.

"Why don't you return to Apple?"

"But we never met!"

"That's not important. Your former staff all say that you are a good boss. They told me that I should get Kai-Fu Lee back."

"But . . ."

"Don't 'but.' Come here to visit me before you take the offer from Microsoft."

"But I have accepted the offer from Microsoft already."

"Then why are you going to China?"

"I am a Chinese. It is a huge market with so many computer users there. I can do many things for China and also do many things for Microsoft."

"It seems that you have decided?"

"Yes."

Jobs accepted defeat and said goodbye.

When Kai-Fu Lee arrived in Beijing in July 1998, Microsoft's China business office had recently moved to the upscale Sigma Center—the same building where the research lab is today. All told, some 4,500 computer and electronics enterprises were crowded into the Haidian district's busy thoroughfares, mainly occupying a vast, T-shaped area. The Sigma center was set back a few streets from the main branch of the T. But while many large and respected corporations had a sub-stantial presence in the area, it was also home to many fly-by-night operations. The Chinese journalist Zhijun Ling noted that Zhong-guancun had many disreputable nicknames and associations: "Many sarcastic sayings were spread among the industry insiders in Beijing," he writes in Chinese. "They describe it as the 'awkward Zhongguan-cun,' saying that 'there are only peddlers in Zhongguancun . . . They even say that 'it is not a street full of electronics but a street full of swindlers.'"

The Sigma Center, with its sparkling blue-glass façade, represented an oasis of modern calm and repute in its bustling, contradictory neighborhood. Its local nickname was "Computer Mansion," and other tenants included Mitsubishi on the first floor, Chinese com-puter maker Lenovo (then known as Legend) on the second, and Hewlett-Packard on the third and fourth. Lee's plan was to establish the lab on part of the fifth floor, but the space was months away from being ready. So he took an office on the sixth floor, inside the Micro-soft business office. The general manager of Microsoft China was Juliet Shihong Wu, a dynamic but controversial businesswoman who would later leave the company amid mutual hard feelings. She and the others in the sales office were welcoming, but Lee felt they didn't recognize the significance of what he was doing. "They thought yet another product group is coming out here. That's great, welcome," Lee says.

It was not going to be easy. Shen-Ling and their two daughters, ages six and two at the time, were still back in California. Shen-Ling had to pack up the house there and sell it. She was also from Taiwan, and a bit stressed-out about the long move across the Pacific.

More importantly for the lab, there was Microsoft's image in China, which hadn't exactly lit a fire of cooperation. Any lingering problems over the first Bill Gates visit had long since been corrected. The Microsoft chairman had arrived for another tour the previous December—his fourth visit in four years—and had received a hero's welcome before an overflow crowd of students and faculty at Tsinghua University. Some said his reception there convinced him to give the go-ahead to a China lab, but at most it seems to have been a contributing factor.

But on the wider stage, Microsoft was still Microsoft. Back in the States, the antitrust trial over the company's alleged monopolistic practices was only a few months away. Inside China, people charged that Microsoft's product prices were too high for the Chinese economy, and the company faced the usual complaints about its heavy-handed marketing. There is a story Nathan Myhrvold tells about a minor scandal a year or so earlier with the Chinese version of Word. By his account, Microsoft's Chinese software subsidiary had hired a company in Taiwan to "localize" the dictionary inside Word, in part by translating terms into Mandarin—and someone inserted a few "politically incorrect" definitions for some words. According to Myhrvold, "This was discovered and the police surrounded the building where the Microsoft subsidiary was."

Lee wasn't fully aware of these issues at the time—he later confirmed Myhrvold's general account though doubts police really surrounded the building—but he knew he had his work cut out for him. His main strategy for making the lab successful was to pursue *guanxi*—building long-term relationships based on mutual trust, not exactly a Microsoft strong point. "Part of being successful in doing business in China is to be viewed as sincere, trying to do something positive," Lee says. "[There's] no substitute for that. If you look at successful foreign companies in China, Coke is wildly successful over Pepsi, Kodak over Fuji, Volkswagen over Toyota. It's not necessarily the better product, but they were in there saying to the government, 'We're doing things to help your country. When I prove I'm sincere, I hope you'll treat me equally or preferentially.'"

Lee describes a certain paranoia about foreigners in China that he feels is rooted in history. He waxes eloquent about various European invasions—most notably in the mid-1800s during the Qing Dynasty, when European countries forced opium on the Chinese. "The government was too weak to fight back," Lee says. "One general had the courage to burn the opium in his city. The British invaded the city, killed a lot of people, demanded China give up parts of cities to European powers. That caused outrage, the Boxer Rebellion. Then eight countries invaded China, burned down the imperial palace, a huge embarrassment to China. It had to give up more land, pay huge amounts of money. The general belief in China is that foreigners are people we have to be careful about.

"This phobia of foreign countries and companies still exists, though in the last twenty years it's dropped dramatically. So, an approach the government has taken and Chinese companies have taken, is first build a relationship, show me you're sincere—when I see the sincerity I'll reciprocate. China has this market size that entitles it to do that."

To show that sincerity, to build that trust, Lee took the approach of hiring great technical people who exhibited the same passion he felt. Microsoft's philosophy in building its research lab in Redmond, as well as the Cambridge facility, was to start by hiring absolutely top-tier researchers, and then build around them. Lee put it another way: "A's" hire "A's." "B's" hire "C's." He only wanted the A-team.

Things started very slowly. Lee had been accompanied to Beijing by Dan Ling, Microsoft's research director and by most accounts the day-to-day driving force in getting the lab going from the Redmond end. Ling was born in Rome to Chinese parents and had grown up in the United States. His English was perfect and unaccented—and his Italian was good as well. He was also fluent in the Shanghai dialect, but that did him little good in Beijing, where everyone spoke Mandarin: the two dialects were virtually incomprehensible to each other.

Ling had never even visited China until the mid-1990s. But he had been tremendously impressed by the talent and energy he found in universities around the country. "That got me really excited with China," he recalls. "It was an exciting place where we needed to become engaged."

Returning to open a research lab in mid-1998, Ling gamely joined Lee on field visits to Tsinghua University and Peking University, as well as other institutions in the area: Zhongguancun was home to 148 research institutes that every year produced the majority of China's 300-odd computer-science Ph.D.s. But despite what should have been a ready-made audience for anything Microsoft was doing, the duo had been met with lukewarm responses, or outright standoffishness. As journalist Zhijun Ling's account of their early activities puts it: "It was midsummer. But the two were fully dressed up. The Chinese university presidents were no fools. Looking at these two yellow-skinned Americans, trying to figure out their purpose for coming, their countenance changed. The expression in their eyes was also strange. No wonder. You called it 'follow talents.' The Chinese called it 'grab talents.'"

Lee was also having limited luck trying to recruit China-born researchers in the United States—people who knew the country far better than he did—to join him in their native land. Many thought they would be swallowed up and rendered ineffective by China's bureaucracy. Others just loved the U.S. way of life and did not want to go back for what seemed like hardship duty. They had plenty of money, good friends, good jobs—why return and slog it out in a dubious political and economic environment? As one friend told him, "Go back? Then you have to deal with those officials all day, smile obsequiously and say sweet words."

Fortunately, Lee says, there was another group of rising Chinese stars in the United States who really wanted to go to China. "They loved technology, and also loved China," he says. "They loved the U.S. for how it supports innovation. They loved China because that's where they were born. Most of them working in software were waiting for the equivalent of MSRA [Microsoft Research Asia] to be born. We were very lucky to be in the right place, right time, to be able to offer the right kind of research environment, support and empowerment, to connect to universities, as well as having a reasonable compensation package. This group of people was naturally sincere; they wouldn't have come our way if they just wanted to get rich or didn't care about China, or if they wanted to forget their Chinese roots. That desire to give back to their origins caused them to come our way."

A few "expat" recruits from Microsoft itself helped get the lab off the ground. First came George Chen and Xiaoning Ling. Both worked in Redmond and had heard about the Beijing lab through the Chinese Microsoft Employees association, CHIME. Both contacted Lee out of the blue. The hard-charging, entrepreneurial Chen was a software test manager in one of the product groups. He had a doctorate in mathematics, but sold himself to Lee as a jack-of-all-trades, not a researcher. He had started his own real estate business on the side, and owned several Seattle buildings. He told Lee he could help with real estate in Beijing, government relations, liaisons to Chinese universities, anything—he just burned to get back to China. Lee hired him on the spot.

Ling was equally passionate about returning to his native country. He had come to the U.S. to get his Ph.D. in artificial intelligence at Oregon State, and afterward had joined a small multimedia company, GPS Continuum, privately owned by Bill Gates. Among his jobs: help design the "smart" infrastructure for the Microsoft founder's showcase home on Lake Washington, including the preprogrammed digital photography displays and climate control that automatically adjusted to the preferences of whoever was in the room. After the company was merged into Microsoft, Ling had become a software development manager, specializing in helping turn research advances into products, a skill that he argued would be needed in Beijing.

Neither of them was a researcher, though, and a research lab needed researchers. So, with Chen and Ling lined up sometime in the summer or early fall of 1998, Lee tried even harder to lure a few Microsoft Research stars currently in Redmond. At the top of the list was Harry Shum, yet another CMU grad and student of Raj Reddy who had interned under Lee at Apple. Since then, Shum had gone on to specialize in computer vision and graphics, and would soon have more than 100 refereed papers and 20 patents to his name. Shum hadn't said yes, but he and his wife had visited Beijing to check it out—encountering four days of glorious weather that seemed to ease any qualms they felt. Lee was optimistic that he would soon have his first true researcher in the fold.

Slowly, very slowly, those sincere souls Kai-Fu Lee had been hoping to attract were setting their sights on Beijing.

•　　•　　•

The hills west of Beijing were shaded in red, the tree leaves resplendent in their colorful migration toward winter. Down in the city, however, the poplars lining JianGuomenwai Dajie, or boulevard, around the Beijing International Club were already sparse. It was Thursday, November 5, 1998, time for the public debut of what was originally called Microsoft Research China. (Its name would be changed to Microsoft Research Asia a few years later.) For months, the true nature of Microsoft's plans in Beijing had been a closely guarded secret outside the company: to hide what he was doing Kai-Fu Lee had even been given an innocuous title—Director of Interactive Systems. Now, it was time to reveal all.

It didn't get more high-class than the historic International Club, which just a few years later would be taken over by the St. Regis luxury hotel chain. Located on a quiet (for Beijing) street on the west side of downtown, a fifteen-minute walk from the Forbidden City and Tiananmen Square, it is a haven of luxury in the busy, grimy, noisy city—with spacious grounds, a suite of top restaurants, and a spa and indoor pool that would do Roman emperors proud. Inside the expansive lobby, atop a wide, glamorous staircase leading to its conference rooms, high-heeled courtesy girls waited by the guest register arranged on a large desk. By the end of the afternoon, some 300 visitors had signed in—a who's who of China's higher education and computer elite. By one count, the notables included 4 university presidents, 9 college deans, 18 academicians, 56 professors, 27 researchers, 7 institute heads, 29 government officials, nearly 100 journalists, and a lone diplomat from the U.S. Embassy. As guests waded into the big meeting room dressed in their business best, they saw a head table surrounded by twenty-two flower baskets—presented to Microsoft by the Ministry of Information Industry, the Chinese Academy of Sciences, and other organizations.

A century earlier, the Year of Waxu in the Chinese lunar calendar, Zhijun Ling observed, China had seen a brief uprising known as the Reform of 100 Days. During his short reign, reform leader Sitong Tan visited a friend in Shanghai and saw an amazing calculating machine. It had six gears, each with grooves representing the numbers "0" to

"9." When a crank was turned, each gear in succession ran 10 times faster than its predecessor, making it possible to calculate figures up to 999,999. Tan reportedly tried the machine 100 times, and never found an error. He was told the device had been invented by a Frenchman named Pascal.

"Unfortunately, history only recorded Sitong Tan's political allegation and his sacrifice as a martyr," the journalist noted. "Whereas for this small incident, which has far-reaching influence, people in the future know very little." Now, however, in 1998, China was in the midst of another, longer-lasting reform that had begun with the economic opening of the country some twenty years earlier and had sparked a mad rush of capitalism into the once-insular communist nation. And here in this room, if Microsoft was to be believed, China was going to be introduced to a new era in computing—one in which computers would be friendlier, easier to use, and more affordable for millions of people.

The seats were lined up in rows, auditorium style. In the front row, Kai-Fu Lee was beaming, greeting guests and chatting with Rick Rashid and Dan Ling, who had flown in from Redmond for the event. Harry Shum was there, though he still had not formally agreed to join the lab. Also on hand were three other Chinese-speaking Redmond researchers: Lee's good friend Hsiao-Wuen Hon, who had helped recruit him to the Dark Side; Hon's boss, X. D. Huang; and Zicheng Liu, from the graphics group. The Beijing lab's first few staffers rounded out the Microsoft contingent, including George Chen, Xiaoning Ling, and Lee's new secretary, Eileen Chen. The two Chens, who were not related, argued good-naturedly for years about who was the first employee of the new lab: each claimed the title.

Xiaoning Ling had come in separately from the main Redmond contingent a few days before the opening ceremony. Lee had been out with Rick Rashid's assistant, Mary Hoisington, doing some advance scouting for the event. When they returned to the office, the receptionist informed Lee he had a visitor. "He's been waiting for you for a while."

Lee had looked at Xiaoning, blank-faced. "Who are you?" he asked.

"I'm Xiaoning Ling. You hired me."

The penny dropped. Lee had been so consumed by matters in Beijing, he had temporarily forgotten all about Ling. "I could not remember who this guy was," he recalls.

And now they were all at the posh International Club, bristling with youth and energy among China's old guard of computing. Xiaoning Ling looked over the crowd and spotted his former professor from Peking University some twenty years earlier. "The professor was as vigorous as before but graying at the temples," wrote Zhijun Ling.* "When he saw his student coming back from overseas, thinking back, he could not help sighing with emotion. At that time, these young people now standing in front of him used to be simple and ignorant children. Now they were known as 'world-class experts,' with lots of patents, theses, and colorful certificates in their pockets. They talked nothing but the most updated progress in the world of computer technology."

The scene spoke volumes about the changes confronting China. More than 100 reporters, three-quarters of them from newspapers, the rest from radio and TV, had come to digest and analyze the event, taking their press packets to assigned tables at the back of the room. A Chinese emcee hired for the occasion opened the event and introduced Lee. Speaking in Mandarin, Lee affirmed the company's commitment to China and promised Chinese customers "a better computer experience." Microsoft, he related, promised to invest $80 million in the lab over the next six years, and hire 100 researchers. Then he turned things over to Rick Rashid, the most senior Microsoft official present: the audience listened to a live translation of Rashid's words through headphones placed on every seat. Rashid then cued in a video clip from Bill Gates with Chinese subtitles:

Good afternoon, ladies and gentlemen. I am Bill Gates, chairman and CEO of Microsoft. I'm very excited to announce the opening of Microsoft Research in China.

---

* Journalist Zhijun Ling is Xiaoning Ling's brother.

Research continues to be incredibly important for Microsoft. Every major Microsoft product has incorporated work from our Research group and I expect this contribution to increase in the years to come. The Microsoft Research Group is building the technology that will enable PCs to see, listen, speak, and learn so that customers can interact with their computers as naturally as they interact with other people.

We chose China as our first Research Center in Asia because of the tremendous talent that we've seen there. I've had the opportunity to talk with developers in my recent visits to China and I'm continually impressed with the caliber of people I meet.

All in all, it was a wonderful day. Nathan Myhrvold had also taped a brief address that stressed his views about the importance of research and the need to go where the brilliant people were. At one point, Harry Shum was stunned when Rashid intoned, "I am pleased to announce that the computer scientist Harry Shum has also joined the lab." Recalls Shum, who was sitting in the first row, "I turned to Dan Ling and said, 'Wait a second. I have not joined.'" But Ling just shrugged and told him not to worry about it. Besides, Shum had pretty much decided to join by then, though he couldn't help wondering if he was making the right choice. "Kai-Fu was smiling all day," he recalls. "He was so confident that we were going to make it. I was not so confident."

Lee was especially pleased at the turnout from government and academe. In China, he notes, even senior officials don't firm up their calendars until about a week before an event, so although he had spent weeks paying courtesy calls and issuing personal invitations, he wasn't sure until late in the game who would show up. But in the end, he says, "We managed to get the minister of science and technology, vice minister of education, and vice president of the Chinese Academy of Sciences. They all said very nice things."

Not every observer saw it that way. A series of speeches and welcomes by academic and government officials praised the lab, though often in guarded terms. The most glowing support came from Yu Wei, the vice minister of education, who had studied in Germany, and said

Chinese education had a lot to learn from the West. Wei pledged to work with the new lab, and said: "When the Chinese people mention the knowledge economy, they would mention Microsoft. Microsoft is a very influential company and Bill Gates is a legendary hero in the heart of the Chinese youth."

But others were far more reserved. Lilan Zhu, the minister of science and technology, was the highest-ranking official present. As Zhi-jun Ling put it, "She said what interested her most was the tenet of Microsoft Research China: 'to provide an open environment.' She also said . . . what Microsoft was doing deserves 'high appreciation from us . . .' She did not show any hostility. The Americans felt somewhat relaxed. But she did not give any warm praise either. At the very beginning, she even said that she was not fully prepared to deliver a speech on the occasion."

Lee later disputed the interpretation of Zhu's remarks, which he felt were encouraging. But he agreed with how Ling's summary continued: "Mr. Bai Chunli, vice president of the Chinese Academy of Sciences, said, 'I hope we can strengthen cooperation and join hands to do a better job and serve the people.' These words offended no one but were superficial and perfunctory."

And there was one official notable for his absence: Jichuan Wu, head of the Ministry of Information Industry (MII). Rashid and Lee had paid a special visit to the ministry, and extended a personal invitation, but to no avail, though Wu did provide a quote for the press release. Coincidentally—or maybe it was no coincidence—Wu was the only Chinese official Bill Gates had singled out for criticism in his book *The Road Ahead.* Referring to Wu's statements to the press that China saw no conflicts between allowing its citizens Internet access while maintaining censorship, Gates wrote: "He may not understand that to implement full Internet access and maintain censorship, you would almost have to have someone looking over the shoulder of every user."

For whatever reasons, in the end Wu sent two lower-grade officials and a couple of congratulatory flower baskets to the Beijing lab's opening ceremony. Neither official delivered a speech, causing a reporter to ask why. One of the officials put it bluntly: "MII first had contact with Microsoft, but no agreement was reached. Later they made an agreement with the Ministry of Technology . . . The Ministry of Technology has its own ideas. They consider cooperation with Microsoft from the perspective of scientific research, while we consider the issue from the perspective of the industry as a whole."

That had to be seen as at least a mild rebuke. Still, when everything was considered, the day had been a success. The following weeks, though, were not as kind to the lab. Some of the press, not taken by Microsoft's promises of goodwill and suspicious of its motives, reveled in the opportunity to fire salvos at Gates and company. One headline proclaimed, "The Wolf is Here." Another publication reported that Kai-Fu Lee had told his new hires, "You're lucky to work for Microsoft." And *Computer Life* quoted from *BusinessWeek*, where an American foe of Microsoft had said: "Microsoft is a big liar. They always say, 'We don't do this, we don't do that.' But later we found that they do everything."

Some other headlines and key phrases:

"Microsoft fought into China's Silicon Valley with huge investment"

"Zhongguancun in war flames again"

"What does Microsoft want to do in China?"

"'A technology enclosure movement' . . . also a 'talent enclosure movement'"

Over the next two weeks, Microsoft's public relations staff counted some fifty-six articles in the Chinese press about the lab. The vast majority were positive. But the harsh comments stung, and Lee grimaces remembering them. "Because journalism is new to China, there will be those five percent on the fringes trying to get attention, make a name for themselves. Probably my toughest time was reading those newspaper articles: with all the good things we're doing, why are they saying this about us?"

China was extremely complex. It did not escape Lee's attention that he had a lot of *guanxi* to build with government and university officials. When he went back to his office the day after the opening ceremony, he began writing personal notes to all the officials who had attended. To Lilan Zhu, of the Ministry of Science and Technology, he penned: "I truly believe that in the coming few years, we can show you the sincerity of Microsoft to open scientific research and we will not fail to meet your expectation of us." Similar notes went to vice president Chunli Bai of the Chinese Academy and, of course, to the friendly Yu Wei.

And although he might have been snubbed by information minister Jichuan Wu, Lee dared not forget him as well. He wrote, "Your wisdom and your understanding and mastery of the information industry greatly impressed us."

Maybe proving one's sincerity didn't mean you were always sincere.

3

From Beijing to Bill G.

November 1998–October 1999

That was the moment that people thought, "Okay, from now on, we mean business."

—KAI-FU LEE

One of Kai-Fu Lee's motives for inviting notable Chinese-speaking researchers from Microsoft headquarters to the opening ceremony, beyond lending weight to the event itself, was to put them on the ground in China, where they could help with recruiting and hiring. Lee was wooing Chinese natives like Harry Shum from the States—setting up interviews with potential recruits for when he returned to Redmond in a few weeks and in the meantime relying on Microsoft colleagues there to do some wining and dining in his absence. But to make serious headway in China, he had to couple a few returning, big-name veterans with local researchers from the nation's top universities. That's where the special guests really came in. Beginning just before the opening ceremony and continuing for nearly two weeks after it, remembers Hsiao-Wuen "Dark Side" Hon, "Kai-Fu put us on this incredible interview schedule."

Thanks to some early positive press coverage, coupled with Lee's previous visits to Chinese universities, the lab had received roughly

500 résumés by the time of the opening ceremony. As Lee had slogged through them, Rick Rashid had given him just one admonishment: whether it was bringing in Chinese from the U.S. or hiring new talent in China, Lee could not lower his standards, no matter how much difficulty he was having. "You cannot compromise," Rashid told Lee.

Now Lee's elite visitors were being asked to help him hold the line on quality. Recalling this critical period, Lee describes himself as confident but aware of pitfalls all around. China in many ways was his oyster, but contradictions abounded, both in terms of the country and Microsoft's image in it. On the positive side of the ledger, the country was producing more than 300 computer-science Ph.D.s a year. And that didn't count the literally tens of thousands of Chinese computer-science undergraduates, probably more than any nation on Earth, or the estimated 10,000 other talented individuals who returned to the country each year after studying abroad. Tapping into all this represented an incredible opportunity.

Another piece of good news was that Microsoft appeared to be ahead of the software development curve. Local competition for software talent was still at a minimum. The Chinese personal computer industry was led by Legend (later Lenovo), Beida Founder, and Tsinghua Tongfang. These companies had some success landing top graduates, mostly in computer hardware and engineering. But on the software side, there was quite simply no equivalent to Microsoft, not even a worthy rival. Case in point: in 1998, when Microsoft opened its Beijing lab, computer hardware sales in China rose more than 30 percent, while software sales *declined* by the same amount. Piracy, not legitimate business, seemed the main outlet for software talent. Relative to hardware sales, the software industry in China was a fraction the size of most other nations'—essentially nonexistent.

A few Western companies did offer some competition. Nortel had set up a telecommunications research center in 1994. The following year, IBM inaugurated its China Research Lab in Beijing. In information technology alone, Lucent, Fujitsu, Intel, NEC, Ericsson, and Hewlett-Packard had all launched small Chinese R&D arms by the time of the Microsoft lab's opening ceremony in November 1998. Many were even located in or near the Zhongguancun district. But, as Nathan Myhrvold had suspected, most did little more than advanced development. When it came to pursuing farther-out research horizons, publishing freely in academic journals, and taking part in worldwide academic collaborations, only IBM and the newly formed Intel lab loomed as formidable direct competitors—and neither planned to build an operation as big and intensely focused on software as Microsoft.

So much for the good news. While Bill Gates remained widely admired as a technology entrepreneur and self-made man, and Windows was by far the most popular operating system in China, many distrusted the Seattle juggernaut. Part of its image troubles stemmed from the aggressive marketing practices that dogged it everywhere. At the same time, while largely ignoring the other foreign research and development operations in the country, some Chinese papers seemed to single out the Microsoft lab for trying to "steal" local talent. "Because we're Microsoft, the first thing people ask is 'Why are you doing this?'" Rick Rashid later recalled. "One of the concerns the Chinese had was, is this some American company coming in to take the best minds from China and put them in a place where nobody ever hears from them again?"

Confounding the situation was that neither Microsoft nor personal computing in general was highly regarded in computer-science graduate schools, where the great professors of the day still focused on mainframes and supercomputing. As Nathan Myhrvold remembers, "Microsoft did not have a great rep in computer-science departments, because we had little pathetic PCs."

Lee dived into this maelstrom with gusto in the days around the opening ceremony, bolstered by his temporary reinforcements. Beginning two days before the event, and picking up again right after it, his team interviewed nearly 50 job candidates. In general, the students proved more open-minded than many press or government officials. Some seemed generally intrigued and wanted to check out the new lab, even if they didn't really understand what Microsoft meant by "research." Others had heard of Kai-Fu Lee and knew that at Microsoft, despite its controversial image, they had a chance to do work that would touch millions of people. A senior at Peking University was quoted as saying: "Of course it is a good thing for Microsoft to establish a research [lab] in China. I don't care whether it is imperialism or not. At least it has more advanced methodology and management skills."

Most of the interviews took place in the still-unfinished sixth-floor business office, where the odor of fresh paint permeated the air. An exception was made for interviews conducted by Hsiao-Wuen Hon, who had severely wrenched his back picking up a load of heavy computer equipment. "I could not even stand," he recalls. Lee had ordered a masseur and a chiropractor to Hon's hotel room to try to ease the pain. The chiropractor performed acupuncture and vacuum tube cupping—a traditional Chinese treatment for back pain that involves lighting small fires inside glass tubes to suck out all the air inside and then placing the heated tubes on the patient's back. The suction created by the vacuum is meant to improve circulation in the affected area and often leaves a person black and blue. Hon did several interviews over the phone, lying in bed during the procedures. Sometimes in the midst of the conversation, the acupuncture needles or vacuum tube cupping would strike a nerve and he would cry out in pain, "Ahhhh!"

"The student would hear and wonder, 'Did I say something wrong?'" Hon relates. After he put down the phone, Hon would scream again, to let the tension out of his back.

Lee also tapped his visitors for help with recruiting. He and George Chen, the jack-of-all-trades from Redmond who had taken the formal title of recruiting and university relations manager, had put together a list of the top ten universities around China. A local public relations company helped arrange visits. Not long after the opening ceremony, Lee dispatched his colleagues in two-person teams to visit the schools and "do some propaganda," as Harry Shum put it. There hadn't been time to mail the lab's new brochures, so the recruiters carried hundreds of them on the plane rides.

Only a year or so later, Beijing lab researchers would be greeted with open arms at the same schools. But those early days were tough slogging. To the Westernized Microsoft team, China was really a sleeping giant; even in many of the country's top computer-science schools, remembers Shum, "No one knew what Microsoft Research was."

Typically, when a speaker visits a Chinese university, he is hosted by a professor—introduced around and taken out to dinner as an honored guest. But the Microsoft group often got a cool reception. Just before the opening ceremony, executives Rick Rashid and Dan Ling visited Tsinghua University, along with Chen and X. D. Huang. "Nobody hosted!" says an amazed Chen, who was waiting for the others at the university. That's when Huang stepped in. Realizing that Chen was still unknown to Rashid, he quickly corralled his colleague to help correct the oversight out of a sense of honor. "I went out to be the host!" recalls Chen. " 'Welcome, Rick Rashid.' He didn't know I was from Microsoft; he thought I was from Tsinghua." The students were lukewarm, as well, Chen remembers. "News media gave them some bad impression of Microsoft. Only presidents or Bill Gates could make them excited."

Things weren't much different as Kai-Fu Lee's emissaries scattered across China right after the opening ceremony: everyone came back with stories to tell. When X. D. Huang and George Chen finished speaking at the National Defense University in the Hunan province city of Changsha, their host, a general, asked if they were hungry. When they answered eagerly in the affirmative, the general pointed down the street. "There are some restaurants there. Why don't you just go and get some food." Huang looked at him in shock, thinking: "Wow, I give a speech and I don't even get a dinner." He and Chen wandered around aimlessly for more than a half-hour, carrying all their presentation material and laptops, before they gave up and found a taxi to take them back to their hotel.

Harry Shum and Zicheng Liu got even shorter thrift at Nanjing University, where their "host" didn't even bother to introduce them to their audience. Recalls Shum, "I introduced Zicheng, and Zicheng introduced me. No one even pointed out the cafeteria. Fortunately, I knew it well, and we had some really wonderful food."

They came back recounting other types of adventures—or misadventures. Chen went off by himself to Wuhan University in Hubei province, near the center of the country. During the visit, he wanted to look up a woman doctoral student in artificial intelligence, Qian Zhang, who was destined to become one of the brightest young stars of the new research lab. Zhang was the only person from Wuhan to even send a résumé to Microsoft. Once in town, Chen telephoned and asked her to come to his hotel to take a brief written test. "She got scared—wondering why is this guy calling me to his hotel," Chen laughs. "I asked her to my room, gave her the paper, and said: 'Now I'll leave for one hour. You finish it.' I went out [in the hall] and found her boyfriend waiting out there." She had brought protection.

Their efforts all seemed worth it after a week on the road, when the recruiting teams met in commerce-conscious Shanghai and were greeted by packed auditoriums at Shanghai Jiaotong University and Fudan University. "People couldn't get in, it was so crowded," Chen says. Tech-savvy Shanghai was naturally more attuned to news about Microsoft than other parts of the country, including Beijing. It was nice to end on a high note.

In January, with the number of résumés coming into the lab surpassing 1,000, the pace of life picked up tremendously. By far the most critical change was the arrival of the first two bona fide researchers, both China-born superstars returning from the United States. One was Harry Shum, who had formalized his decision to join the lab. The other—the icing on Kai-Fu Lee's cake—was Ya-Qin (pronounced "Yah-chin") Zhang of Sarnoff Laboratories in Princeton, New Jersey.

Zhang had been a child prodigy, entering the University of Science and Technology of China, then the country's top school, at the age of twelve. He had never slowed down. After coming to the United States to earn his doctorate, he had joined Sarnoff, birthplace of modern television, and risen to head a world-class multimedia group doing work on image processing and communications. In 1997, at age thirty-one, he had been named the youngest fellow in the hundred-year history of the IEEE, the Institute of Electrical and Electronics Engineers, the top engineering and computer-science society in the United States. The next year, just before Kai-Fu Lee recruited him, Zhang had been named the IEEE's Young Engineer of the Year. A framed letter of congratulations from President Bill Clinton hung on his office wall.

Shum, for his part, had been a prodigy as well. Born and raised in Nanjing, he went to the Nanjing Institute of Technology (now called Southeast University) when he was thirteen, and then attended graduate school in electrical and electronic engineering at the University of Hong Kong. From there, he, too, had journeyed to the United States, earning his Ph.D. at Carnegie Mellon under Raj Reddy and Katsushi Ikeuchi, another pioneer in computer vision and robotics. After graduating in 1995, he turned down a faculty job at CMU to join a start-up called Real Space in Silicon Valley. By the time Shum signed on at Microsoft Research in Redmond the next year, his achievements in vision and graphics had earned him international recognition as a rising young star. One of Lee's hopes for the lab was, "Can we find ten more Harry Shums in China?"

Zhang and Shum had met each other a few times. In fact, Shum had helped wine and dine Zhang in Redmond after Kai-Fu Lee moved to Beijing. On one occasion, he and two other Microsoft researchers had taken Zhang out to dinner at a local Chinese restaurant not far from the Microsoft campus. It wasn't a very good restaurant, Shum relates, but the Microsoft group had been blown away by Zhang's personality and knowledge. "After we said goodbye," he remembers, "we all looked at each other and said: 'How could we find anyone better?'"

By pure coincidence, Zhang and Shum moved to Beijing on the same day—January 15, 1999—and shared a connecting flight out of Tokyo. They ran into each other at Narita airport and had instantly been struck by the excitement of their adventure. They found a sake bar and started drinking—carrying the party to the plane. As their voices grew louder, a Japanese government official sitting near them finally shouted in Chinese, "Will you guys shut up!"

The pair were put up in a two-bedroom apartment on the outskirts of Beijing, near Kai-Fu Lee's house. The next morning, Lee knocked on their door. "I'm going to fix you guys. Both you guys are going to take haircut. I will pay because you are going to see the reporters."

As the articles from that day's press conference showed, Zhang was arguably a bigger name even than Kai-Fu Lee. A's attract A's. George Chen had recently been on a recruiting trip to Shanghai Jiaotong University, touting plans to build a world-class lab in computer science and mentioning multimedia as one potential area. As one skeptical student had told him, "The best scientist in the field is Ya-Qin Zhang. If you can get him, then you will be the best lab." Chen knew Zhang was coming, but it had not been formally announced, so he bit his tongue. But with the veil of silence lifted, Zhang instantly gave the lab greater credibility, both in China and among Chinese in the United States. He became a magnet for talent from around the world.

Immediately, Lee named multimedia a core focus of the lab, expanding the original charter, which focused on Chinese language processing and next-generation speech interfaces. Ya-Qin Zhang didn't know it then, but he had also advanced Microsoft on a path to applying multimedia to cell phones and other mobile devices—soon to become a separate business division and important growth area for Microsoft. Within a few years, he would be back in Redmond, running the effort.

With the arrival of Zhang and Shum, Lee had the critical mass to form a viable interview committee. He had waited until more help arrived to sort though the latest pile of résumés pouring into the lab. "So many résumés, we couldn't handle them," says George Chen. In January, Lee worked out the first standardized written exam to help winnow the field. Far more comprehensive than the one given to Qian Zhang in Wuhan, it took roughly two hours to complete.

———

Largely based on the test, about 100 people were selected for the next round of interviews. Almost every day for two months, a procession of nervous young faces arrived at the Sigma building—at least four or five, but sometimes as many as twenty. For a short while, all the interviews continued to take place on the sixth floor. In early February, though, the lab moved into its own space on the fifth story, taking up half the floor. This would be its base for years, even as the facility grew rapidly, eventually taking up the entire floor and sprawling to other parts of the building.

The new digs were as professional and fully equipped as any Western computer laboratory, with conference rooms, library, kitchen stocked with free sodas, juices, tea, and coffee, and all the hardware and software a researcher could desire. Lee also created a series of interactive tea and coffee tables in the lounge area; a white board formed the main surface of each table, with slots cut in the wood around the tables' edges to hold Magic Markers. That way, researchers coming together on breaks could scribble notes or diagrams on the tables themselves to preserve their ideas should a chance conversation spark a key insight. Unlike in Redmond, though, where all Microsoft researchers, no matter how junior, had their own offices with outdoor views, in China such egalitarianism was unthinkable. Most of the researchers got semiprivate cubicles. Only research managers and senior management rated their own offices. Lee himself had a luxurious suite, with a huge curved wooden desk and small meeting table in one room and an adjoining private conference room—far nicer than even Rick Rashid's space back home. All in all, it was a splendid place to impress new recruits.

The interview process, though, was grueling for candidates and interviewers alike. Each applicant was questioned by as many as eight Microsoft staff in a series of hour-long sessions. Hirees described a sinking feeling when they saw their schedule for the day: one interview after another, including during the lunch hour. For the Microsoft managers, it felt like they never had time to do any research, just meet and greet job hunters.

Interviews were conducted in Mandarin, but sometimes the managers would check out a candidate's English. Mostly they asked standard questions about background, areas of expertise, and future ambitions. But Kai-Fu Lee was looking for more than standout students. He wanted creativity, self-confidence, and team spirit—and that sincerity he valued so much. To get at these intangibles, the Microsoft group developed some special questions. Among the favorites:

Why are manhole covers round?

Please estimate how many gas stations are in Beijing.

What if you had a different opinion from your teacher?

If I gave you a very difficult question, how would you solve it?

Please evaluate the user interface in Microsoft's elevator.

There are two irregular ropes. Each takes one hour to burn. Please burn the two ropes in exactly 45 minutes.

As Lee summed up, "These questions don't necessarily have correct answers, but we can use them to gain an understanding of how someone thinks and how original that thinking is." For example, one examinee breezed through all but the third question. Here, he told his interviewer a tale of woe and frustration about his advisor—how the instructor had failed to properly utilize his talent. He didn't make the cut.

The burning-rope question was designed to test one's ability to think out of the box. It became so famous that candidates posted it on a Tsinghua University Web site. The problem actually had several solutions:* what was most interesting to the Microsoft managers was *how* the candidate approached the problem, so they didn't really care

---

* One solution would be to light both ends of one rope and one end of the other. When the two flames on the first rope meet, 30 minutes will have elapsed. At that moment, light the free end of the second rope. When the two flames on the second rope meet, 15 more minutes will have elapsed, marking a total of 45 minutes used to burn both ropes.

if people came forewarned. Harry Shum had his own favorite question: "Why did you choose your Ph.D. topic?" If a candidate said their advisor had dictated the subject—and many of them did say that—he or she got low marks from Shum.

As an interviewee navigated this potential minefield of questions, Lee set up a formal process behind the scenes. He wrote it up in a memo to the lab: "After each staff member conducts an interview, he or she will send e-mail to the next interviewer regarding his or her opinions, decision (must hire, should hire, could hire, weak hire, or don't hire), information about what areas he or she has already thoroughly covered, plus recommendations as to what directions the next person might want to explore." As time went on, a kind of shorthand evolved, where candidates were ranked on a scale of 1 to 5, with the higher number corresponding to "must hire" and the lower to "don't hire."

Of the 100 people interviewed early in 1999, the lab made about 20 offers; almost everyone accepted and would start after school finished in June. Indeed, some of the lab's biggest stars came from those first rounds of interviews.

One was Qian Zhang, the woman from Wuhan University who had been hesitant to visit George Chen's hotel room. She had done very well on the written test, and so a more extensive phone interview was set up. She was incredibly nervous. "This was the first time I received such an interview," Zhang recalls. To prepare, she adds, "I locked myself in my small room and was very serious in there." The interview, it turned out, was far more casual than she had imagined. But soon thereafter, the Wuhan student was asked to Beijing for the daylong interviews, and she ran the gamut of six successive hourlong meetings with the lab's hierarchy. "You just get exhausted," Zhang says. Still, she was excited about the prospect of working at the lab. "I had this feeling that they are really great people, and I could learn a lot of great things from them."

Lee's adage—and it was really the charge from Rick Rashid—was not to risk lowering the lab's standards by taking an ambiguous choice. So, usually a split decision from the interview committee ended without an offer being extended. But the Wuhan coed, the first woman interviewed, proved a rare exception. "Two people gave her 5's, two gave her a 1," remembers Ya-Qin Zhang, no relation to Qian. "I gave her 5, and Kai-Fu gave her 5."

That was enough for Lee, who soon made her an offer. By then, Qian Zhang had mastered the interview process and had fielded offers from Bell Labs and IBM, both of which had labs in Beijing. Concluding Microsoft was more of a classic research center, she joined Zhang's multimedia and Internet group. Later, she became the manager of an important wireless networking project for cell phones. "She was a great hire," says Ya-Qin Zhang.

Another star-to-be was Jian Wang. A studious sort with an infectious smile to whom people instantly warmed, Wang had been born and schooled in the garden city of Hangzhou, about 100 miles southwest of Shanghai—"from kindergarten to Ph.D.," as he put it. He had received his doctorate in an unusual field—engineering psychology—for which he had to specially petition the Ministry of Education. "The first one and probably the last one to get an engineering Ph.D. in psychology," was how he described himself. But he had built on that core to become an expert in human-computer interfaces, specializing in virtual reality and 3-D graphics. As the Beijing lab was being formed, Wang was a professor at Hangzhou University, one of four previously separate schools that united later in 1998 to form Zhejiang University, the largest college in China. Wang had been the youngest person ever to chair the psychology department.

Wang was pondering a career crossroads. He felt tired of university politics, and also wanted a change of research horizons. He had determined that the virtual reality interfaces he had been pursuing were at least another decade away from becoming practical. Kai-Fu Lee had sent him an e-mail before the opening ceremony, but he had ignored it. "I didn't know Kai-Fu. I didn't even know what is Microsoft in China." Lee telephoned to follow up, again inviting Wang to the ceremony, but Wang demurred (he later found out that an everhopeful Lee had nevertheless reserved a chair for him at the event). Reading a newspaper article recounting the ceremony, though, he grew more intrigued. Then Lee sent him another e-mail—this time saying if Wang didn't want to join the lab, perhaps he would consider a collaboration. "So I said, Okay, I would be happy to meet you," Wang remembers.

Wang visited the Sigma Center on his next trip to Beijing. It was late 1998, before Harry Shum and Ya-Qin Zhang had arrived. He and Lee had a great chat that lasted for almost an hour. The next day, rather than a typical collaboration, Wang proposed that he spend a few months at the Microsoft lab, to get the lay of the land. "I'm the first visiting researcher in this organization, so I'm very proud of that," he says. Wang made the move that March, on a six-month leave from the university. He never went back.

Three additional prize recruits—two living in the U.S.—solidified the new lab's standing. First came Changning Huang, a professor at Tsinghua University and China's number one expert in language processing. Huang was sixty-three years old, a revered figure. Lee remembers asking him, "Professor Huang, what should we call you?"

"Well, if you call me Professor Huang, that's too formal, not like Microsoft," Huang replied. Calling him by his given Chinese name was also out—it would be unspeakably rude to call someone so senior by his first name. But Huang noted that when he had become a Christian, he had taken a second first name, Tom. "Call me Tom," he said.

Another coup was landing HongJiang Zhang, no relation to Ya-Qin. He was a notable figure in information processing who had probably come the most circuitous route to get back to his birthplace—with stints studying and working in Denmark, Singapore, and the United States. He had spent the last several years at Hewlett-Packard Labs in Palo Alto, and in addition to his standout research had become skilled at bringing lab advances into products. Ya-Qin had tried to get him to come to Sarnoff as a department head, "but he was too expensive." Beijing, though, was another story. HongJiang's mother, still in China, had recently suffered a heart attack: he wanted to be closer to her. So he flew out for an interview that spring, arriving in the middle of a sandstorm. HongJiang had not wanted word to get out at HP that he was job-hunting, but he ran into a colleague on the flight. To make matters worse, when he got off the plane, there was a driver holding a sign that read: "Microsoft: HongJiang Zhang." He started that April.

On his heels came multimedia and image compression expert Jin Li, who had gotten his bachelor's, master's, and doctorate degrees at Tsinghua University, all with honors. Li, immersed in postdoctoral studies in integrated media and mathematics at the University of Southern California, was Ya-Qin Zhang's first hands-on recruit. Zhang flew back to the States that February to attend an information-processing conference in San Jose, which he knew Li was also attending. There, Zhang targeted the brilliant up-and-comer, offering him a job with no formal interview process.

Li was renowned around China. As a schoolboy in early 1984, he had been a computer prodigy. Chinese leader Deng Xiaoping visited a Shanghai science fair where Li's school computer club had an exhibit. He placed his hand on Li's head, proclaiming how such brilliant youth were the future of China, and that computer education should begin with children. The scene had been captured by a photographer and turned into a poster that went up around the country, in a massive campaign to boost science and technology education. Tens of millions of Chinese knew the poster—and Li—as "Deng touched my head."

The initial recruiting thrust, coupled with efforts to forge good relationships with Chinese universities, dominated the lab's agenda well into the new year. "To be honest, for the first six months we didn't do any real research," remembers Lee. "The most important thing we needed to do was establish credibility." Meaning, build a world-class staff. It wasn't until late spring of 1999 that Lee began to shape and define the direction of the research his lab would undertake. "The research we engage in today should be in areas that will have become mainstream five years from now," he told his small but energized group. Later, Lee put it this way: "I tried to think of each day as not what can I do this day, but what's the five-year impact? Sure, we could hire super thinkers and have them think great thoughts, but that wouldn't accomplish the long-term goal." Lee promised Rick Rashid he would stay in Beijing at least five years—to see the fruits of that original work make it into Microsoft products.

This was the heyday of the Internet. Back in the States, dot-coms had shot out of the cannon, spouting buzz phrases and promises about the new economy, e-commerce, and pervasive computing, where everything and everyone would be interconnected 24/7. Some of the start-ups went public and soared to incredible valuations that were at least temporarily on a par with mainstays like IBM or General Electric or Microsoft. Everyone knew people less talented than themselves who had become stinking rich.

Almost everybody in information technology bought into the hype to some degree. This held true for Lee as well. Still, in looking back over his musings at the time about the future of computing, he shows a remarkably level-headed and prescient view of what the next five years would bring. Every few months Lee would issue reports or overviews, in English and Chinese, that laid out his thinking for the staff. One, delivered in the spring of 1999, was entitled "The Direction of Our Research."

Lee got the growth of the Internet pretty much right. "Five years from now," he wrote, "the Internet will be ubiquitous. There will be multitudes of users, a vast array of Web pages, abundant bandwidth, and a rich selection of intelligent appliances . . . Text, images, speech, video, and other forms of information delivery that do not exist today will be accessible on the Web at any time. New forms of information might include lectures, programs, meetings, the locations (GPS) of each individual in the network, and a complete record of each person's and company's activities. For the first time in history, a complete portrait of contemporary life will be available, on the Web."

He was mostly on target as well about the PC of the future. He correctly predicted 1-gigabyte-per-second wired connections to the Internet and 10-megabyte wireless links. Personal computers, he foresaw, would boast a gigabyte or so of random-access memory and a 50-gigabyte hard drive. Lee also forecast an explosion in "so-called 'intelligent appliances'" such as smart cell phones and PDAs, even if he was overoptimistic in adding electronic books to his list. This trend would result, he asserted, in a vast array of wired and wireless devices and networks operating at different speeds and with varying stability that somehow had to be seamlessly connected and supported by the same applications across the board.

Perhaps his biggest miscalculations concerned TV, since he seemed to buy straight into the "interactivity" hoopla of the times. "In the future, a television might be able to recommend programs that its owner would like. People also want a television to be more like a computer in that a computer is something people use interactively rather than just watching passively. For instance, a television user might place himself or herself into the plot of a movie or browse in a marketplace filled with eye-catching products." Lee also turned out to be overly optimistic about progress in his own field, speech, which he asserted would bring about the demise of the PC's desktop user interface. "The greatly expanded hard disk and data capacity of tomorrow's computers will render the current system of menu commands and lists obsolete . . ." he wrote. "Users will require a more natural and more intelligent user interface . . . Out of all of the kinds of human communication, speech requires the least special training and is the most direct."

He was most prescient about the importance of search technology. "Because the information on the Web is vast and unstructured, searching is extremely difficult. Another problem is that most of the information on the Web today is English-language text, but in five years there will be materials in many more languages and much more multimedia on the Web. There will also be many more users and much larger hard disks. These factors will contribute to a more than 100-fold projected increase of information on the Web. If things continue in this direction, five years from now a simple search will be even more frustrating and confusing than it is now."

All in all, it proved an impressive forecast. But more important than any specific prediction was Lee's focus on speech interfaces, natural language processing, and multimedia, including search. He correctly intuited that these three areas would form the basis for much of Microsoft's plans for growth in the years ahead. And it was in these fields that he concentrated his resources.

Lee planned to personally direct the speech work, long his area of expertise. "Our goal is to develop new technologies that will enable people to 'talk' to their machines more naturally and in a greater variety of ways, so that using a computer will be similar to conversing with another person . . ." he wrote. "We plan to research speech technologies, with a particular stress on improving speech technology in ways that will make it better suited to Chinese."

Related to this was natural language processing, which focused on inputting and understanding text. The goal here was to bring together linguistics, information theory, probability theory, and statistical methodologies "that will enable Chinese users to use Chinese computers with the same ease and convenience that Americans use English-language computers." Lee put "Tom" Huang in charge of that work.

Next-generation multimedia, not even contemplated until Ya-Qin Zhang, HongJiang Zhang, and Harry Shum showed up, now formed the biggest area of research. Lee divided it between his three stars.

What was called Internet multimedia became the domain of Ya-Qin Zhang. His challenge was to find new ways to compress and stream multimedia content—video, music, voice, graphics—over the Internet on both wired and wireless networks. Among other things, Lee predicted that this field would spawn high-quality videoconferencing, ubiquitous wireless television, and 3-D interactive electronic shopping.

The formidable problem of unstructured data—how to order and present the chaotic array of information on the Web so that it could be readily searched and organized—fell to HongJiang Zhang. Harry Shum, meanwhile, turned his expertise in computer vision and graphics to produce new algorithms for automatic and rapid synthesis of graphic environments, characters, and animations that it was hoped would spark a revolution in games and a host of other areas. Predicted Lee: "Ten years from now, these results may have radically transformed e-commerce (where customers may enter a virtual store and try on clothing), and interpersonal communications (where users may participate in meetings or meet with friends by way of a virtual self in a virtual environment). The entire human-computer interface may even become three-dimensional."

A sense of urgency pervaded this early work. Even though Microsoft was taking the long view, Lee felt that the lab needed to move quickly to prove the company's planned $80 million investment in China was worth it. That spring, he told his charges to put together some cool demos showing off their research. "These demos were built on very little technology," he now acknowledges. "We basically said for the next six months, half the lab was going to focus on a couple of 'instant gratification' projects." This would help attract publicity in China—and hopefully generate excitement in Redmond. Even then, he wasn't just thinking of other research colleagues or his bosses Dan Ling and Rick Rashid—he meant Bill Gates himself.

Surveying the Microsoft headquarters campus, Kai-Fu Lee had to admit it: he was nervous. At a recent all-company meeting, Bill Gates had generously praised the China lab to 30,000 Microsoft employees, saying: "We've opened a research center in Beijing, and their research is off to a great start." Now, in mid-October 1999, still less than a year since the lab had opened, Lee and his core researchers had been invited to Redmond to showcase their first demos for the Microsoft chairman and offer solid proof that his statement wasn't far off the mark. It was an honor to be asked to present before Gates, for which Lee was truly grateful. But talk about pressure. Talk about a rush.

The sessions were a tried-and-true Research tradition. Gates was known for his passion for new technology, and a few times a year he loved to check in and see some of the most promising projects from the various labs. A select team of researchers, accompanied by Nathan Myhrvold, Rick Rashid, and Dan Ling, would brief Gates on Research issues and run through some demos. Gates would watch carefully and ask questions—sometimes lots of questions. Everyone called them "Bill G. Reviews."

The Beijing contingent had been going full throttle on the demos for months, almost since springtime, when Lee had decided to build them in the first place. They had brainstormed a list of possible projects to highlight, and narrowed it down from there. Says Lee, "We came up with three or four such things, some of which we thought might stand up to a Bill G. review."

At the top of the list was a demo showing a new interface for inputting Chinese characters into a computer. The current state of the art was to type what you wanted to say phonetically, in Pinyin. Then software would make a best guess—from a limited "vocabulary"—about what Chinese characters they likely represented and convert them to Chinese. For instance, typing in "Kai-Fu Lee" would be translated into three Chinese characters: "Kai," "Fu," and "Lee." The problem was, there was lots of room for error. "Lee" alone could be represented by four or five different characters. The framework for this effort had been proposed by X. D. Huang before Lee even joined the company. Lee's team had adopted the idea, taking existing English "speech language models"—mathematical representations of common word orders, grammar, and so forth—and training them extensively on Chinese. Lee's background in speech recognition helped a lot. "It was pretty obvious we would get a huge jump in conversion accuracy," he says. That's because the language models worked by examining the context of what a person was saying and then employing statistical algorithms to predict the most likely next words.

To ensure the greatest possible accuracy, they needed to train the system on a vast corpus of Chinese-language text: the more real-life wordings the system saw, the better its predictions of what was coming next. So, they dispatched staff members to purchase Chinese newspaper data, mainly from the *People's Daily*. "They were delighted to sell us CD-ROMs for thousands of U.S. dollars," laughs Lee. At the same time, Lee rounded up some smart student interns and detailed them to write code for statistical language models. This was a relatively simple job, because the mathematical framework already existed for other languages; they would need only to plug in the rules of Chinese grammar, which were straightforward. They then trained those models on the newspaper copy, letting the system digest the ebb and flow of Chinese sentences until it could predict which words, or characters, generally followed from others. Lee calls it "instant research." It wasn't really research—there was no scientific investigation, just hard labor. But within three months, he says, "we had a system that was working much better than any implement you could find on the market. So we prepared that as the primary thing to show Bill."

The system only handled written text. But with a text model in hand, Lee decided, he might as well show a speech recognizer as well, since that would work on the same principles. For help, he sought out X. D. Huang, who was leading Microsoft's speech recognition and language processing research. In fact, he had built Microsoft's technology partly based on Lee's doctoral thesis. The system only dealt with English speech recognition, as Microsoft scrambled to catch up with IBM's ViaVoice dictation software and others on the market— but Lee still remembered the code. Give us a recognizer, and we'll make it work for Chinese, he told Huang. The system the Beijing crew put together was crude; it didn't understand subtle Chinese tones very well, so they left that part out (the way Mandarin teachers sometimes tell beginners to stop worrying about tones). But with Lee and a half-dozen colleagues working on it for three solid months, they successfully retrained the core system to handle basic Mandarin. That demo was also earmarked for Gates.

For a third demo, they videotaped several staff members and built a crude interactive system where if you clicked on someone in a still image, he or she began to move around and talk: in one scene, researcher Jin Li flew through the air on a magic carpet after his image was clicked.

"You should see that demo, it's so flimsy!" says Lee. "It's kind of cool for people who don't get it. But from a technology point of view, anyone working on [next-generation video coding standard] MPEG4 would say, Why are you showing this? We didn't show Bill. We wouldn't dare do that." Instead, they reserved it for the Chinese press. Laughs Lee, "They thought, that's so cool."

In the weeks leading up to the review, the staff had flown into even higher gear in an all-out attempt to vanquish the last bugs from the demos. But two days before their flight to Seattle, the text conversion demo—the prime exhibit—still wasn't working right. Jian Wang, the interface guru with a degree in engineering psychology, headed the effort. His small team was pulling all-nighters, eating meals in the lab, to get it done. The group kept on working, even as Wang left with Lee and a few others to check in at the Beijing airport. Just before they were about to board, a student ran up and handed over a CD with the debugged software.

A small group made the trip across the Pacific. Besides Lee and Wang, five other Beijing lab members were on the flight: Ya-Qin Zhang, already named assistant director; Harry Shum; HongJiang Zhang; Xiaoning Ling; and Frank Yang, a computer support specialist. They connected through Tokyo and billeted in a three-bedroom apartment Lee had rented in Redmond, five minutes from the Microsoft campus. He would later keep the apartment there year-round to save money on hotel costs for the constant flow of researchers visiting Redmond.

The Beijing team had an hour for its presentation. Lee himself had spent most of the National Day holiday (China celebrates its government's October 1 birthday in a weeklong series of events) drafting his report. His only break came in attending October 1 celebrations. He had made many calls to Ling and Rashid and other Bill G. review veterans for some tips. His list of To-Dos:

- When talking about a particular project, explain the challenges this project faces and its importance to Microsoft.
- Describe in detail what is innovative about our work. (Unlike most company CEOs, Bill understands almost all technical details. Of course, you can't go into too much detail, because Bill's time is much too valuable.)
- As much as possible, be prepared to answer the tough questions Bill will ask.
- Bill's knowledge is very broad, so you won't be able to get away with ambiguous statements.

Armed with a wealth of supporting materials—backgrounder briefs, newspaper articles and commentaries, a list of published research papers—Lee had broken his presentation into two major components. First, he would provide an overview on MSR China and its progress. Then would come the demos.

On October 17, the night before the review, team members were still practicing the presentation in their rooms. The next morning everyone gathered in a large conference room next to Gates's office. In those days, the chairman worked out of Building 8, a two-story wood-trimmed structure in the center of the Microsoft campus, across from the long quad and the little pond known as Lake Bill. Besides Gates, they would be presenting before Myhrvold, Rashid, Ling, and a handful of other Microsoft officials, including Craig Mundie, a senior vice president then in charge of all consumer electronics. The principal actors found places at the main table; the others sat in chairs along the walls.

The Beijing crew's nerves were on fire. Says Lee, "This was the first time anyone showed Bill research that was done in six months! Usually it's three to five years. They were in awe. They couldn't believe it. When they went into computer science as undergrads, they thought they'd probably be a programmer in some state-owned enterprise, and now they're in the room with Bill Gates."

Gates was in fine form. He greeted everyone cheerfully and gave the visitors positive feedback throughout. Lee began with his overview of the lab, detailing the opening ceremony and the top researchers he had hired, including those in the room. He also laid out his "6 P" strategy for the lab: people, programs, publications, patents, prototypes, and product impact. (In Mandarin, the sound "pee" is the word for "fart"—so lab members joked about Lee's "six farts" presentation; Gates was oblivious to this.) The lab, he reported, had already published 28 articles in international journals, presented 11 featured talks at international and domestic conferences, and was preparing 49 patent applications.

His focus on people impressed Gates. The Microsoft chairman beamed over the story of Jin Li and "Deng touched my head," for which Lee even trotted out the famous poster. Gates, in turn, impressed his visitors with his knowledge of China and the requirement for *hukous,* or residency permits, before anyone could move to Beijing from another city. Says Lee, "He asked, 'When you hired these people, didn't they have residency problems?' He knew you have to get approval to move from city to city, to avoid Beijing being overrun with immigrants. I told him of the tremendous changes that have been sweeping the country over the past few years. Only a decade ago, it was nearly impossible for people who wanted to change jobs to do so. But now, under the reforms, people's needs to realize their potential come first."

Gates also asked how Lee was balancing his recruitment of top Chinese computer scientists—including some professors like Jian Wang—with the need to maintain good relations with local universities. In response, Lee detailed his strategy: "As I told him, the great majority of our hires are very young and full of potential," he once remembered. "For them to be able to stay in China and conduct basic research is something that most everyone wants to see happen. I explained that we have never tried to actively recruit the most valuable people from top-level universities or from other research institutes; but if such people take the initiative and apply to us for positions, we will take their applications as seriously as we do all others." Lee also took Gates's question as an opportunity to talk about some of the research collaborations he had started with Chinese universities, and a few projects he had helped fund in conjunction with the National Natural Science Foundation of China.

Throughout the overview, the Microsoft chairman took copious notes, often making comments to Rick Rashid and others in the room, or asking Lee follow-up questions. As Lee summarizes, "He asked me in particular about the state of information sharing and collaboration between MSR in Beijing and in Redmond, while especially emphasizing that the headquarters in America needed to take full advantage of the Beijing research center's superiority in talented multimedia researchers and also had to find ways to overcome the difficulties posed by the physical distance. He also expressed the hope that through the efforts of its superior multimedia talent, Beijing could make breakthroughs in multimedia for the whole company."

Finally, it was time for the demos. As Lee and Wang prepared to put the Chinese text-processing technology through its paces, Lee was surprised to discover that Gates already understood the basics of both Pinyin and the rival *wuhua* (five-stroke) inputting methods—and why it was still excruciatingly slow to input English spellings and wait for the corresponding Chinese characters to appear.

"A billion minutes is wasted in China each year from slow timing of these systems," Lee summarized.

At which point Gates interrupted, cracking everybody up with: "Hey that's even more time than waiting for Windows to start up!"

Gates couldn't read Chinese characters, of course. So they had rigged the demo to highlight every character that was incorrectly translated in red. The demo took Chinese newspaper text, converted it to Pinyin, translated it back to Chinese characters, and then compared that to the original newspaper article to see how many mistakes there were. Three existing products were stacked against the lab creation. The commercial systems came back all full of red, while the Beijing lab system proved almost error-free. An impressed Gates especially liked the neat user interface Jian Wang had invented to correct the errors. It consisted of a small wheel that appeared on the screen, with alternate characters (for example, the many alternatives for "Lee") spaced around the wheel. Users could simply scroll around the wheel to select the correct character, a vast improvement over other systems that required users to hunt laboriously through long lists of possibilities.

To avoid making errors in the first place, the system relied on a proprietary search algorithm modeled on machine learning techniques. As the user typed in a Pinyin phonetic spelling, it labored behind the scenes to make sure the spelling was correct—automatically correcting any phonetic spellings that seemed to call up the wrong character. When told of this, Gates immediately saw broader implications.

"Why can't we use this Pinyin technology to search databases and set up a model for correcting [English] typing errors?" he queried Lee.

Lee was astonished. As he once related, "As a matter of fact, this very method was precisely the new algorithm that I was going to discuss on the next page of my outline! Because this part of the report touched on many technical and product-related problems, Bill and I spent a long time discussing it." The core technology would later be introduced in Microsoft Office 2003.

The speech recognition demo went smoothly as well. In the midst of all this, Lee chewed up his entire hour-long slot. Rashid asked Gates whether they should wrap it up, but Gates declined, opting to use some of his lunchtime to hear more. Lee took the opportunity to discuss speech as a revolutionary replacement for the user interface of computers and information appliances—something he was glad to hear Gates agree with wholeheartedly. Gates also stressed his understanding that such a transformation took time, and made it clear that Microsoft was willing to support years of research to make it happen.

When the Bill G. review finally finished, Gates was effusive. "Super-impressive. That's really amazing, and you guys just started. Super!" The Beijing team then corralled everyone present, including Gates, and took two pictures to commemorate the scene. As Lee was leaving the room, Gates said to him warmly: "It must be the greatest thing to bring in so many outstanding researchers and get to work with them." Lee felt deeply proud.

Afterward, Lee took his team out to dinner at a local Chinese restaurant. Later, back at the apartment complex, he brought out Cuban cigars to celebrate: the cigars became a ritual after every Bill G. session.

"That review was probably one of the defining moments of this lab," Shum relates. "People realized that those guys in Beijing can really do something."

Agrees Lee, "That was the moment that people thought, 'Okay, from now on, we mean business.'"

4

Microsoft's Chinese Heart

November 1999–August 2000

> *Mountains and rivers only appeared in dreams,*
> *I haven't been to my homeland for many years,*
> *But whatever happened, my Chinese heart would*
> *never change.*
>
> —"MY CHINESE HEART,"
> TRADITIONAL CHINESE BALLAD

The success of the Bill G. review blew wind into the Beijing lab's sails. By the first anniversary, barely two weeks after the Redmond trip, the rapidly swelling Microsoft Research China counted 58 employees. A palpable feeling of excitement and a growing confidence charged the atmosphere. Remembers Harry Shum, "By the first-year anniversary I think we started to realize that we can actually do something great."

A birthday party was in order. Lee rented out the China Club, a legendary dining and meeting space with ancient Chinese architecture in the heart of Beijing, near Tiananmen Square. The Sichuan restaurant perched in one corner of the classic Chinese Quadrangle was rumored to have been Deng Xiaoping's favorite; the former leader had entertained many state visitors in its confines, where the attentive staff scurried to keep every glass full and changed silverware with each dish served. The space had since been purchased by a Hong Kong businessman and turned into an exclusive private club, and the service remained impeccable.

Sheila Shang, the lab's dynamic public relations director, planned the event. Shang had started out on loan from the business office to help orchestrate the opening ceremony but had soon asked to switch over full-time, volunteering for what seemed like a demotion. But with her standout people skills, friendly shrewdness, and excellent English, she had become indispensable, turning her new position into an asset. Kai-Fu Lee called her "a gift from the Gods."

For the party, Shang explains, "We wanted to do everything very creative. We wanted something new and fresh, where people had never been." The China Club, with its famous restaurant and beautiful courtyard decorated with fresh flowers, ancient red pillars, and traditional Chinese lanterns, exuded the feeling of old Beijing—"the sense of China," as Shang puts it.

The party was held on November 5, exactly one year after the opening ceremony. Unlike the first ceremony, no media were invited. But a host of dignitaries from government and academia brought the attendance to nearly 200. "This was really a relationship-building event," says Shang. "To show our grateful feeling, to celebrate our achievement and say thanks to everyone."

After a multicourse sit-down dinner, served by waiters and waitresses in classic Chinese dress and featuring Peking duck, Sichuan spicy shrimp, and lots of wine, the entertainment started. In addition to a Chinese opera and traditional dance troupe, Shang had brought in Kun Jiang, a popular television entertainer who specialized in the humorous performance art style known as *xiang sheng*. Jiang had started one of the first personalized Web sites in China and had become a friend of the lab when he visited to learn more about computing. Everyone at Microsoft Research China, and millions around the country, worshipped him.

The most formal part of the evening was Kai-Fu Lee's presentation. He was throwing a party, not speaking at a conference, so he had vowed "no bullet points." Instead, he showed photos of the opening ceremony and the noted researchers and dignitaries who had come through in the last twelve months. It was a Year in the Life presentation, depicting the lab's progression from an unknown upstart to a world-class research center—or at the least the makings of one.

Lee was still pumped up about the Bill G. review and launched into a vivid description of the visit, complete with a screen shot of the speech recognition interface they had demonstrated for the chairman. He also talked excitedly about the lab's famed recruits, especially those like Harry Shum, HongJiang Zhang, and Ya-Qin Zhang who had come back to help both Microsoft and China. To reinforce the point, he introduced several brand-new hires. One was Baining Guo, a well-known graphics expert whom Shum had lured away from Intel. Guo had gone to Redmond for his employee orientation only a few days earlier and would have stayed another week in the United States, but Lee had pushed him to make it to the party. "They really wanted me there, to show overseas returnees," Guo recalls.

During his presentation, Lee was asked to describe what he liked most about coming to Beijing. His response: "In the last twelve months, I had the opportunity to work with the most excellent people in the world. This made me happiest."

If his words seemed overly sentimental to some, even more blatant heartstring pulling lay ahead. Toward the end of the evening, Shang gathered a group of lab staff members who had agreed beforehand to come on stage to sing "My Chinese Heart," a traditional song about what it means to be Chinese.

> *Mountains and rivers only appeared in dreams,*
> *I haven't been to my homeland for many years,*
> *But whatever happened, my Chinese heart*
> *would never change.*
> *Yangzi River, Great Wall, Huangshan*
> *Mountain, and Huang River,*
> *They mean a lot to me,*
> *No matter when, no matter where,*
> *My heart belongs to China.*
> *The blood flowing in my heart*
> *Echoes with Chinese pulses . . .*

Some of the veteran professors in the audience were moved almost to tears, and most of the audience applauded warmly, but someone must have been offended. Even though no press had been invited, a very accurate description of the event—and the song—appeared a few days later in *Science Times*. The article intimated that Microsoft had gone too far by pretending to be Chinese itself. The headline read roughly: "Microsoft sings aloud about Chinese heart." It doesn't sound bad in English. But in Mandarin, explains Shang, it came across as sarcastic—and condemnatory. Lab members, especially Lee, were stung by the criticism. The silver lining in the cloud was that the rest of the article generally praised the lab for its first-year accomplishments.

As Lee had known going in, pitfalls lurked everywhere. It was too bad an anniversary party had proved to hold another one. Still, a little controversy wasn't going to slow things down for the Microsoft team. When Lee had described the Bill G. review for the partygoers, he had presented a blowup image of Gates, over which he superimposed a gigantic thumb pointing skyward—symbolizing the chairman's endorsement of the lab. A speech balloon coming out of Gates's mouth read: "Super. Super."

The party served as a nice respite from the long hours and whirlwind days everyone had been putting in. But all the recent good news only seemed to reinforce the idea that much needed to be done—and no one let up. Many staff members ate and occasionally even slept in the lab. For Xiaoning Ling, who had worked for Bill Gates's privately owned company and helped build the Microsoft founder's house, it reminded him of life in a start-up. "Everybody worked very, very hard. Everybody was very passionate. Day and night—it was very much like a family. Everybody worked together, ate together, had fun together."

Amidst the group meals and all-out pace, the lab also developed a split personality not found in Microsoft's other research centers. In ancient Chinese philosophy and metaphysics, yin and yang are complementary but opposing forces. Fittingly, when examining the lab's efforts, it's easy to describe a yin-yang balance to its affairs. The yin, which can represent inward focus, lay in shaping a research agenda and blazing new horizons in computer science that would ultimately help Microsoft. The outward-facing, more extroverted side of the lab—its yang—concentrated on building relations with Chinese universities and both national and local governments, with an eye to strengthening collaborations, recruiting researchers, and building the trust the lab would need to become a successful, world-class research facility. Both efforts existed in parallel, and to a degree all Microsoft labs had this dual aspect to their existence. But far more outreach was needed in China than in other venues. Lee had made a big initial push on establishing outward ties for months after the lab was formed, then concentrated more on developing the first demos and prototypes to show Bill Gates and Microsoft's business groups. Beginning after the Bill G. review and continuing into his second year, he again put more weight on recruiting and enhancing relations with Chinese education and government officials.

Lee and his top lieutenants—Ya-Qin Zhang, Harry Shum, and HongJiang Zhang—worked tirelessly to improve the lab's ties to government ministries and universities. All three men had been invited to serve as guest professors at a number of institutions, including Peking University, Zhejiang University in Hangzhou, Xi'an Jiaotong University, and the Chinese Academy of Sciences. In addition, a steady stream of distinguished visiting professors came through the lab from around the world—Cambridge University, the University of Tokyo, Berkeley, Princeton, MIT, and of course Carnegie Mellon—to meet and interact with staff members as well as Chinese university professors.

In an inspirational move that seemed to lift Microsoft's standing in China, Lee also inaugurated a gala annual conference dubbed "Computing in the 21st Century." For the first event, held in late June 1999 at Peking University, he brought in two winners of the Turing Award. One was Microsoft's own Butler Lampson, a pioneer from the early days of computing at Xerox's Palo Alto Research Center. Raj

Reddy, Lee's mentor from Carnegie Mellon, was the second. Breakout technical sessions featured such notables as natural-language and speech guru Victor Zue of MIT and X. D. Huang from Microsoft's speech product group in Redmond. Rick Rashid, Dan Ling, and Roger Needham, the venerable founding director of Microsoft's lab in Cambridge, England, also jetted in for the event. Some 3,000 students and faculty members from Peking University attended the daylong extravaganza.

Finally, in addition to a number of smaller research collaborations with individual professors, just before the first anniversary Lee signed an agreement with the Chinese National Natural Science Foundation to co-sponsor fundamental research projects at universities around the country. Microsoft would aid basic research in such fields as mathematics that underpinned many areas of computer science but that Lee did not have the manpower to pursue in the Beijing lab. The investment helped his host country by advancing the state of Chinese science, and it provided Microsoft a window into early-stage research on important fundamental topics, as well as a leg up on identifying potential recruits. Under the terms of the agreement, Microsoft's funding—anywhere from $10,000 to a few million dollars a year, depending on the scope of the undertaking—would be matched by the federal government, with projects lasting between one and three years.

Lee had dutifully reported on all this at the first Gates review. Now, in the last days of 1999 and the cold first few months of 2000, he put the pedal to the metal. It didn't help that Microsoft's China business office was in turmoil. Earlier in 1999, the company had released its Venus set-top box, a roughly $300 gadget equipped with the Windows CE (for consumer electronics) operating system designed to let people surf the Web via their televisions. It was good thinking: the Venus box was far more affordable than a PC, and China's TV penetration was many times the size of the computer market. But Microsoft had violated some basic principles of good *guanxi*—plowing ahead without full government cooperation or a complete understanding of local market demands. After an initial period of good press, it all fell apart, and the company endured scathing criticism for allegedly trying to carve out another monopoly for itself. To make matters worse, its famous president and general manager Juliet Wu, perhaps China's most popular woman executive, had left the company on unfriendly terms. In a few months she would unleash her own criticism of Microsoft's high software prices and other business practices in her book, *Flying Against the Wind: Microsoft, IBM, and Me.* Wu's replacement, Jack Gao, started work on January 1, 2000.

The Beijing lab acted as a foil for all the bad business news. In April 2000, Lee put on the second Computing in the 21st Century conference, making sure it was bigger and better than the first, with twin events in Beijing and Shanghai. Keynoters included another Turing Award winner, database trailblazer Jim Gray of Microsoft's small research lab in San Francisco, and laser printer inventor Gary Starkweather, another prize from Xerox PARC brought into the Microsoft lair. Lee expanded the number of technical sessions from four to six, focusing on many of the same areas his own lab pursued: user interfaces, multimedia, speech, and advanced networking. Some 7,000 people attended the two events, which were widely covered in the Chinese press.

All these efforts built Microsoft's standing as a corporate citizen and, Lee felt, contributed greatly to a sea change in how the research lab was viewed on university campuses. When Microsoft Research China was formed, Lee and his colleagues had received an ambiguous, sometimes outright rude, welcome in academe. But within less than a year, things changed dramatically. When Ya-Qin Zhang visited the University of Science and Technology of China, his alma mater, students packed the auditorium, spilling onto the stage. Latecomers jammed into the corridor outside the hall, crowding so tightly together to get into the room that a glass door was broken.

At Harbin Institute of Technology, in the far northeast of the country near Mongolia, 600 people jockeyed into a 300-capacity auditorium to hear Kai-Fu Lee and George Chen speak. Afterward, the students clamored around them, gushing questions for two hours.

When Lee and Chen finally tried to break the impasse and leave, Chen remembers, "Students surrounded us in the hallway and wouldn't let us go . . . They said, 'Please give us an opportunity. Come more, we really want to listen to talks—that was so great.'" A few students had tears in their eyes. When the Microsoft men finally emerged from the building, Chen saw a mist in Lee's eyes as well. "George, help those students. Help those students," Lee pleaded. "Do whatever you want, as long as you help Chinese students and don't hurt Microsoft."

Later, Lee and Chen received the royal treatment from their hosts—a group dinner featuring true "northern hospitality," with lots of drinking and toasts. Chen didn't imbibe much alcohol, so it was up to Lee to uphold the lab's honor, as one university official after the other raised his glass and cried, *"Ganbei!"* Lee matched each toast, drawing compliments from his dinner companions. "This is nothing," Lee responded. "My mom is from Mongolia."

The late fall and first several weeks of January leading up to the Chinese New Year constitute job-hunting season for students looking to line up permanent work following their graduation the next summer—hiring time for companies vying for the best and brightest from Chinese universities. For the lab's second hiring season, the number of résumés submitted soared to nearly 5,000—so many that Lee instituted written screening tests on ten campuses around the country.

As he and his colleagues pored over stacks of CVs and ground through scores of interviews, Lee was more struck than ever by the vast chasm in the level of education and professionalism between Chinese and Western universities. He summed it up in a missive to the lab. "Since my return to China, I have had frequent conversations with Chinese scholars, leading technology experts, and officials of organizations that administer research. All of these people have expressed a common awareness that there is still a sizeable gap between the level of the best research being conducted in China and the best research being conducted internationally. Furthermore, the level of basic research lags even farther behind than that of the work being done in development and applications. People may believe that these disparities can be attributed to factors such as the scientific research environment, the facilities, and the salaries that are offered in China. But in my opinion, there are even more important causes of these disparities."

In heartfelt terms, Lee continued. "The Chinese people are one of the most intelligent peoples on the face of the earth, and there are many outstanding Chinese scholars and scholars of Chinese heritage in computer-science research. However, a sizeable percentage of these accomplished individuals have achieved their successes outside of China . . . Why is this? Could it be that computer scientists have to leave China in order to do first rate work? Of course not. But Chinese researchers have a very serious problem—namely a lack of information about international research trends in their field. I believe that only by enhancing scholarly communication can we get a firm handle on the general direction of scientific research . . ."

Lee expounded on his thoughts in a controversial open letter to Chinese students that was widely reprinted in newspapers and magazines. In it, he boldly offered his views about the future of research and the level of creativity and collaboration necessary for Chinese scholars to be successful on the world stage. Integrity, he stressed, was the most important thing for a researcher. But on a more mundane level, it shocked him that many of the students he met had no clue about how to put together résumés or how to dress and conduct themselves professionally in interviews—givens in most parts of the West. He didn't sugarcoat the truth—and he blamed both educators and parents.

Sheila Shang says the letter sent shock waves around Chinese higher education and government circles. "That was just like a bomb, actually, back then," she notes. "Before that nobody talked so openly about what they thought the Chinese students needed." But Lee's communiqué was generally well taken. At the University of Science and Technology of China, the president even read excerpts of the letter to the entire student body.

Even as he pushed for more professionalism from Chinese students, Lee balanced that formality with the need to create a loose, creative atmosphere in the lab. As he wrote in late 1999 in another of his periodic musings to the staff: "Many people think that the key to hiring good people is compensation. Even more people think that when Microsoft came to China, it could simply 'buy the best minds with high salaries.' Naturally, everyone ought to receive appropriate compensation, and at MSR China we can offer competitive (but reasonable) salaries. However, what is even more important to a researcher is the research environment."

Lee then proceeded to list a half-dozen steps needed to create an attractive research climate, including ample support resources, open communication and collaboration, and "the space and freedom for each individual to develop his or her own abilities and pursue his or her dreams."

The Beijing lab director was serious about the need to not always be serious, and he applied this philosophy to the dozens of student interns coming into the lab in late 1999 and early 2000. For some of his workers, Lee may have taken "freedom" too far. Lee bought five or six sleeping bags for the students, so they could crash more comfortably when pulling late-nighters. He also tolerated their playing video and computer games in the lab. Harry Shum, for one, wasn't so pleased by this. He spoke to his boss quietly, questioning whether it was professional.

Lee brushed off Shum's concerns, countering: "If I don't let them play games, am I still allowed to?"

Less than two weeks after the first anniversary party, Lee called a two-day management retreat at Longyuan, or Dragon Villa, a recreation center with hotel facilities attached to an exclusive community development about ninety minutes northeast of the Sigma Center. Despite all the recent good news, the gulf between the culture created by the Chinese education system and what was expected in the research arm of a Western company like Microsoft dominated the agenda—sparking one of the few management and personnel crises in the Beijing lab's history.

Everything came to a head at Dragon Villa. On hand were Ya-Qin Zhang, HongJiang Zhang, Harry Shum, "Tom" Huang, George Chen, Jian Wang, and Sheila Shang. Lee had prepared an aggressive agenda: full-force work combined with full-force play. Everyone gathered at eight in the morning in a comfortable meeting room with several tables, a sofa, and leather-bound chairs. They huddled and paced and brainstormed for four straight hours, breaking promptly at noon for lunch in an adjacent dining room. Then, with only an hour set aside to eat, they went back at it for another six hours, until dinner. At that point, the liquor flowed and the games began: darts, bowling, billiards, karaoke, and "pushing-pig," a Chinese card game not unlike Spades that requires the loser of each hand to crawl under the table. The party didn't break up until 3:30 A.M. But everyone shuffled into the meeting room at eight the next morning and put in another full day of strategizing and self-assessment. Finally, at 5:30 that evening Lee called it quits—and the exhausted colleagues piled into sedans waiting to take them back to Beijing.

A variety of topics came up during the marathon retreat—everything from the research agenda to public relations. By far the biggest issue, though, centered on the clash of cultures between Microsoft and its young Chinese researchers. Everyone agreed that the recruits were extremely talented. But they commonly lacked an assertiveness and independence found in top U.S.-trained Ph.D.s, who had no problem conducting research on their own and seemed fearless about making mistakes. By contrast, many newly hired Chinese researchers were timid, so worried about making errors that they couldn't bring themselves to push the envelope of their research unless specifically directed by a manager.

Kai-Fu Lee had insisted many times that he didn't care if researchers made mistakes, so long as they were trying to stretch the boundaries of computer science. "Making mistakes is no problem, but doing nothing is no good," he had stressed. But his words seemed to have fallen on deaf ears. It was such a problem that the lab had created a new position—"associate researcher"—not found elsewhere in Microsoft Research. Instead of being hired outright as full-time staff researchers, Chinese Ph.D. graduates were given a two-year appointment as associate researcher. Only if they demonstrated the independence Lee was looking for would they be offered permanent jobs (this position exists to this day). At the time of the Dragon Villa session, no one had yet made the transition to full-time researcher.

One source of confusion for the associates was the lab's stated mission to do basic research in computer science that would also help Microsoft. As Ya-Qin Zhang explained to his colleagues at the Dragon Villa: "The Chinese think that basic study is to ruminate and meditate sitting in a room. A university professor once expressed his idea to me: We give him some money, and he sends some scholars to our research lab; we don't ask them to do anything but thinking. One year later, they report to us what they thought about."

That, of course, wasn't what Microsoft was looking for, but the associate researchers didn't understand the company's idea of basic research any better than the professor in Zhang's example. Two key aspects of the term needed to be better explained, he asserted. "If we do a lot that benefits our society but is useless to our company, we fail. If we do something that benefits our company, but is ineffective to our society, it is not a research institute any longer."

As Lee later explained the central issues raised at Dragon Villa: "The associates were sure they were smart and working hard. But they were not really clear on what success looked like. They were still looking at it the way they always looked at things—which is their boss or professor tells them what to do and they follow orders and execute perfectly. That's what they had done their whole lives." The associates also had a hard time taking things at face value—instead reading between the lines of what the lab leaders said to guess their manager's "true" intentions.

One particular example came up—the case of a very bright associate researcher who had resigned from a tenure-track assistant professor's job to join the lab and work with managers he considered the best and brightest in their fields. The associate had met with Lee to discuss the research topic he wanted to pursue. Lee didn't much like the topic and laid out his reasons. However, he had told the researcher, "If you want to do it, go ahead."

It was not unlike the situation Lee had found himself in as a Ph.D. student at Carnegie Mellon. His advisor, Raj Reddy, had disagreed with Lee over which course of research to pursue for his thesis—but had supported him in the decision anyway. But the young associate researcher in the Beijing lab wasn't used to this kind of attitude from an advisor. As Lee relates, the associate processed the meeting this way: "He thought, 'You don't agree with me but you said to go do it anyway, so you must be setting me up for failure.' He felt doomed to failure and thought he would never get support, because I would be losing face if I reversed my opinion."

The same researcher had once asked for time off to visit his family, who had not yet been able to move to Beijing. He asked Lee if he should take the train or a plane. "Either way is fine," Lee had responded. But the associate had read between the lines of that comment, thinking: "The plane is more expensive, and if that were really okay, you would have just said to take the plane. So by giving me the choice between a plane or train, you really meant train—you just wanted to appear generous by giving me a choice." He took the train.

Only a few weeks before the Dragon Villa session, the associate had quit the lab, unable to resolve the cultural differences. His was an extreme case, but still typical of the confusion many associate researchers felt—and no one wanted that to happen again. Perhaps none of the Microsoft managers had done as good a job as they should have in conveying exactly what was expected of the associates, in other words, what it would take for them to be permanently hired.

The more they discussed the issue, the more the Microsoft team began to see the other side of the coin. "We didn't really empathize enough with the plight of the associate researchers," says Lee. "I think we left the program a bit too opaque. They had a two-year appointment, but they were not clear on what they needed to do to become full-time. They thought, 'After a year, should I try to move on? Or will you tell me how things are going—God knows what the selection process will be. Maybe I will be on the street and I won't even know why.'"

It was funny in a way, because all the research managers except Lee had grown up in mainland China and should have given the cultural differences more thought. But all except Tom Huang had spent a decade or more in the United States and had completely assimilated into the U.S. approach to research management. Now, they realized, both managers and associate researchers needed to adjust a bit, and Lee himself needed to start the healing process. As one of the managers present summarizes: "The students didn't know how to work in an environment like MSR China. The management team realized that some issues needed to be taken more seriously—that the associate researchers had issues, too. We said, 'Kai-Fu, you have to talk to them.'"

Lee started right in to meet the challenge, determined to clearly explain the difference between open-ended basic research and basic research strategically targeted on areas likely to benefit Microsoft in the long run. The managers also brainstormed a list of specific goals or milestones for each research team. They hoped this would make things more concrete for the associate researchers than the admittedly fuzzy target of "advancing computer science" that had been stressed in the past. "Okay everybody," Lee said. "Let's set a January goal and a June 2000 goal, and another relatively long-term goal." In that way, they assigned targets for the next eighteen months for every research project then on the books.

Finally, and most importantly, they painted a detailed picture of what a successful researcher looked like: someone who took initiative, openly discussed issues with senior managers and even disagreed with them, and led by example. Because Chinese students seemed to thrive on concrete examples rather than general terms, the managers decided to showcase YingQing Xu, an associate researcher who had blossomed at the lab. He had come up with great ideas, written papers, submitted patent applications, and generally hadn't waited to be told what to do. Indeed, Xu would become the first associate promoted to full researcher.

Lee laid everything out in a presentation, complete with a Power-

Point slideshow with the straightforward title "My Expectations of Associate Researchers." He gave the talk a few days later, speaking for forty-five minutes and then taking questions for another half-hour. During the discussion period, some associates were very direct; it was the first time they had ever challenged the lab director. Lee saw that as a good sign and promised that the management team would do its share to overcome the lab's cultural gap—though he stressed that both sides had to do better. He advised researchers and managers alike to commit to speaking their minds and not wasting time reading between the lines of a colleague's comments. As Lee put it to the lab: "Cut to the chase and say what you mean and mean what you say and not dance around and make people guess."

While no one pretended the problem was solved, the session seems to have cleared the air and signaled that communication between Chinese researchers and their Westernized managers would from then on be much more of a two-way street.

And train or plane were really both okay.

Amid all the politicking, hobnobbing, recruiting, and hashing out of culture clashes, the lab's research agenda blazed along. True, most of the early projects were aimed at paying off five years or so in the future. But no sooner had Lee gotten through one Bill Gates review than he began thinking about the next. Another aspect of the Dragon Villa retreat was what to do for an encore.

In their first meeting, Lee had told Gates about the lab's main areas of focus: human computer interaction (encompassing speech recognition and natural language understanding) and multimedia. But because the multimedia work was a late addition spurred by the arrival of Ya-Qin Zhang, HongJiang Zhang, and Harry Shum, the initial demos were all from the human-computer interaction work. Lee had promised Gates that the next review would feature "amazing" multimedia.

At the Dragon Villa, he had reminded his managers of this promise. Then he had turned to Harry Shum.

"What have you got?"

A bit nonplussed, Shum replied that he could probably show something on concentric mosaics, a graphics-based visualization algorithm that enabled 3-D views of a computer environment—a room, say, or outdoor scene—that were so realistic that a user could wander around and experience the natural effect of being there, complete with lighting changes due to shadows or sun position.

The powerful system, it was hoped, could dramatically enhance the graphics in video games as well as a host of other applications such as architectural design. Though Shum had started this work while he was in Redmond, it was still early going. Shum gave it a 70 percent probability of success by mid-2000. That was good enough for Lee. Next, he had turned to Ya-Qin Zhang.

"Ya-Qin, what do you have?"

Zhang named four possible demos from his multimedia research, each with a 40 to 70 percent chance of success. He figured to narrow it down to two or three early in the New Year.

Finally, it was HongJiang Zhang's turn. He estimated he had a 90 percent chance of completing a demo showing technology for turning unstructured Web data into a structured, searchable format.

"Okay, it's going to happen," said Lee, referring to the next Bill G. review. "I'm going to reserve the date."

Ya-Qin Zhang objected. "Kai-Fu, usually you have the whole thing done before you agree to show Bill!"

"Well, in this case we know we'll have two things working. You do believe in expected probability, don't you?"

Soon thereafter, Lee had notified research director Dan Ling of his intentions, and a second Bill G. review had been set for June 15, 2000, nine months after the inaugural session. Once again, the Beijing team flew into Seattle a few days early. The core members of the first presentation contingent returned: Lee, HongJiang Zhang, Harry Shum, and Ya-Qin Zhang. They were joined by most of Ya-Qin's multimedia team, including his former Sarnoff colleague Shipeng Li, and Jin Li of "Deng touched my head" fame. All had flown in from Beijing, except for Ya-Qin. He had been with his family in Princeton on paternity leave; his second child, Brandon, had been born less than two weeks earlier.

The Beijing lab had ended up with three demo slots. Shum was showcasing concentric mosaic graphics. Ya-Qin Zhang would talk about a new video compression technique called scalable wavelet coding. HongJiang Zhang covered ways to structure and index Web data, enabling people to retrieve a group of photos showing similar scenes or locate football highlights in a mass of sports video, for example. Unlike before the first Bill G. review, Lee had no real worries with his three stars presenting. "I'm sure they were a bit nervous," he says. "But I knew they would do great."

The session took place in the same Building 8 conference room as the first review. After light rain the day before, this day, a Thursday, was typical early Seattle summer: partly cloudy with temperatures in the 60s. As before, the principals sat at the main table, while observers took seats along the wall. Ling and Rick Rashid were at the center table, and from the business side of the company came Craig Mundie and Eric Rudder, Gates's technical assistant. Rudder was a kind of aide-de-camp who would soon become senior vice president in charge of the Servers and Tools business group. In that capacity, he would lead the launch of Microsoft's .NET initiative, the company's strategy for sharing information across a variety of applications, operating systems, and platforms such as PCs, cell phones, PDAs, and smart appliances.

One of the wall-huggers was Lie Gu, who had earned a master's degree from Peking University and was doing tech transfer work in Redmond before going on to get his Ph.D. at Carnegie Mellon. Gu, to the endless future amusement of his colleagues, seemed paralyzed by the prospect of an audience with Gates. Beijing lab members describe him as "frozen," unable to utter a word. Linda Stone, a Microsoft vice president who was passing by, looked in, assessed the situation, and patted him warmly on the shoulder. "Loosen up," she smiled.

The meeting proved another rousing success. It was supposed to last an hour, but it went over by fifteen minutes. Gates arrived about twenty minutes after they had started but caught up with relish. At one point, as Harry Shum was presenting some of his concentric mosaics results, Gates correctly predicted his next slide. But what really lit Gates's fire was Ya-Qin Zhang's briefing on scalable wavelet coding, an area Zhang had helped pioneer. In its essence scalable coding was a superefficient technique for compressing video images such as maps and photos that maintained enough of the original data that images could be transmitted and reproduced on the receiving end with far higher quality than conventional data compression methods. As Zhang began talking about wavelets and signal decomposition, Gates jumped to his feet and approached the display screen. "Okay, wavelet decomposition, these are the frequencies . . . but how are you doing the compression?"

"I was really amazed at how much he understood about compression," remembers Zhang. "So I spent some time explaining how this stuff works, and he shared some in-depth observations."

Gates was still asking questions after the session had formally broken up. They later heard he went straight from the review to a senior executive meeting and bragged that the company had the world's best multimedia people in Beijing.

Again the Beijing team emerged from Building 8 walking on air. That night, Lee took them out to dinner and trotted out more celebratory cigars. Both he and Ya-Qin Zhang soon fired off e-mails to their colleagues in China.

From: Ya-Qin Zhang
To: Research-Beijing, China (ALL)
Cc: Kai-Fu Lee
Subject: BillG review super successful!!!
Importance: High

Dear MSRCNers [Microsoft Research China researchers],

I thought you all wanted to know the great news that we just had a fabulous, flawless, and impeccable review this afternoon w/ BillG!!! Everybody just did a super job in preparations, presentations, and demos.

He was VERY interested in our technologies and made extremely positive comments on our work. He asked many questions and even stood up and came to stage once to ask some technical details.

He was happy to see how fast we have built such a world-class multimedia team.

He especially pointed out the relevance and importance of our work for the new .NET (formerly NGWS) strategy in several occasions.

He concluded with a series of comments like:

"Great!"

"Great stuff!"

"Just perfect."

I think you all understand how difficult it is to grab a full hour of his time and attention (we actually got 75 minutes because of his interest), especially in the midst of the .NET announcement, antitrust case, among many other major events.

This represents the best recognition and endorsement for the great work we have done in our lab, especially on the multimedia area. I want to congratulate the members in Visual computing group, Internet Media group, and Media Computing group for the "great stuff" and the dedication and hard work from the RSDE team for making this happen! Special thanks go to Kai-Fu's coaching, "staging" and relentless pursuit for perfection (you have no idea how many times I had to change my vugraphs :-))

For now, we'll focus on the celebration party. I'll send a more detailed note early next week.

Cheers,

Ya-Qin

$\bullet \quad \bullet \quad \bullet$

From: "Kai-Fu Lee"
To: "Ya-Qin Zhang", "Research-Beijing, China (ALL)"
Subject: RE: BillG review super successful!!!

Ya-Qin, Hong-Jiang, and Harry did a really superb job.

Bill was very very interested and engaged (we think maybe he ate a pencil during the presentation :-)). We also got a lot of good feedback that will help our work in the future.

You can all look forward to a "亚勤话题" [Ya-Qin Zhang's report] on this review shortly.

Rick and Dan both told me afterwards that they thought the review went really well.

Congratulations!

Kai-Fu

P.S.—Hope you all enjoyed the parties we had after the review.

P.P.S.—Now I have to delay my annual health/blood test—too much wine + beer + cigar + beef in my blood now :-)

A couple days later, after half the group had already returned to Beijing, Lee's team rented a speedboat and took it out on Lake Washington, the long and narrow, glacier-sculpted waterway that separates Redmond from downtown Seattle.

Ya-Qin Zhang took the helm on a gloriously sunny day, with highs hitting 80 degrees. Lee, Xiaoning Ling, Jin Li, and a few others roared out with him to enjoy the fine weather. Zhang threw the throttle open, at one point getting the speed up enough to momentarily bring the bow out of the water. With Ling as their guide, the group cruised around the scenic lake. They tooled past the house of Microsoft co-founder Paul Allen, then spent several minutes idling off Gates's far more famous enclave, the one for which Ling had helped build the multimedia infrastructure. From the water, sightseers could get a splendid view of the multilevel, timber and frame, glass-walled mansion that cost an estimated $97 million to build. Easily visible were its two docks, boathouse, pool building and adjacent exercise facility, sport court, and office and reception area that peered out over the lake. Farther back, almost hidden from view, rose the domed library that harbored the *Codex Leicest,* Leonardo da Vinci's 16th-century notebook, for which Gates paid $30.8 million.

A powerboat ride soon became the lab's second post–Bill G. review tradition, along with the cigars. Laughing and chatting and just reveling in the summer day, the Beijing contingent brought out more stogies. Zhang recalls a huge burden slipping off his shoulders in the pleasure of the moment. "I felt so relieved. I had been stressed for several months, being the point person for the review, and with the new baby."

Little did he know that everything was about to change—for himself perhaps most of all.

In late May 2000, some two weeks before the Bill G. review, Ya-Qin Zhang had gone on his paternity leave. His wife Jenny and daughter Sophie, then six, had stayed behind in Princeton after Zhang had joined the Beijing lab. Zhang had spent the last year and a half traveling back and forth, for most of the time living out of the Shangri-La, a first-rate business hotel on the west side of town, when he wasn't in New Jersey. "Check in, check out! Month here, month there," is how he puts it. Brandon had been born on June 3. Zhang had flown to Seattle for the review, then returned immediately to Princeton, planning to stay through July with a combination of paternity leave and accrued vacation time. (Leaving family in the States to work at the lab was not uncommon for China-born recruits. The lab later created a tongue-in-cheek award for those who endured this hardship—the "MBA" degree, for Married But Available. Zhang was one of the first recipients.)

The phone call from Kai-Fu Lee came on the evening of July 20, not long before Zhang was due back in Beijing. Right away, Zhang felt apprehensive. His boss had only called him once in all the time he had known him—and that was to tender a job offer. Otherwise, all their communication had come in person or over e-mail. Neither Zhang nor Lee recalls Lee's exact words, but they were terse, along the lines of: "Ya-Qin, I need to go back to Redmond. You will be in charge of the lab." It soon became clear that Lee was moving on to bigger and better things in the company—and so was Zhang. The friends spent a half-hour discussing the implications of the change and how to inform lab staffers and the Chinese press. Lee asked Zhang to return to Beijing at once to strategize.

The Microsoft hierarchy, all the way up to CEO Steve Ballmer, had been watching Lee for months. The company's system for spotting and rewarding talent in its own ranks was straightforward. The dynamic executive duo of Gates and Ballmer—Bill and Steve to almost everyone—expected to be aware of the top 600 to 1,000 people out of the company's 55,000-odd employees. To help identify this talent, they required each member of their senior management team to know the top few percent in their groups; those managers in turn relied on their key personnel to spot younger talent, and so on down the line. Executives would lay out the strengths and weaknesses of the most elite group to Bill and Steve, putting talented employees on their radar screens for higher duty should that become a possibility.

One day in late 1999 or early 2000, Rick Rashid had sent Lee an e-mail saying Ballmer wanted to see him. A meeting was scheduled, and Lee soon found himself face to face with the chief executive. Ballmer started off by reminding Lee they had met in China briefly about nine months earlier—impressing the Beijing lab head, who had figured the short encounter wouldn't even have registered with the CEO. "Steve has an amazing memory," Lee relates.

The Microsoft president then proceeded to ask a flurry of questions, soaking up the answers, taking Lee's measure. How does Microsoft become successful in China—do you have any suggestions? How can natural user interfaces become products? How do you feel about our efforts so far?

"Tell me what excites you," Ballmer then queried.

"My whole career has been between research and products," Lee responded. "I love doing research that can become products or doing products that just came from research."

"If there's something in Redmond, would you be interested?"

"Yes, maybe," a slightly flummoxed Lee replied. After all, he had promised to stay at the Beijing lab for at least five years, so such talk seemed premature. Ballmer concluded by telling Lee to come and see him every six months or so.

Not long before the second Bill G. review, Lee went back for another meeting. Ballmer explained some details behind Microsoft's forthcoming .NET initiative and its goal of moving digital information across a wide range of often incompatible devices and systems. A lot of the desired seamless connectivity could be achieved through the user interface, Lee's own area of specialty. "Is that something you'd be interested in coming back and turning into products?" Ballmer asked.

Lee admitted being intrigued. Ballmer then handed Lee off to Bob Muglia, the senior vice president in charge of the Windows Server Division and a key shaper of Microsoft's business and technical strategy, including .NET. Says Lee, "I had a good chat with Bob. Bob told me, 'We're looking at the organization. In the next month or so, expect a call from me about a very senior position we'd like you to consider.'"

So Lee had known change was in the air. After his first meeting with Ballmer, he had sought out Rick Rashid's advice. The Research executive told Lee not to think about it too much. "You're still pretty new," he said. "You have great potential, but stay focused and do a good job."

After the second meeting with Ballmer, Lee checked back in with Rashid. "I told Rick, 'When I took the job, I gave you my word I'd do it for five years, maybe longer.' He said, 'There's a greater calling. I support it—you should take it. I don't think no is an option for you.' I said, great!"

A few weeks later Muglia called and offered Lee a job as corporate vice president in the newly formed Servers and Tools group under

Eric Rudder. All language-based technologies—such as those for searching files, spell-checking and grammar, speech synthesis, and help functions—would come under Lee's direction. The basic charge was to supply natural interactive software and future user interfaces that would become part of a variety of Microsoft products.

It was all heady stuff for Lee. For those at the Beijing lab, the change was just as dizzying, but not in a good way. Harry Shum was in Redmond, visiting some research colleagues when someone mentioned almost in passing: "I hear your boss is leaving. He's going to be promoted to VP."

Shum went numb. "That was a shock," he says. "That was actually a shock." Shum immediately called Ya-Qin Zhang in New Jersey, probably the day after Lee had called him. Zhang, still a bit dazed by the magnitude of his new challenge, seemed just as nervous and uncertain about the future as Shum. The two agreed to meet in Beijing as soon as possible and hung up the phone with heavy hearts. Shum couldn't shake the bad feeling all the way back—wondering what the still-neophyte lab would do without its founder's wisdom and experience. The flight home was a far cry from when he had joined the lab, drinking sake with Ya-Qin and exhilarating over their new adventure together.

The very next day, Shum and Zhang joined Lee and HongJiang Zhang for brunch at the Shangri-La. Lee was upbeat, confident of the lab's future and the managers' abilities, but his colleagues were still feeling gloomy. Finally, Lee solemnly leaned across the table and began shaking hands with each man in turn:

To Ya-Qin Zhang, he said: "Congratulations, managing director Zhang."

"Congratulations, assistant managing director Shum."

And then to HongJiang Zhang: "Congratulations, assistant managing director Zhang."

The news hit the rest of the lab like a brick. It was announced at an all-hands meeting called the last week of July, with everyone gathered in a large conference room on the sixth floor, in the business office space. Rick Rashid, Dan Ling, and X. D. Huang back in Redmond were patched in via a conference call, listening in through the big speaker, shaped like a Klingon warship, in the center of the meeting table.

Lee spoke briefly about his new role, and stressed his belief in the lab's bright future. Then it was Ya-Qin Zhang's turn as the new managing director. In a low voice, he began talking about Lee as if he had died, almost eulogizing him. They later joked that you could hear an acupuncture needle drop in the room. Remembers Shum, "Ya-Qin spoke very quietly, sad and solemn. People actually started crying." By most accounts, Shum was one of those whose eyes welled up. So did Lee's. Listening over the speakerphone back in Redmond, or so the story went, people actually heard some sobs. One of those listening in pushed the "mute" button and said: "People are crying!"

Rashid and Ling then jumped in and tried to speak encouraging words about the lab's future and its new leadership.

Lee was leaving on August 3, so there wasn't much time to plan his goodbye. Still, Sheila Shang and Lee's executive assistant Eileen Chen organized three farewell parties, each successively more private. The first was at the Shangri-La hotel, by now well-known to the Microsoft crew. A dozen or more reporters were invited, along with various academics and government officials. One famous reporter from the *People's Daily* stood up and addressed Lee in congratulatory terms no "objective" American reporter would utter: "Although people think you did a political job, you strike us as a true scholar, and you care about Chinese education, science, and technology."

The second party, held at the Jade Palace hotel just a block from the lab, was for staff members and a few visiting students and friends, about 100 people in all. It was more upbeat. In one emotional moment, Lee gave his badge to a middle-school student who interned at the lab. When the boy, whom Lee later helped get into college in the U.S., began crying and hugging Lee, many adults teared up as well, including the lab founder. But the moment was balanced by a tongue-in-cheek PowerPoint presentation by Ya-Qin Zhang. The lab's new director had taken Lee's standard overview talk and altered some of the images and captions to poke fun at the outgoing leader. In one slide about recruiting top talent, he had replaced a picture of Lee in a crowd of mostly male students with a scene showing him superimposed among a group of female models.

The last farewell—an intimate gathering for the management team and Lee's family—took place at the Hong-Tse Lon Ba restaurant, also not too far from the lab. As the wine flowed, guests took turns at what had become a Chinese party favorite: karaoke. Most of it was in good fun. But at one point, someone selected a very sad Chinese song by Xinshui Zhao about friends separating to go off to war, prompting about a half-dozen people to join in.

Loosely translated, the song's title meant "Farewell my comrade." Those present would vividly remember the moment and find meaning in the title and lyrics:

> Come on brothers and sisters, rise up in our great
>   moment.
> A great battle lies ahead, and our life is for the
>   revolution.
> Things are in disorder. We go ahead blindly into
>   the fog of war.
> Although we will be separated, we are all
>   together in spirit.
> . . . .
> In the spring wind, it will be a better time.
> My comrades in arms, we will meet again.

5
Ya-Qin Dynasty
August 2000–July 2001

Asia is a market and a source of talent. The Beijing lab became a center of expertise for Microsoft.

—YA-QIN ZHANG

I n July 2001, all was green in the city of eternal spring. While Beijing sweltered though its summer heat, humidity, and sandstorms, Kunming enjoyed a breezy, semitropical climate. The capital of the southwestern province of Yunnan is a three-hour plane ride from Beijing and a top vacation spot, owing to its year-round flora and natural attractions. Perched atop a mile-high plateau, visitors can take in scenic vistas of mountains on three sides and the ocean-like Dianchi Lake to the south. The spectacular Stone Forest, Shilin, and other popular tourist destinations are within a day's drive.

It was a perfect spot for Microsoft's Beijing lab, now in full bloom, to hold its first true offsite, or working session away from the lab. Previous retreats had taken place in and around Beijing. This time, the whole lab made the cross-country flight aboard two commercial jets. The exact number of staff on the trip was 108. That number held some significance. In *Shui Hu Zhuan* (*Outlaws of the Marsh*), a popular novel set in 14th-century China, a band of 108 rebels escaped to a mountain hideaway to wage battle against a tyrannical government.

The researchers joked that they could play that part in Kunming—planning an all-out assault to help Microsoft win the future of computing. They would help ensure this goal by spending a day and a half in intensive team-building meetings and another day sightseeing and recharging. The first night featured Yunnan dinner theater, including a traditional ethnic-minority wedding skit that had lab managers carry a "bride" across the stage with marbles placed underfoot to try to make them lose their balance.

The next morning, in the ballroom of the Kunming Jia Hua, one of the best hotels in town, Ya-Qin Zhang stood on a grander stage to address the lab. Nearly a year had passed since Kai-Fu Lee's departure, and Microsoft Research China, having established its credibility as a research center, was coming into its own. As the lab's new managing director, Zhang still remembered the loneliness he had felt the day after Lee left, when he first sat by himself in his friend's old office. Back then, staff members knew each other like family. Now the lab felt much larger and less personal. Many new faces stood out in the crowd.

Dressed in a casual shirt and slacks, Zhang exuded an air of gentle confidence. As he saw it, the lab faced three main challenges. The first was geographic and cultural separation from Redmond headquarters—a constant struggle to avoid being marginalized. The second was its growing size. All of these fresh-faced researchers were talented and hardworking, but they needed careful and experienced mentoring, which would be increasingly difficult to achieve as their ranks swelled. And the third challenge, true for all corporate research organizations no matter their size or location, lay in making sure the lab's research stayed relevant to its company's future products. But Zhang's first order of business—the underpinning necessary to meet the challenges ahead—was keeping the lines of communication strong through the ranks. This talk, he felt, marked a great opportunity to unite the lab.

Zhang never met an analogy he didn't like. "Imagine the lab is a car," he began, putting up a cartoon slide of a shiny red vehicle. "Researchers are like the engine. You make the whole thing go. The management team sets the direction." The animated car started to drive forward. "PR is the horn," he continued, pointing to a freakishly large air horn on the car roof that flashed on the screen to the sound of a loud honk. For days afterward, lab members would call PR head Sheila Shang *da la ba*—"big horn." Finishing off the analogy, Zhang explained that the four wheels of the car represented technology transfer, university relations, software development, and support staff. If any of these broke down, the car would go nowhere. In this way, he "drove" home the idea that each person's job was crucial to lab performance.

Looking ahead, Zhang then turned to the overarching theme of this offsite: having impact on the company. He provided some context by discussing Microsoft's quarterly profits and its product pipeline, and by summarizing what he and the top brass saw as the lab's key objectives. First, advance the state of the art in computer science. Second, become an incubator of disruptive technologies. And third, serve as a think tank to help the company strategize five to ten years down the road. These goals were not new—they had been hashed out and reiterated from the Redmond boardroom to the Dragon Villa. Still, the whole lab, especially the newcomers, needed to hear them again. What was new was Zhang's emphasis on how to bridge the gap between research and products. He called it "finding your home." As he explained, "We should position ourselves as an owner of technology strategy. So tell me, if you succeed in your research, where is your home? Which business group will it be transferred to? Who's your partner on the other side?"

The questions resonated with many researchers in the audience. Some felt happy—after some reflection, they found their target on the business side, perhaps for the first time. But others felt frustrated—their research was too far removed from any product group. In that case, Zhang urged them to think through the problem and discuss options with their research managers. If a project was compelling enough, he explained, it might spawn a new product area or home on the business side that didn't yet exist. And if it wasn't compelling, it might be possible to sharpen its focus. With Zhang, every problem seemed like an opportunity, seemed solvable. He kept things lively and positive. Years later, staff members still remembered his last slide. It read simply, "The best is yet to come."

To get down to the nuts and bolts of implementing his vision, Zhang turned things over to assistant managing directors Harry Shum and HongJiang Zhang, who proceeded to perform a researcher's version of good cop, bad cop. Shum, the graphics and vision expert who seemed to take Kai-Fu Lee's departure the hardest, acted as the good cop. He spoke on how to be a first-rate researcher: how to choose a topic, solve problems, write a scientific paper, and so forth. Most memorably, he made his points with charts, graphs, and equations, all with an animated delivery as if he were giving a research talk himself.

HongJiang Zhang, the bad cop, followed. He looked a little older and sterner than Shum and Ya-Qin Zhang. He didn't smile as much. His talk covered professional conduct and even workplace hygiene. Some researchers called it his "spoiled kids" routine: wash your hands when you go to the bathroom; bathe regularly; don't sleep in public; respect your colleagues; take responsibility for your projects. It sounded basic, but this was the sort of mentoring the young associate researchers needed. Roughly a year earlier, Lee had noticed the same shortcomings, prompting him to write the open letter to Chinese students that had caused such a splash. Some progress had been made, but too many kids still lacked role models for proper workplace behavior, let alone doing research and collaborating on projects. While the lab was open and researchers had enviable freedom to work on what they wanted, certain nonnegotiable rules of decorum and conduct were necessary.

As he watched his deputies in action, the magnitude of the challenge before him swept over Ya-Qin Zhang. He thought about how the lab's start-up mentality was necessarily changing as it grew, he hoped, into a world-class research center. He also thought about how to position the lab as Microsoft's center of expertise in Asia—and how it must eventually do a lot more to ensure the company's global future. Despite his apprehension, Zhang wasn't really worried. He had a quiet but supreme confidence in what the lab could accomplish. His certainty was born from personal experience. In the face of great adversity, he had always found success.

Ya-Qin Zhang was born in January 1966, the Year of the Snake in Chinese astrology. His hometown, Taiyuan, capital of coal-rich Shanxi province, sat in a wide plateau about 250 miles southwest of Beijing. It was one year before the start of the Cultural Revolution, a period of ten tumultuous years that would shake China to its core. When Ya-Qin was a toddler, Mao's Red Guard spirited his father away to a labor camp for what was chillingly called "reeducation." He never came back. It is unclear exactly what happened there—Ya-Qin doesn't talk about it today—but his father passed away when he was five years old. Ya-Qin's mother, Juan-Shang Bi, was left to raise her only son.

When Ya-Qin was six, his mother sent him to live with his maternal grandmother in Yuncheng, a small town in the south of Shanxi province. Over the next few years, he was shuttled around to live with relatives in various cities across China: Beijing, Xi'an, and finally back to Taiyuan at age eleven. The experiences taught Ya-Qin to be adaptable and self-sufficient.

The young Zhang also proved to be a superbly gifted student. Most would call him a genius or nerd—the Doogie Howser of China. He skipped five grades in elementary school and high school. But to this day, he deflects all personal credit, chalking his successes up to luck and the people around him. "Every time I moved to a new city," he remembers, "it was the middle of the school year, so I either had to skip a grade or retreat. So I skipped ahead."

In 1978, at the age of twelve, Zhang became the youngest college student in the entire country, enrolling in the gifted program of the prestigious University of Science and Technology of China in Hefei, west of Nanjing. But he wasn't just a bookworm. He had already developed serious hobbies, ranging from the Asian strategy game Go to classical oil painting ("in case I needed to find a job," he says). Intensely curious about all branches of science and engineering, he chose between majoring in mathematics or electrical engineering by flipping a coin. It came up engineering—and Zhang proceeded to graduate with honors and complete a master's degree.

In the fall of 1986, Zhang moved to Washington, D.C., to pursue his doctorate in electrical engineering at George Washington University. He turned down MIT and Princeton for the opportunity to work with Raymond Pickholtz, a renowned expert in communications and a pioneer of spread-spectrum radio, which is now an integral part of the CDMA standard for wireless communication. Pickholtz could tell right away that the kid was special—"brilliant, hardworking, and very thoughtful," he relates. On Zhang's second day, Pickholtz gave his new doctoral student eight books and a dozen papers to read. Zhang came back after a week and asked for more. From then on, Pickholtz would give his student piles of technical problems and reading material; Zhang would disappear for a few days and always come back with something new—observations, critiques, ideas, computed results. Pickholtz soon put him on two of his top research grants, one to develop secure satellite communications, the other to build a database to network and retrieve medical images.

One day Zhang didn't show up for a meeting, and Pickholtz grew worried. It turned out Zhang was in the hospital with a bleeding ulcer. He had been living on Coca-Cola and junk food, working at all hours, sleeping only a little bit here and there in the lab. "I got annoyed at him and had to start monitoring his diet and making sure he was getting rest," says Pickholtz. It would be the beginning of a long and fruitful collaboration and friendship. Zhang blazed through his dissertation research, passing his qualifying exams with a perfect score and finishing his Ph.D. in 1989. "Ya-Qin is by far the best student I ever had—and I have had many great students," gushes Pickholtz. "He is what I'd call a treasure of the world."

Out in the professional world, Zhang never slowed down. He spent his early career in telecommunications research at Contel Corporation and GTE Laboratories in Waltham, Massachusetts. In 1994, he moved to the research and development house Sarnoff (formerly RCA Laboratories) in Princeton. There, he quickly ascended the ranks, becoming the director of the Multimedia Technology Lab, where he was in charge of 50 researchers, many of them internationally renowned. Zhang's team was best known for its work on multimedia coding and communication, contributing heavily to the widely used MPEG-2 and MPEG-4 international standards for audio and video data compression and U.S. standards for HDTV. By 1998, Zhang had become one of the world's leading experts on digital television, video, and low-bit-rate communication—and had won seemingly every award in his field. (Years later, after he joined Microsoft in China, Eileen Chen, the Beijing lab's head administrator, dug some of these awards out of storage and put them up around the office. The ever-modest Zhang asked her to take them down.)

In the fall of that year, just weeks before the opening ceremony of Microsoft Research China, Kai-Fu Lee had telephoned from Beijing, offering Zhang the opportunity to join the lab. Lee made his case in a strong and compelling manner. "Kai-Fu was so convincing, so persuasive. He really sold me on the future of the lab," Zhang recalls. "He said, 'It's a challenge to start a research lab in China. It's never been done before. You can make history.'" After visiting with Rick Rashid and Dan Ling in Redmond, and blowing away Harry Shum and other interviewers during their dinner meeting, Zhang decided to take the plunge.

His decision stunned many at Sarnoff and in the wider multimedia research community. "It was a surprise to most people that I was going back to China," says Zhang. "Back then, it was not so popular. Today, it's considered an upgrade!" The concern among his U.S. colleagues was also what made it so intriguing: there was no precedent for doing world-class research in his field in China. Says Zhang, "My mentor at Sarnoff, [then] CEO Jim Carnes, said, 'I understand you want to make a change after five years, but going back to China? That's out of the mainstream, especially for doing research. You might do well, but you might be forgotten.' Lots of people, including my wife, had the same concern."

But when the thirty-two-year-old Zhang decided to move to Beijing to work for Microsoft after fourteen years in the U.S., his old advisor Pickholtz was one person who wasn't surprised. "When he was a student, he had to leave his mom behind in China," says Pickholtz. "He always said he wanted to give back to China."

In spite of the hardships he and his family had suffered, Zhang yearned to go back to his homeland and help improve the state of education and research training. And when he met up with his all-star lineup of new colleagues—starting with sake-drinking Harry Shum in the Tokyo airport—he knew he had made the right choice.

In the eleven months leading up to the Kunming retreat, Zhang concentrated on laying the groundwork for his term as managing director. It was a time of transition, and what the lab needed most was strong leadership. Carrying on Kai-Fu Lee's tradition, he focused on communicating his ideas in a series of lab-wide talks and essays. But he would do it in a style all his own.

If Zhang liked analogies, he loved equations. The former child prodigy delighted in using popular formulas from different fields—and some of his own creation—to frame his philosophies on research and management. Putting his principles in terms of equations got his point across in simple language that students and scientists could immediately grasp. This symbolized another kind of "low-bit-rate communication": transmitting complex ideas and imagery with a minimum of words. Plus, he says, it was easier for *him*. "Every few months, 'Ya-Qin's message' went out in a newsletter," he relates. "I had to write something!"

The catchiest—some might say kitschiest—of his written principles came to be known as "Ya-Qin's management equations." They consisted of five "formulas" that he felt people needed to know to run a successful research lab. It helped tremendously that his attitude in presenting them was playful and paternal, not arrogant or condescending:

1. $IT = IQ + IP$. In Zhang's view, becoming a world leader in information technology required raw talent and brainpower—but it also

required enforcing laws on intellectual property and patents. This latter point was a sticky matter in China, given the rampant piracy of Microsoft's software that was largely ignored by the government. Zhang referred to this equation extensively in his talks with the Chinese media and government officials.

2. $E = mc^2$. A takeoff on Einstein's famous equation relating energy, mass, and the speed of light. Here, it meant that an institution needed to reach critical mass and be moving fast enough to fulfill its potential and release its energy. ("I didn't win a prize for it," quips Zhang.)

3. $\Delta x \, \Delta p > \hbar/2$. Heisenberg's Uncertainty Principle. In the original equation, a quantum particle's position (x) and momentum (p) can only be known to within a tolerance called Planck's constant ($\hbar$). For Zhang, that represented the tradeoff between speed and precision in research. "It reflects two kinds of cultures," he says. "One is, you're very careful, you move very slow, you don't make mistakes. The other culture is, you move very fast, take risks, but make mistakes. For the lab, we encouraged the second culture. Because, if everything is successful, you fail—you didn't take enough risks."

4. $S \to \infty$. The Second Law of Thermodynamics states that the entropy (S) of any closed system, a measure of its disorder, grows infinitely. In Zhang's "parallel" equation, the idea was that the lab should be kept open to allow the free exchange of ideas with both industry and academia. "If a lab is closed in culture, eventually you're going to die," says Zhang.

5. $1 + 1 > 3$. The point of this mathematically incorrect relation was that research collaboration should only happen if it seems extremely worthwhile. Zhang believed in collaborating when it felt natural and, most importantly, when the whole was greater than the sum of its parts. "If one plus one is less than three, don't collaborate, because there's always a collaboration tax," he explains. "You shouldn't force people to work together."

The Chinese press and local government officials lapped up "Ya-Qin's management equations." His formulas for success were reprinted in technical journals and newspapers, circulated in academia, and widely cited by educators and policymakers intent on establishing the nation as a global technology leader.

All of this philosophizing, though, would have meant little without a backbone of technical excellence. The lab's bread and butter was research—advancing the state of the art in computer science. In that regard, Microsoft Research China was also making its mark. In early 2001, Zhang began to schedule two or three Bill G. demos a year: the reviews were becoming as routine as a face-to-face meeting with the world's richest man could be.

Bolstered by the foundation laid by Lee, the new managing director charted an even more ambitious research course for the lab. On Lee's watch, the enterprise had successfully wrestled with start-up issues—how to balance basic versus applied research, and how to communicate more effectively with young Chinese researchers. Under Zhang, the top priority shifted to excellence in research. "Zero tolerance for mediocrity," was how Zhang explained his standards. To make clear what he meant, he wheeled out another catchphrase: his "5/5" rule. With this, he decreed that in order to be considered world-class, the lab should contribute at least 5 percent of the papers to each of the top five journals and conferences in its areas of expertise.

Achieving the "5/5" benchmark would be a tall order for any research organization; no Chinese infotech lab had ever come close to filling it. But by mid-2001, behind scores of high-profile papers and patents in its original core areas of speech interfaces and multimedia, the Beijing lab was well on its way to success.

Lee had passed his own group specializing in Chinese speech recognition and text-to-speech synthesis on to Eric Chang, an MIT graduate who had been born in Taipei but had spent much of his youth in Beverly Hills: "Yes, it was 90210," he says. In the MIT vernacular, Chang was a "lifer"—meaning he had done his undergraduate, master's, and doctoral degrees at the school. And he had never stopped "drinking from a firehose," another MIT term for going all-out in both work and play. In mid-1998, Microsoft had hired Chang away from Nuance Communications, a hot start-up in Menlo Park, California, that provided much of the speech recognition engine behind automated airline reservations. (The company was later purchased by ScanSoft, which in October 2005 rebranded itself as Nuance.) Less than a year later, Lee had plucked him away from Redmond to join the Beijing lab.

Wiry and bespectacled, Chang brought a jittery intensity to the lab. He talked fast, asked lots of questions, and seemed to know what you were going to say before you said it—a living speech recognizer. He quickly distinguished himself as a major force in the speech world. In 2001, his group developed a number of cutting-edge prototypes, including a Web browser for mobile devices that worked with speech input instead of a keyboard or number pad, and quality control software that quantified how "natural" synthesized speech sounded. Both projects garnered "Best Paper" awards from prestigious international conferences, and supported Microsoft's long-range efforts to build user-friendly speech interfaces.

Ya-Qin Zhang's own area, multimedia coding and compression, was also coming on strong. His team's "scalable" coding scheme—which he presented at the second Bill G. review in June 2000—won its own Best Paper award, this one from a prestigious IEEE journal. The technology turned out to work well for a wide range of band-widths and devices, so in theory it could be used to improve everything from videoconferencing over cell phones to Internet video streaming to HDTV.

Some tricks used in this type of coding came from the image-processing algorithms being developed in HongJiang Zhang's media computing and information processing group. The group's goal was to enable computers to analyze, understand, and retrieve multimedia—useful for automatically searching for digital photos, video, and audio files on a hard drive or across the World Wide Web. HongJiang Zhang's group was even more prolific than the others. Every year, the Beijing researchers would rank themselves by how many papers they published; Zhang would invariably come out on top—as he did in 2001, with more than a dozen to his name. "Always number one," he would say.

Still in his first year as managing director, Ya-Qin Zhang seized the opportunity to move the lab into key new areas that would help transform research results into products. Early in 2001, he formalized two new research thrusts that drew naturally on the lab's existing areas of expertise and meshed tightly with the latest interests of Microsoft's business units back in Redmond.

The first area was digital entertainment. In January, Bill Gates had unveiled the Xbox game platform to the public at the annual Consumer Electronics Show in Las Vegas; researchers in Microsoft's labs worldwide were already scrambling to put technologies in the pipeline that could help game developers in time for the actual product launch that fall. Zhang's idea was to split off a separate entertainment graphics group from the visual computing group led by Harry Shum. "We already had lots of great results with graphics. Harry gave us a lot of expertise. The talent base was there," he explains. "And look at the company business. Xbox was taking off. There was a need to develop new technologies in the platform and the tools and games. It was an opportunity for us to help the business group."

While the new Beijing effort was designed to complement the existing graphics research group in Redmond, Zhang felt that combining his lab's unique strengths in vision, graphics, and digital multimedia would soon establish it as a center of excellence for the company. Baining Guo, the former Intel researcher who had rushed to Beijing just in time for the first anniversary ceremony, was named manager of the new graphics group. Guo had already juiced up the lab's creative flair. He didn't chit-chat much and put on a bit of a mysterious air when he took visitors around the lab. He kept a large and rather menacing monkey wrench in the corner of his lab area, he said, "in case things aren't working." Now, he and Shum put their heads together and hired half a dozen top researchers to fill out the new group. Guo even set aside a special room along an inner hallway for Xbox research. For years, its windows would remain papered over, the sign on the door reading: "Xbox: confidential." Guo seemed to delight in the mystique it created. "Some of our best people work in there," was all he would say about what went on behind the door.

Guo and Shum launched a variety of projects designed to make next-generation video games more realistic. One tapped principles from computer vision such as Shum's concentric mosaics to enable 3-D visualization of virtual environments. Others sought realistic simulation of natural phenomena like water flow, new ways to render complex textures like tree bark quickly and efficiently, and better simulation of human movements and facial expressions. Continuing the balance of basic and applied research, the groups also focused on fundamental advances that pushed the state of the art in graphics. The key benchmark on this front was SIGGRAPH, the world's largest and most prestigious computer graphics conference, which drew 10,000 people a year. Only about one of ten papers submitted was accepted. In 2001, the lab had two papers approved by the conference—a strong start for a lab effort barely two years old.

While graphics research was taking off, a second area—wireless networking—also heated up amid a confluence of favorable factors. As Zhang explains, "One reason to start wireless was we had a lot of people working on networking and low-bit-rate communication"—the study of how to transmit and receive information under severe constraints. Wireless was basically an extreme case of low-bit-rate communication, in which the conditions for sending bits over a cellular network, for example, could change at any time depending on location, weather conditions, traffic volume, and other factors. "The second thing," Zhang continues, "was that in China, the largest mobile market, there was lots of excitement and lots of talent. Many universities have wireless and telecom as majors, so there's affinity to the market."

So Zhang split off a wireless networking group from his main multimedia effort. The new research team was not to concentrate on traditional wireless communication—the logistics of modems, radios, and cell towers. Instead, Zhang positioned it to develop cutting-edge software that could allow developers to model the changing conditions of a network, and allow cell phones and handheld computers to send and receive any kind of data—voice, text, video—from anywhere. Here, unlike with the digital entertainment group, the Beijing lab found almost no overlap with work going on elsewhere in the company. "Microsoft did not have a huge research group focused on wireless, so there was a need to create such a group," Zhang says. "We could be the center of expertise because of our talent base and the market. I always felt Microsoft should get into the cellular communication and software business."

Getting wireless off the ground was up to a pair of rising stars out of Zhang's group. One was Qian Zhang, the Wuhan University graduate who had nervously gone to George Chen's hotel room for an interview. She had never worked on wireless or multimedia in school. But before joining the lab, she had asked Ya-Qin Zhang to recommend books and papers to get herself up to speed. Some were difficult to find in her university library in Wuhan, but she came back with in-depth comments and questions. She was like a young Ya-Qin, when he would go off to absorb the weekly readings assigned by Raymond Pickholtz.

Tapped to manage the new wireless networking group was Wenwu Zhu. Tall, lanky, and originally from Qiqihar in northern China, Zhu had been a star researcher at Lucent Technologies' Bell Labs in New Jersey and had collaborated with Ya-Qin Zhang for years. In the summer of 1999, he was talking to Zhang about a paper they were writing on wireless multimedia when he learned about the Beijing lab. "Before I thought, 'China? Why go to China?'" he relates. "Then I saw Ya-Qin, HongJiang [Zhang], and Shipeng [Li] were all there! It was the people that attracted me."

Zhu quickly bought into the lab's start-up mentality. After dinner, the researchers would frequently go back to work, even on weekends. "It wasn't like that at Lucent," says Zhu. But that was okay—things were different here, and he never forgot the way Kai-Fu Lee had introduced him to the press when he had first started at the lab.

"This is Wenwu Zhu, a 'Nobel' award winner," Lee had dead-panned. "No-Bell Labs anymore."

The yin and yang of running the lab continued. And from the start of his tenure Ya-Qin Zhang strived to take the relationship-building aspect of his job to an even higher level.

It didn't help that Microsoft's image abroad was flagging, especially in light of the U.S. Department of Justice's antitrust case, which was coming to a head. The trial had begun just before Microsoft Research China had formally opened—throwing shadows over the company's image-building efforts even then. In June 2000, just a month before Zhang took over as managing director, U.S. District Judge Thomas Penfield Jackson announced that in light of what he perceived as Microsoft's unfair business practices, he would grant the Justice Department its long-standing request to split the company into two separate firms. Microsoft's lawyers would appeal the decision—and eventually get it overturned—but in China a lot of damage was done. As Sheila Shang explains, the news triggered more suspicion and bad press across the Pacific than it had in the United States. "In China, the government is holy," she says. "What kind of company fights with its own government? You must have done something very bad."

Zhang understood the environment in which the lab's young Chinese researchers and their peers were raised. Their parents had grown up, as he had, during the Cultural Revolution of the 1960s and 1970s. As the novelist Shuo Wang wrote in *Time* magazine, "Back then, children sang, 'Mommy and Daddy can't compare with Chairman Mao, the greatness of heaven and earth can't compare with the great kindness of the Party.' The slogan board on the door of the police headquarters read in big red characters, 'Resolutely support the righteous anti-imperialist, anti-colonial struggles of all the peoples of the world.'"

The lab would need to be even more proactive in building *guanxi*. Interestingly, while Zhang and Kai-Fu Lee were both highly accomplished scientists and managers returning to their families' roots in China, their personalities and social strengths were quite different. Where Lee was formal and meticulous in his preparation, Zhang tended to be looser and more apt to get ahead of himself. Journalist Zhijun Ling described Zhang as "charmingly naïve. He speaks softly and always to the point no matter how complicated the question is. Lee cares about his appearance, is good at PR, and always speaks with propriety to the journalists. While Zhang never cares about what others think of him."

Still, Zhang did hold a trump card: having grown up and gone to college in mainland China, as opposed to Taiwan and the U.S. like Lee, he may have been more comfortable dealing with Chinese politics. At least, he knew how to fit in. "Be modest, be humble, respect others," was his mantra. Coming from someone with his level of accomplishment, that meant a lot. He showed an ability to relate to starving students and high officials alike. On his own time, Zhang gave seminars, advised students, and took part in discussions that went beyond his Microsoft job description. "Ya-Qin has been quite active in academia here, giving many keynote speeches," says Shiqiang Yang, executive vice chair of the Department of Computer Science and Technology at Tsinghua University. When Chinese officials looked at Zhang, they didn't see Microsoft so much as they saw a world-class scientist returning to help educate his homeland.

Zhang's academic achievements earned the respect of university presidents, deans, and the Chinese Academy of Sciences—the government-run research and funding institution with far greater power than its namesake in the U.S. With some 80,000 employees, the Chinese academy was something like a merger between the U.S. National Academy of Sciences, the National Institutes of Health, the National Science Foundation, and the Department of Energy's national laboratories. Its president was a member of the thirty-person Chinese cabinet, with the same rank and privileges as the minister of personnel, minister of education, and minister of science and technology.

But it was Zhang's efforts to engage local city officials that paid off first. Since the early days of the lab, he had served on Beijing's city planning teams, including the committee in charge of construction and development in the high-tech Zhongguancun district. He used that service to learn the ins and outs of municipal laws. Beijing had strict residency rules to control overcrowding; people who wanted to move to the city from other parts of China had to receive *hukou*s, the residency permits Gates had asked Kai-Fu Lee about in the first Bill G. review.

At the time, Lee had explained to the chairman that China's reform policies made this less of an issue than in the past. But the story wasn't really that simple. In early 2001, as the Microsoft lab's numbers swelled to nearly 100 researchers, residency permits became a thorn in the lab's side. To get a permit, a new hire had to submit rigorous paperwork, which was time-consuming and could be denied for any number of reasons—especially if the researcher wanted to move with a spouse or family. The lab faced the daunting task of seeking approval for each new hire.

Fortunately for Microsoft, Zhang had gotten to know some people in high places. He had become good friends with the deputy mayor of Beijing, Zhihua Liu. In his mid-fifties, Liu had a weathered countenance; he had been a mine worker for eight years before getting into politics. Now he was in charge of science, technology, and culture in Beijing. He would later be credited with helping to stop the spread of SARS in the city. Zhang also knew Liu's boss, the mayor of Beijing. Qi Liu (no relation to Zhihua) was a boyish-looking hotshot in his early fifties who often wore a black leather jacket over a freshly pressed suit. The men had visited the lab several times. "They both went overboard to help us because we helped bring world-class talent to Beijing," relates Zhang.

One day in the spring of 2001, Zhang picked up the phone and called Zhihua Liu. Zhang explained that he had a dozen new hires who needed permits. For the lab to do the applications itself would take several days of back and forth messaging and paper-pushing for each person. "Can you help?" he asked. The next day Liu sent his director of personnel to the lab. He spent the afternoon going through the recruits case by case to finish the paperwork on the spot. "Problem solved," beams Zhang.

The biggest coup by far in Zhang's early tenure was establishing Microsoft Research China as a postdoctoral degree–granting institution. In China, a postdoctoral certificate is the highest, most respected formal degree: earning a postdoc typically guarantees not only a good state job but also employment for your spouse and schooling for your kids. In Europe and the U.S., by contrast, a postdoc is a research position—not a degree at all—and confers few benefits other than experience. Zhang, who had never been a postdoctoral researcher or student, jokes that his mother told him, "You haven't finished your education yet. When are you getting your postdoc?"

Under Kai-Fu Lee, the lab had begun hiring fresh Ph.D.s from Chinese universities as associate researchers, in effect giving them a two-year probationary period to prove themselves. Zhang's idea was that after the two interim years, they should receive a postdoctoral degree—whether or not they became permanent hires. That would add prestige to the position and offer a more concrete benefit even to those researchers who weren't hired—and therefore would be good for Microsoft, the students, and the state of Chinese industry and education. But as Zhang puts it, "The idea was not hard to conceive. The execution was hard."

Setting up a postdoctoral program in the lab would take serious negotiations with the government, which strictly regulated academic degrees and who could award them. Zhang laid the groundwork in a series of meetings with officials at the Ministry of Personnel in central Beijing. "We always went to meet them there, to show the respect," says Sheila Shang. In the meetings, Zhang was open about how he thought the program would help Chinese education as well as Microsoft. The early discussions centered on how to adapt the existing postdoc guidelines to what Microsoft wanted to do. For instance, Microsoft could not provide jobs for postdoc spouses or school for their children. But it could pay postdocs a higher salary than they would receive at a university or a Chinese firm.

The ministry at first wasn't buying it. Officials might have perceived Microsoft as a foreign entity trying to dictate its own rules. The breakthrough meeting occurred in the early spring of 2001. Zhang and a handful of his colleagues met with three representatives from the Ministry of Personnel. Zhang proposed that they kindly consider the Microsoft postdoc as a "pilot program," an experiment that the ministry would review after a two-year probationary period. It gave the government the final authority—you judge our students, we judge you—and that seemed to do the trick.

Still, the deal would require a policy change and the creation of a new category of postdoc, no small feat considering China's many layers of bureaucracy. Zhang credits his university relations manager, George Chen, and his government-savvy assistant Cherry Han with deftly navigating the hundreds of pages of paperwork needed to seal the deal. The final terms of the agreement were agreed on at a dinner meeting between Zhang and the minister of personnel, Songtao Xu.

In April 2001, just before the Kunming offsite, the lab officially became a postdoctoral degree-granting institution—the first and so far only foreign company's lab to be awarded such status. But one more hurdle remained: public perception. At a signing ceremony and press conference on the fifth floor of the Sigma building, a reporter from *China Daily* asked the minister Songtao Xu point-blank, "Are you afraid that Microsoft is stealing talent?" The lab's PR staff cringed at the question—fearing the worst—and was prepared to do some damage control. Xu, an older gentleman with white hair and a severe look about him, cut an intimidating figure; what he said would influence what a lot of higher-ups thought of Microsoft and its program.

To their surprise and relief, Minister Xu paused and then replied, "No, not at all. I believe their slogan, 'While working at Microsoft, serving the people of China.'"

6

The Great Wall and Other
Microsoft Creations

October 2001–January 2004

Microsoft is the first company to put together such a comprehensive program to help China.
—JI ZHOU, CHINESE MINISTER OF EDUCATION

O n a crisp, sunny morning that October, Ya-Qin Zhang found himself pacing the lobby of the Pudong Shangri-La hotel in Shanghai. He was waiting for Bill Gates, who was staying in the same hotel, on the same floor as Zhang. Microsoft Research China was hosting one leg of its third annual conference on Computing in the 21st Century at Shanghai Jiaotong, arguably the most prestigious university outside of Beijing. No less than Chinese President Jiang Zemin had done his undergraduate study there, finishing in 1947 with a degree in electrical engineering. The conference, which opened in Beijing but moved to a different second city each year, had become quite the popular ticket. Even more so in this case, because for the first time, Gates himself was going to speak.

Microsoft's operations in China were entering a new phase in the fall of 2001. Gates and company still saw the country as an emerging infotech power, if not yet a particularly profitable market. Although China made up less than 1 percent of its sales, Microsoft was willing to start pouring more resources into product testing, training for software developers, and tech support for small businesses.* Its hope, of course, was that a new generation of Chinese software would be built on Microsoft platforms such as Windows. During his visit to Shanghai, Gates was quoted in *People's Daily* as saying, "Microsoft sees huge market potential here in China and its incredible human resources, if developed properly."

It helped that at home, Microsoft had finally turned the corner on its antitrust case. Under the new Bush administration, the Justice Department no longer threatened to break up the corporation, opting instead to enforce restrictions and monetary settlements over the next few years. Things were looking up for the company.

When Gates emerged from the elevator, he wore a big grin on his face. He told Zhang that he had enjoyed a wonderful dinner with President Jiang Zemin the night before. They had discussed a wide range of topics, including music, education, technology, the state of Chinese software development, and even Microsoft's employee policies. The Asian Pacific Economic Cooperation summit, one of the world's largest, was taking place in the city later that week, and President Jiang was the host. Gates would attend the summit in good company—the distinguished guest list included the likes of President Bush, Russian President Vladimir Putin, and Japanese Prime Minister Junichiro Koizumi.

Outside the hotel, Gates and Zhang joined Michael Rawding, Microsoft's vice president in charge of the Greater China region, for the car ride to Shanghai Jiaotong. Rawding had been doing sales and marketing in China, Hong Kong, and Taiwan since 1998 and would later become president of Microsoft Japan—a much larger market despite its smaller geographic size. The car ride was smoother than Zhang expected. Shanghai was generally more Westernized, more commercial, and more crowded even than Beijing. But that morning the streets were quiet, because officials had shut down traffic and busi-

---

* Despite an estimated 6 million PCs sold in China in 2000, software sales for Microsoft China were only slightly higher than Microsoft Argentina, where just 400,000 personal computers had been sold.

nesses for three days in preparation for the economic summit. It was barely a month after the terrorist attacks of September 11, so security was extra tight.

Zhang briefed the chairman on the conference agenda. Gates seemed in an uncommonly good mood and asked many questions. "How many students will be there?" he inquired excitedly. "Will they be graduate, undergraduates, computer-science students?" A total of about 3,000 graduate and undergraduates, replied Zhang. And not only from Shanghai Jiaotong. They would also come from other parts of southern China, from as far away as the University of Science and Technology in Hefei and Zhejiang University in Hangzhou. The men proceeded to talk about the Beijing lab and Zhang's new research programs in graphics and wireless multimedia, even getting into some technical details of coding schemes. "Bill was amazed at the trajectory of the lab and the caliber of talent we had hired," Zhang later recalled.

By nine o'clock that morning, all eyes were on Shanghai Jiaotong's main campus. Outside the Jinjing auditorium, a crowd of about 2,000 people awaited the arrival of the world's richest man. That didn't count the 1,500 already in their seats inside. Microsoft had distributed free tickets to selected faculty and students. But because of overflowing demand, scalpers were reportedly getting 400 yuan a pop (about fifty U.S. dollars), a hefty sum for a Chinese university student. Huge TV screens were set up outside for the overflow crowd. Security had cleared the streets and cordoned off a few blocks around the building. Across the street, a long glass wall about two meters high, in front of a library, held back onlookers trying to catch a glimpse of Gates. As the time for his arrival approached, Microsoft staffers recall, it became a wall of faces, as students and passers-by squeezed in and pressed their noses to the glass. Some students even climbed nearby trees to get a better view.

Finally, the motorcade pulled up in front of the auditorium. A shiny black Mercedes stopped at the curb, followed by a van and a few other official-looking vehicles. A small welcoming contingent was waiting for Gates and Zhang. They included Microsoft senior vice president and chief technology officer Craig Mundie, Rick Rashid,

HongJiang Zhang, Harry Shum, and Shengwu Xie, the president of Shanghai Jiaotong. As the Mercedes door opened, they all moved forward to greet the chairman—but Gates was not inside. At that point Shum, standing near the back of the car, heard a door slam and a familiar voice behind him say, "Hey!" It was Gates, stepping out of the ordinary-looking van, with almost nobody noticing him.

Campus security hustled Gates and his entourage through a back entrance and into a VIP lounge, where they chatted with university officials and took pictures together. A few minutes later, Ya-Qin Zhang went onstage to kick off the conference, addressing the crowd of 3,500 students, faculty, and guests. After thanking university officials and the National Natural Science Foundation of China for co-sponsoring the event, he summarized the day's speakers and then turned things over to the Microsoft chairman.

Gates took the stage to a raucous ovation. His hour-long talk, titled "The Last 10 Years . . . and Shaping the Next," highlighted Microsoft's contributions to computing and spelled out how information technology would transform daily life, especially in rapidly developing economies like China's. He vowed to partner with Chinese academia, government, and software developers to make the transformation happen. Ever the consummate businessman, Gates then plugged the imminent worldwide release of Windows XP (for "Experience"), just one week away. It would be the first new PC operating system from Microsoft in three years. He also made a plug for Microsoft's Xbox video-game system, which would debut that November.

The Microsoft chairman looked relaxed and comfortable, in his element. Looking back, Zhang once remarked: "Bill always loves China. He loves the talents, the culture. Every time he talks with Chinese students, he feels energized."

The Gates talk proved a watershed event for the Beijing lab. For starters, it marked the first time the chairman showcased the lab's technology onstage. The task of giving the seven-minute demos on graphics and multimedia fell to Shum and HongJiang Zhang, respectively. The preparation had been nerve-wracking. At nine o'clock the night before, the researchers were in the auditorium testing the demos when security officers barged in with bomb-sniffing dogs and told them they had to leave. The demos were in good shape, but the managers hadn't had time to check the timing of an important file download Gates would use during his talk. If Gates pushed the button himself, he'd have to endure a half-minute of dead time; but if someone else did it too early, Gates would be caught off-guard. So the morning of the talk, Shum arranged for an IT manager to hide behind a curtain onstage, Wizard of Oz–style, and practice triggering the download ahead of time so it would pop up at just the right moment in the chairman's talk.

In the end, Shum pulled off the timing without a hitch and even hammed it up during his demo, telling the audience, "This is my homecoming"—he grew up in Shanghai's Pudong neighborhood— and incorporating the "beautiful Pudong river and skyline" in his demo of computer-generated raindrops hitting the water. The crowd ate it up. None of this was lost on Gates, who seemed very pleased with the warm reception.

Something else happened that day that spoke volumes about Microsoft's commitment to the region, and the soaring importance of the lab. In his talk, Gates announced that Microsoft Research China was changing its name to Microsoft Research Asia. It might have seemed a minor point—semantics really—but the decision had been mulled over for months. The previous summer, Ya-Qin Zhang had visited several universities in Japan and South Korea. In meetings with officials, he had found it awkward to propose "joint laboratories"—formal research collaborations in which Microsoft would fund students and projects—without having a more inclusive mantle for the Beijing lab. No one would say it outright, but there was reluctance on the part of officials in Japan and South Korea to be seen as so closely tied with something "China." Zhang had felt some of the cross-cultural tensions and discussed it with the lab's management team and with Rick Rashid; they agreed a name change was in order.

It proved a subtle but important move. "Initially we targeted China because lots of research was on speech recognition and user interfaces for China," explains Zhang. "As we grew, we wanted to expand our engagement to the whole region. We found it's a lot easier to attract talent if we have a more global, regional agenda." Within two years, Microsoft would formalize joint labs at the University of Tokyo, Korea Advanced Institute of Science and Technology, National University of Singapore, Hong Kong University of Science and Technology, National Taiwan University, and the University of Sydney.

"The last thing we wanted was to be perceived as a local lab," Shum said later.

The winds of change were swirling again in the spring of 2002. One blustery morning, Zhang was riding in a private car from his home to visit the Chinese Ministry of Education. He had received a call earlier that week from the secretary of the recently appointed minister of education, Ji Zhou. The minister wanted to know if Zhang was available to meet for breakfast or tea. It wasn't a great week for Zhang—he had a slew of papers and presentations to prepare—but he made time anyway. Minister Zhou had summoned him to discuss a new idea that Zhang was pushing—a proposal that would become Microsoft's largest and most important collaboration with China to date.

Things were changing for Zhang on a personal level as well. In November, his wife Jenny had quit her job as a financial analyst at Dow Jones and sold their house and cars in New Jersey to move to Beijing. Their two children, Sophie and Brandon—the boy was now almost two—had never lived in China. His family's arrival meant no more staying in hotels. Microsoft arranged for Zhang to rent a modest house in a secluded subdivision on the outskirts of Beijing. It was the same neighborhood in which Kai-Fu Lee's family had resided. The commute was longer, but worth it.

It was a dusty day with little traffic, and Zhang enjoyed the ride over to the minister's office in central Beijing. He liked to joke that, as usual, he spent the commute taking a nap. In reality, he read his e-mail and gathered his thoughts. Zhang called his proposal the "Great Wall Plan." The name, born from a late-night lab brainstorming session, was meant to convey a strong alliance or coalition. The idea was for Microsoft Research Asia to invest in Chinese software development and education on a far grander scale than it ever had before. First, Zhang had obtained the tentative support of the National Reform and Development Commission, which was in charge of state planning and reform. The commission had proposed an initiative in which Microsoft would provide training for professional software developers—basically teach them how to write better code and deliver product-ready software. Zhang made clear he supported such an initiative, but he didn't agree with the notion of only supporting what he called "blue-collar" developers. "China needs not only programmers, but also program managers," he insisted, pushing for management training to be part of the deal.

Now he was trying to work out details of the training with the Ministry of Education. The meeting was set for eight o'clock. George Chen from university relations met Zhang at the minister's office, where, they later recounted, a secretary offered them a choice of half a dozen different teas. After a few minutes of chitchat—Ya-Qin had met Minister Zhou when he was president of Huazhong University of Science and Technology and mayor of Wuhan—the men got down to business. The minister proposed that the best way for Microsoft to help train software developers was to sponsor China's recently created "software colleges"—specialized computer-science departments that focused on development. That was fine with Zhang, but he again insisted that the plan should cover project management as well. It could have been taken the wrong way—as Microsoft trying to gain deeper control of China's IT infrastructure by training its own future managers. But Zhang's point was that investing in professional managerial education would pay dividends for the nation as it struggled to develop its economy. To his surprise, Zhou proved very supportive. "The minister's enthusiasm was much more than I expected," recalls Zhang.

Toward the end of the two-hour meeting, Minister Zhou commented, "Microsoft is the first company to put together such a comprehensive program to help China. On behalf of the Ministry of Education, I personally would like to be involved. Please update me in three to six months." The meeting concluded, as these encounters typically did, with a friendly photo session.

A series of summits with business managers, lawyers, and education and government officials was needed to finalize the deal. But the essence was agreed upon that morning. In the end, the Great Wall Plan called for Microsoft to invest 200 million yuan (about $25 million) over three years, with an option to renew for another three years starting in 2005. The bulk of the money would be spent on software curriculum development, faculty and managerial training, equipment, and textbooks for the 35 existing software colleges, which were housed at top universities around China. Some funds would also be used to sponsor the newly created Microsoft postdoctoral fellowships, as well as lab internships for undergraduate and graduate students.

Zhou had not exaggerated when he spoke of the precedent-setting magnitude of the Great Wall Plan. Another signing ceremony was in order. It took place on a hot afternoon in June at the St. Regis Hotel, the lavish site of the lab's opening ceremony (when it was known as the International Club). A horde of about 150 journalists showed up for the televised event. Steve Ballmer attended in person. Minister Zhou himself could not make it that day—but no slight was intended. In the lobby, Ballmer and Zhang chatted with his top representatives, including vice minister of education Qin-Ping Zhao, and the director general of higher education, Yaoxue Zhang. The Microsoft men also greeted the presidents of the top five Chinese universities: Peking University, Tsinghua, Shanghai Jiaotong, Zhejiang, and the University of Science and Technology of China. Each of these schools housed a software college.

The plan for the signing was for Zhang to sit at the center of a long table, flanked by the five university presidents and ministry officials. Ballmer and vice minister Zhao would stand behind them, in the back center of the stage. In traditional Chinese culture, the center is the position of greatest honor. But before they all sat down, Zhang had an idea. To show more respect for the guests—"these guys are the presidents of the most prestigious universities!" he explained later— he politely requested that they sit at the center of the table, in alphabetical order by university. Zhang then took a place on one end, signifying that he acted as an equal participant.

Nothing was ever said about Zhang's gesture of respect. But he could be assured it didn't go unnoticed. After all, there was even a physical reminder. Zhang notes how the official documents were passed from person to person and signed. Because of the last-minute change in seating order, he laughs, "In the end, the signatures were in the wrong places."

In the months leading up to the Great Wall Plan signing, Microsoft Research Asia was also starting to make its first significant impact on the company's business. From the beginning, Kai-Fu Lee had stressed the importance of doing research that was relevant to products five years down the road. But it was on Zhang's watch—still less than four years into the lab's existence—that Microsoft Research Asia reached critical mass in all of its major research areas. The center had doubled in size to 140 researchers and was pumping out more than 200 scientific papers a year. More to the point, the lab's technologies were beginning to trickle into the product pipeline—with a flood on the way.

One of the earliest successes had been a Chinese dictation system for Office XP that used the same core speech recognition technology Lee had presented at the lab's first Bill G. review in October 1999. In the summer of 2001, X. D. Huang, who had helped recruit Lee and was then the general manager of Microsoft's Speech Platforms product group, demonstrated the system at Tsinghua University. "Some of the students didn't believe what I was saying about the technology," he recalls. "So there was a challenge." The showdown pitted Huang, speaking Mandarin into a microphone and speech recognizer, against an undergraduate typing the characters on a keyboard—in a race to see who could accurately enter a passage of Chinese text the fastest. "I beat him two to one," exults Huang. "I finished everything in half the time, including the corrections I had to go back and make . . . That made a big point right there."

By the time of the Great Wall Plan signing in the spring of 2002, multimedia, graphics, and wireless research projects were also feeding into products. A slew of new image-processing features, including an automatic home video editor, slide show organizer, and photo retrieval system, shipped as part of Windows Movie Maker. A bit later in the year, a graphics package that performed fast rendering of realistic-looking water simulations shipped for Xbox video games. Cross-breeding was also taking place between research groups. For Xbox, the wireless group developed an algorithm to give remote users smoother and more reliable access to peer-to-peer gaming networks—and the speech group created voice-morphing software that let players personalize their characters' voices.

The lab even helped tailor products to specific geographic markets. A version of Office set for release in Japan included Beijing-lab technology that automatically generated stylized cartoon drawings from a person's digital photos. People could use the renderings as "avatars," or digital likenesses, when sending personalized e-mails and greeting cards—applications that were more popular in Japan than elsewhere. And a Chinese version of Office included an "English writing" help feature that checked whether certain groupings of English words made sense together as the user typed—and suggested alternate choices on the fly.

The most mature technologies, however, came from the lab's original focus areas. The user-interface team, led by engineering psychologist Jian Wang, had developed key technology for a handwriting system called "digital ink." Users could take notes and draw charts and tables on a computer screen with a penlike tool; Wang's software would then allow them to edit and store the text and diagrams digitally, as simply as drawing a circle around the notes they wanted to digitize and selecting a pop-up menu command. Gates had seen this digital-ink research demo at one of the increasingly frequent reviews and immediately pegged it for the company's Tablet PC platform, which launched later in 2002, not long after the Great Wall Plan ceremony.

In speech interfaces, Eric Chang's text-to-speech software—which took typed text in Chinese or English and outputted natural-sounding spoken words—had also made a strong impression on the Microsoft chairman. It would allow users to listen to e-mail, for instance, when they were on the road. Text-to-speech was still a few years behind digital ink. But this technology would soon be transferred to a product group and bound for Vista, the company's forthcoming version of Windows.

Though the lab was experiencing more and more success, the grueling workload exacted a personal toll on the researchers—even with a small technology transfer group working full tilt on readying research prototypes for the handoff to development teams. On top of supervising research projects, lab managers like HongJiang Zhang, Eric Chang, and Jian Wang were making the thirteen-hour plane trip to Redmond as often as twice a month to meet with product groups. They attended to conference calls and e-mails at all hours, in part because of the sixteen-hour time difference (fifteen hours when daylight saving is not in effect) from headquarters.

"Researchers sacrificed their personal lives to work with product teams," recalls HongJiang Zhang. "We all realized this would not scale up." He and his colleagues understood that how the lab handled the impending bottleneck of new technology transfers would be key to its ultimate success.

In the spring of 2003, severe acute respiratory syndrome, or SARS, gripped Beijing in a near-panic. Nearly a thousand people died from the disease, mostly in cities across China, and several thousand cases were reported worldwide. For the better part of May and June, theaters, libraries, schools, and businesses in Beijing were closed. Residents were advised to stay indoors. The World Health Organization slapped a travel advisory on all of mainland China—and Beijing in particular. At the Microsoft lab, students and postdocs got orders to stay home. Ya-Qin Zhang remembers coming in one day to find the lab totally empty. "The students are like your own kids," he sighs. "Sometimes they get on your nerves. But when they leave, you realize how much you miss them."

With fewer visitors and meetings, Zhang had more time to focus on government relations and outreach—implementing the Great Wall Plan during this period. By summertime, the quarantine had lifted, and life in the lab returned to normal, with a steady stream of prominent visitors. The highest-ranking official to visit was Jian Song, a former state councilor who was still an iconic figure in Chinese science and politics. Song was then chairman of the State Commission on Science and Technology and had served as Deng Xiaoping's and then Jiang Zemin's top science and technology advisor for the better part of two decades. He was also a mentor of the new president of China, Hu Jintao. Several members of the Chinese cabinet reported to Song, including the minister of science and technology. As if that wasn't enough, Song was also president of the Chinese Academy of Engineering.

Song, a former department chair at the University of Science and Technology, had first met Ya-Qin Zhang in 1978 when the twelve-year-old Zhang arrived on campus to begin his college studies. But it was in 2000, when they served together on a Beijing science advisory board, that they first interacted as colleagues. Song was the chairman, Zhang the newcomer. For years, Song had championed the idea that Chinese innovation should be the domain of the young and talented, not the old and well-connected. Song believed in supporting higher education and independent small companies over large, state-run institutions. He and Zhang hit it off well and had several follow-up meetings to discuss the state of Chinese science education.

In late September 2003, Song came to visit Microsoft Research Asia, together with a few other dignitaries. They arrived that morning a bit early for the appointment, so they went directly up to Zhang's office on the fifth floor of the Sigma building. Zhang walked out of his office and was surprised—and more than a little embarrassed—to see his distinguished visitors standing in the hallway, waiting for him without an escort. But Song wasn't fazed. In his early seventies and sporting thick black glasses, he immediately began asking Zhang lots of questions.

Zhang and his deputies regained their composure and treated

their guests to the full tour. First, Zhang gave an overview of the lab and its mission. He even trotted out his "management equations"; Song got a kick out of them. Harry Shum proceeded to give a more technical talk on graphics and computer vision research. Some of the mathematics he used—ideas such as feedback loops and orders of convergence—were familiar to Song, who had been a leading scientist in cybernetics and control theory. The former state councilor asked some detailed technical questions that impressed everyone. Then it was on to demos of some of the latest research projects under way. The unprecedented four-hour visit concluded with a trademark photo session.

Two weeks later, at Zhang's invitation, Song visited Microsoft's Redmond headquarters. There, he was hosted by Rick Rashid and Kai-Fu Lee and met with Bill Gates and Steve Ballmer. An astute judge of scientific and managerial talent, Song was struck by ways in which Microsoft might serve as a model for Chinese industry, as well as government and academic institutions. The influential advisor stressed this belief and expressed his appreciation of Zhang and Lee in a personal letter sent after his trip. He wrote in Mandarin: "From each of you and the other elites at Microsoft, I see great hope in the future, both for Microsoft China and Microsoft worldwide . . . High IQ alone is far from enough. We all know how important an open, world-leading work environment as well as an excellent team with outstanding management [is] to the good use of one's talent. Otherwise, if one is confined to close surroundings, wisdom just becomes petty tricks for petty actions . . . IQ, honesty, modesty, diligence and teamwork spirit, which were frequently mentioned by Kai-Fu, and the 'management equations' upheld by Ya-Qin constitute the typical characteristics of that orderly open system we found at Microsoft, for which I zealously advocate in the same way like you."

The letter continued, "I should say that I was particularly impressed by the ideal model I saw during my visit to Microsoft Research Asia on 30 September and to Microsoft headquarters on 16 October. Most people there work hard, strive for progress, keep good balance of work and life, and keep up with the times. All these are badly needed by many

Chinese institutions. I do hope the younger generation in China can earnestly learn from this cultural atmosphere, which not only taps personal wisdom but also benefits our country and society. While we should thank Bill Gates for his ambitious strategy, we should also thank you two for your great contributions in establishing Microsoft Research Asia. I believe in many occasions, cultural exchange is more important than technology exchange."

Song concluded, "Please allow me to congratulate you from the bottom of my heart on the fantastic achievements made by Microsoft and Microsoft Research Asia. By launching and leading such a momentous research institution, you have made admirable contributions to the advancement of the world, and of course, Chinese civilization. You should be proud of it . . . Words cannot express my appreciation for both of you."

In the sixth-floor conference room of the Sigma building, champagne corks popped in unison with hearty cheers. The Beijing lab's administrative staff wheeled in a cart bearing a five-layer white cake the size of a tabletop. The lid of the box flipped up to reveal the words "Happy 5th Birthday MSRA," written in frosting. It was November 5, 2003. Lab researchers and visitors mingled and talked excitedly among themselves, holding little plastic cups and plates. All that was missing were party hats.

Not a bad way to finish off a Technical Advisory Board meeting, normally a reserved and businesslike event. At the meeting, senior vice president Rick Rashid stood up and said a few words. When a company starts a research lab, he began, it expects the first real results in five years. But Microsoft Research Asia had far surpassed that expectation—with 170 researchers, 72 technologies transferred, more than 750 scientific papers published, and hundreds of patents filed. Rashid punctuated his remarks with heartfelt praise for the staff. "Congratulations to everyone," he said.

Rashid's words made the management team reflect on what it had accomplished, something it had not had time to do lately. "I felt so proud. The lab was doing so well, momentum was very strong," says Ya-Qin Zhang. His deputies concurred. "Looking around the room, we had tears in our eyes. We thought, 'This is a dream come true. We made history,'" remembers HongJiang Zhang. "We started from nothing," adds Harry Shum, recalling his thoughts from that day. "Kai-Fu said he was going to do a world-class research lab in China. *Nobody* believed him."

The rest of the day was filled with lab demos, coupled with closed-room meetings for the advisory board and staff members to delve into research topics in greater detail. The next day, at the cavernous Kerry Center in downtown Beijing, the lab kicked off the first leg of its fifth annual conference on Computing in the 21st Century. That same night, the management team plus Rashid and Dan Ling flew to Xi'an, some 500 miles southwest of Beijing, to host the second leg of the conference.

Ya-Qin Zhang barely had time to process the week's whirlwind events when his head was sent spinning again. The first morning in Xi'an, Zhang met Rashid for breakfast at their hotel. Unbeknownst to Zhang, his boss had recently spoken with Bill Gates and Steve Ballmer about matching up top people in the company with evolving business priorities, as part of Microsoft's annual review process. Headquarters was reorganizing the mobile and embedded business divisions—which covered software and operating systems for cell phones, PDAs, and wireless handheld computers—and Zhang's name had come up. "Bill and Steve think you're the best person to lead that group," Rashid told him.

His heart in his throat, Zhang felt elated and honored. "This was really recognition of the lab," he says, in characteristic modesty. For Zhang, not only would this be an opportunity to lead a product division as a corporate vice president, but it was also in the emerging area of mobile wireless devices that he had long felt was key to the company's global strategy. But he knew it came with a host of new responsibilities. "I always joke that Bill and Steve and Rick thought I had too much fun here. Time to get a real job!" Zhang laughs.

· · ·

In January 2004, Zhang announced that he was leaving the Beijing lab to become vice president of the Mobile and Embedded Devices division in Redmond. He had been in Beijing for five years, serving as the lab's director for more than half that time. Now, just two years after his family had made the move to Beijing, they would all be heading back to the States. This time, the lab's management team worked to spread the news in person to small groups, so that the whole lab would not be shocked, as it was when Kai-Fu Lee announced his departure. Because many employees had lived through the loss of Lee, they were not as worried about the future. "This time it was not completely unexpected," Zhang says. "And people won't be surprised if it happens again."

Zhang was leaving the lab in good hands. Harry Shum would take over as managing director of Microsoft Research Asia. And Shum wasted no time, continuing the lab's dogged pursuit of top talent by landing a trio of new stars. The first was Feng-Hsiung "C. B." Hsu, the former IBM standout who had built the Deep Blue chess computer that defeated world champion Garry Kasparov in 1997. (C. B. stood for "Crazy Bird," a play on "Feng," which sounds like the Chinese word for "crazy." The "bird" was a friendly high school moniker, something like "dude.") The second was Hsiao-Wuen "Dark Side" Hon, who would move to Beijing after being involved with the lab for six years. The final coup came in the person of Kurt Akeley, the Silicon Graphics co-founder. Akeley had married a Chinese woman in the States and was interested in exposing their children to the land of their heritage. He started at Microsoft Research in Redmond that July, but with the understanding that he would be reassigned to Beijing later in the year, as soon as his family was able to make the move. "I told Rick that hiring Kurt was the last thing I had to do," says Zhang. "Kai-Fu gave us the hint that Kurt might be available. Harry did a great job to close the deal. He was relentless."

Multiple farewell parties were practically a tradition. At the first event for Zhang, a staff party held a block away from the lab at the Tian Hong hotel, the mood wasn't nearly as melancholy as when Lee had left. There were doctored photos of Zhang and plenty of good-natured ribbing. One by one, researchers walked up to the front of the room to tell stories about the departing director and wish him well. Ming Zhou, the research manager of the natural language group, presented Zhang with a scroll of traditional Chinese calligraphy and poems, about ten feet long. Across the top, the characters translated roughly as "Come back often." And when a large group of researchers gathered at the front to sing a familiar refrain—"Farewell My Comrade"—things got emotional. This time Shum's tears were mostly of joy. Life would go on. The lab would ascend to new heights.

The next week featured a larger gathering at the Crowne Plaza Hotel in the Asian Games Village in north Beijing. Jian Song, the former state councilor who had written the glowing endorsement of Microsoft and its China lab, attended the party together with many of Zhang's friends and colleagues, including local university presidents, deans, and ministry officials. People recalled that Song gave a remarkable half-hour speech; normally, such a high-ranking official would not even appear at such a party, let alone give a speech. He told stories about meeting Zhang and Kai-Fu Lee and their many discussions over the years about Chinese education and technology. He reiterated his thoughts that the Microsoft lab could be a role model for research and development and the kind of place where Chinese students could get the world's best training in computing. His words meant a lot to nearly everyone present.

What people remembered best, though, was Song's last line. It was a reference to a famous scene from *Nan Zheng Bei Zhan* (*South Conquest, North Battle*), a classic 1952 Chinese film about the Communist-Nationalist civil war of the 1940s. Toward the end of the film, a doomed Nationalist Party officer radios for help while his platoon is getting bombed. He pleads not to be forgotten in his cause, as his comrades flee to an island called Taiwan.

Song's parting line conjured the idea that even with the success Ya-Qin Zhang and his colleagues enjoyed, they shouldn't forget their homeland—and that their continued help would be welcomed. The rough translation: "As you see the face of the party and the country, Brother, give me your hand."

7

Microsoft Made in China

November 2002–November 2004

China is emerging, but China is no longer just a follower. It is starting to lead.

—HONGJIANG ZHANG

The bustling port city of Zhuhai, on the southeastern coast of China where the South China Sea meets the Pearl River delta, serves as a perfect base camp for tourists and business travelers alike. Its southern land border abuts Macao—making it a short trip to the former Portuguese colony's nonstop nightlife and gambling casinos. The city of nearly 1.5 million is only a short plane ride from Taiwan, an hour's high-speed ferry due west of the hustle and bustle of Hong Kong's business and shopping districts, and an excursion point for slower ferries that cart locals and tourists to the 146 islands, many secluded and scenic, within Zhuhai's borders.

Zhuhai is also its own destination. A former sleepy fishing village, it thrived as a Special Economic Zone created in the late 1970s and early 1980s under the open-door policy of Deng Xiaoping. (Its per capita gross domestic capacity of just over $8,000 in 2003 made it China's third most affluent city.) Millions of visitors annually flock to the metropolis, which long before China entered its more widespread boom emerged as a model for economic expansion. And while the

Pearl River is extremely polluted, causing discerning swimmers to stay off its beaches, the area is also famous for its spas and hot springs.

Another great vacation spot, another Beijing lab retreat. It was the last week of November 2002. The weather was cold and damp in Beijing but dry and warm in the south (back in the U.S., colleagues were just returning from the Thanksgiving holiday weekend). More than a year before he would leave China to become a Redmond vice president, Ya-Qin Zhang had rounded up his managers and flown them down to Zhuhai for a two-day getaway at the Imperial Hot Springs resort, a famous four-star hotel and spa on the outskirts of town. Fifteen staff members made the trip, including the lab's two assistant managing directors, HongJiang Zhang and Harry Shum, and many of the same faces who had been at Dragon Villa three years earlier. Management retreats were getting to be an art form for the lab. Those at Zhuhai enjoyed daily massages and karaoke—lots of karaoke. "That's a must for a management offsite," jokes HongJiang Zhang. "That's where our team building takes place."

The indoor and outdoor hot springs, though, formed the prime recreational attraction for the Beijing contingent. The resort boasts some twenty specialty hot springs, most of them large tiled tubs or pools capable of holding a dozen or more guests. Six Chinese herbal medicines are blended in the herb pool. The bottom of the foot massage pool is lined with cobblestones to promote blood flow and soothe aching feet. The fragrance therapy pool is spiked with flower extracts intended to rid the body of toxins and improve blood circulation. The geothermy pool, heated by a large stone on the pool floor, contains some forty trace elements and is a favorite of those with arthritis or rheumatism. In addition, the spa boasts a light-wave pool laced with infrared rays to protect against diseases, a fruit juice pool whose blend of flavors is changed every four hours, a coffee pool, and pools for female beauty and male virility.

Microsoft staff arrived alone or in small groups over the weekend of November 23. On Sunday, the 24th, a small contingent went off to visit the Zhuhai branch of Zhongshan University. Another group, led by Shum and HongJiang Zhang, flew first from Beijing to Shenzhen, across the mouth of the Pearl River delta from Zhuhai, to tour the sprawling campus of Huawei Technologies, the network equipment and solutions giant dubbed the "Cisco of China." A college classmate of Shum's, who had become a Huawei executive, arranged the excursion. The fusing of an offsite with university, company, and sometimes government visits to help justify the expense of the trip was a standard practice. Says Ya-Qin Zhang, "It's typical that we combine all the things together, try to leverage the time." Their driver got lost on the way to the hot springs after the Huawei visit, and the group found itself at a dead end in a local cemetery. That was good luck in Chinese culture, explains HongJiang Zhang, essentially because "you can't be worse anymore in life."

The retreat began in earnest that Monday. Managers gathered at eight in the morning for breakfast and then moved to a hotel meeting room to hear overview reports on the research groups. But soon it became clear that Ya-Qin had anything but a standard offsite in mind, as he proceeded to address a strange dilemma: could the Beijing lab have too much innovation on its hands?

The answer would prove to be a milestone in the lab's evolution, for in an odd way, the enterprise was becoming too successful. It had gotten up to speed faster than expected and was in the process of transferring several technologies into product groups for development. At the same time, the business units were starting to appreciate the Beijing lab's work, looking for more. But as Zhang looked ahead to what was in the research pipeline, he realized the current system was about to be overwhelmed. So many things were coming down the pike, not always in sync with what the product groups were doing, that they couldn't all be readied for development in timely fashion—and even if they could, the product groups were ill-prepared to handle the rush. The result would be a series of bottlenecks. And anything that threatened the smooth flow of technology threatened the viability of the still-young lab.

On one level, Zhang was confronting a conundrum facing many high-tech companies—how to move more innovations more swiftly and effectively from research to development to market and thereby continue to justify the money poured into R&D in the first place. But central to his thinking were several issues unique to the Beijing lab and China itself.

One was the inherent limit on how big his lab could be—and how that fit into the vast sea of talent that was China. There was a size constraint on any research lab: how many top researchers could be recruited and how many projects could be supported and sustained. But even if the Beijing lab could grow limitlessly, researchers represented only one kind of talent in the world's most populous nation. Indeed, the still largely untapped university and professional community abounded with computer experts who were not researchers, but rather programmers, developers, and engineers. How to bring more of them into the fold as well?

Zhang's idea was to create a novel type of organization that would bridge the gap between R and D by better preparing lab innovations for handoff to the development groups—making sure software was more refined and tested, more suitable for mass production than the often cobbled-together code used in research prototypes. This was typically the job of development groups, but often these groups were too busy with existing products to tackle new things. Consequently, not just at Microsoft but with any industrial research center, stories are legion about tech transfers that never happened.

The new organization, Zhang figured, would help overcome such product development bottlenecks. What's more, if it worked like he imagined, such a center would not only tap a new vein of Chinese talent, it would provide a springboard for introducing brand-new technologies directly into the booming China market. Once proven, those technologies could then be brought to the rest of the world.

He hadn't worked out all the kinks. But Ya-Qin knew in his bones he was on to something potentially very important. In a sense, any company that sets up a development lab in a foreign country is seeking such gains. But what was especially novel in his idea was the coupling of a new advanced development arm with a foreign-based research lab. Microsoft itself had a four-year-old development lab in

Hyderabad, India. But it developed innovations created elsewhere and got them ready for commercial release in the U.S., not India. The idea here was to work side by side with the researchers, readying Beijing lab innovations for the China market as well as the rest of the world—in the process minimizing the geographic and cultural differences that often impede any company doing research on one continent and development on another. In this way, Zhang reasoned, the Beijing lab could be a leader of the entire innovation process.

When Ya-Qin described his idea at Zhuhai, it was the first time most of his managers had heard of his plan. However, he had already tested the concept out on his two lieutenants, Shum and HongJiang Zhang. As Ya-Qin later put it, with perhaps a little exaggeration: "Harry and HongJiang, just like babies, they jump up. They understood there was lots of research—it was a bottleneck."

That same sense of excitement quickly enveloped the Zhuhai crowd. As Ya-Qin scribbled notes on a flip board and animatedly held them up as he spoke to make his points more clear, his passion proved infectious. "From that point on people really started to get into the meeting," says Sheila Shang. "It was no longer a regular meeting. It was really brainstorming." They discussed the shape of the new organization for most of the morning—how to make sure it leveraged the best of the research lab; how many staffers would be needed, and what kinds; which of the Redmond business units would be most supportive? On the spot, the group identified ten projects that might kick off the new organization—projects almost ready for commercialization, for which there would likely be strong demand in the product groups—and worked them into a draft PowerPoint presentation to show managers in Redmond.

The discussion continued that night after dinner, when the managers converged on the hot springs—joking around and keeping a stream of cold sodas and beer coming from the busy waiters. Everyone was upbeat. Besides the getaway, they were celebrating Shang's birthday—Ya-Qin had surprised her during the day by suddenly ushering everyone into the next room, where a cake awaited.

It wasn't just a chance to improve technology transfer that got the lab members excited: just as their director felt, it was the chance to help Microsoft while also making China more of a center of emerging technology. As HongJiang Zhang once put it, "China is emerging, but China is no longer just a follower. It is starting to lead." Microsoft's old approach to technology development was to grow and test in the U.S., "spiral" or tweak new products for introduction in Europe, and then further localize them for the Chinese market. But, the Beijing team reasoned, that was not the right approach anymore.

Microsoft had nothing like the envisioned organization—any-where. "It's an incubation center for new technology," as Ya-Qin Zhang later summed up.

Technology made in China.

In the first few months following the Zhuhai retreat, Ya-Qin and his top aides worked to refine the idea, though they were slowed by the U.S. holidays and Chinese New Year. It was a bit tricky, asking to cre-ate a new organization. Says HongJiang Zhang, "This is something that came from bottom up. We never did this before, and Microsoft is very conservative on company projects. When you ask for headcount and out-of-plan growth [not approved in the annual budget], you have to put a good story together."

Their story, though, encompassing the history of the lab's tech transfer efforts, almost wrote itself. Since it typically takes several years for research projects to yield anything worth commercializ-ing, moving innovations to development (while an important part of Kai-Fu Lee's long-term vision) was hardly a top priority when the lab formed in 1998. Early on, a group was set up to help researchers build demos for showing concept technologies to the business divi-sions and Redmond research colleagues, with two engineers or pro-grammers assigned to each of about a dozen projects. But as the lab grew and its technologies became serious contenders for product development, it became clear that while two engineers or program-mers might be fine for one project, another might require five or more staff to handle the extensive refinement needed to verify that a one-of-a-kind research prototype could be scaled up for mass production.

The initial solution, in late 2001, was to form a centralized, more flexible organization dedicated to technology transfer. Rather than being assigned to specific lab projects, the roughly 25 developers in the newly configured group went where they were needed—in the numbers needed.

Heading the group was Bin Lin, an experienced engineer who had joined the lab in mid-2000 after five years in Redmond development groups: Lin displayed a stack of "Ship It" awards in his office, signifying his extensive track record contributing to Microsoft products. The new group was right for that period of the lab's growth, he says. But even with some developers working on more than one assignment, his team could only handle about thirty projects at a time. As time went on, he says, "The research lab was growing so big and so huge, this thirty projects was only a small number of what was available. I was only able to cover the projects that had the most active and short-term need for tech transfer. And that was the bottleneck."

There was no way the product groups in Redmond were going to pick up the slack. It wasn't just the geographic distance that made it so difficult, it was the nature of R&D. When researchers are ready to hand off an invention or new piece of code to product developers, a lot of refinement and testing is needed to get it ready for commercial release—and product developers aren't always able to do it. They often have their hands full with more pressing jobs such as upgrading conventional features or improving security. And even a great new invention might arrive at the wrong point in a product development cycle to fit easily into the next release. "Which means that for the product group to form a team and take that risk [of developing it] may be too big a risk and too big a distraction," says HongJiang Zhang. "As a researcher," he adds, "if you miss the boat, you may miss four or five years."

Getting around this barrier was central to the Beijing team's thinking, and the group members worked to emphasize the arguments they were certain would strike the most resonant chord back in Redmond. Topping the list was the fact that the company was only tapping a small piece of Chinese talent through its research lab, which could support a limited number of projects and staff members, notes HongJiang Zhang. "But when you look at the talent pool in China, every place you go, the lecture room is always too small. You see people standing in the corridors and outside the windows, peeking in and trying to listen to the talk. You got to have another scheme to tap into this talent."

A few weeks before the Zhuhai retreat, Ya-Qin had briefly described the raw outlines of his idea to Rick Rashid when the two attended Comdex, the gigantic consumer electronics show held each November in Las Vegas. Rashid had been especially intrigued about the opportunity to mine a new vein of engineering talent and asked for a more formal proposal. "Not elaborate. He always wants simple things," Ya-Qin remembers.

The "simple" but now far better thought-out plan submitted to Rashid early in 2003 highlighted four prime goals: tap Chinese talent in a new way; amplify technology transfer by moving more products to development more efficiently; better prepare Microsoft for an emerging China market hungry for cool new software; incubate technology created in China and spread it to the rest of the world.

Rashid loved it.

Late that February, HongJiang Zhang, Harry Shum, and a handful of Beijing lab colleagues were in Redmond for TechFest, the annual event where Microsoft research teams from the headquarters lab and around the world demonstrate projects for their product group colleagues. Just as if they were attending an industry exposition, research teams set up scores of exhibition booths at the company's vast conference center to showcase their wares—and provide a forum for hearing what product personnel might want from Research in the future. Ya-Qin had to stay behind to be with Bill Gates, who was coming to China around the same time (this was the trip when Gates and Kai-Fu Lee visited then-president Jiang Zemin). But a few weeks had passed since they had sent the proposal to Rashid and Ya-Qin asked

HongJiang to personally follow up with the research head to see how it was faring.

"I was there to reiterate the proposal," says HongJiang. But he got a bit of a surprise when it became clear how keen Rashid was on the idea. Indeed, the events that Rashid was putting in play would provide a case study in how even a large, fairly conservative organization like Microsoft can amplify innovation if it has a system to bypass red tape and commit resources to new ideas—when the right people are behind them. No one even dreamed of it at the time, but within two years the new organization would eclipse the Beijing research lab in size.

But that was still far down the road. At the time, Rashid told HongJiang he needed a more complete estimate of how many people would need to be hired, which projects would be supported, and how much the whole thing would cost. "I think he had already talked to Bill in the executive retreat or one-to-one with Bill," HongJiang later surmised.

That wasn't the real surprise, though. HongJiang figured they had days, if not weeks, to work something up and was planning to tackle it with Ya-Qin when he got back to Beijing. But a few hours later he got a call from Rashid's assistant. "I was told by Rick's secretary that Rick actually wanted that memo right away, because he was going off for vacation and wanted it before he left to put on Bill's table."

That evening, after dinner, HongJiang called Ya-Qin in China, where it was late morning or early afternoon of the next day. Harry Shum joined him on the teleconference from one of the guest offices in Building 112, the Redmond lab headquarters. How many people would the new center require? Fifty, they decided. Next they winnowed the ten projects presented at the Zhuhai offsite to seven, assigning a headcount to each project. Three of the projects were aimed at creating internal software tools to help developers and testers do their jobs more efficiently. Another involved a promising technology to better link paid advertisements to consumer search terms. It aimed to ensure that when a person launched a search on MSN—say for cashmere sweaters or digital cameras—the ads that popped up under "sponsored sites" on the Web page linked to the items they were seeking. This would benefit consumers and advertisers alike, and was a key part of the plan to help the MSN division compete with a juggernaut called Google.

The fifth project was an improved interface and management system for entertainment files—videos, music, photos, TV—for Microsoft's forthcoming Media Center software. And the remaining pair—a souped-up graphics engine and a more accurate text-to-speech technology—were both targeted for Vista, the next version of Windows. Ya-Qin wrote it all up in an e-mail and beamed it to Rashid, whose office was on the same floor as where HongJiang and Shum were then seated.

Two key things happened in the interactive process surrounding the initiative, as the budget-conscious Rashid, who traces his fiscally conservative roots to his Iowa childhood, exchanged several e-mails on the subject with Gates and CEO Steve Ballmer, who had to approve personnel additions of this magnitude. First, Rashid determined that since the product groups would be the main beneficiaries of the new center, they should pay for most of its costs—not the Research organization. He also eliminated the fifty-person ceiling on staff for the enterprise.

The funding suggestion got at a fundamental roadblock to innovation in big companies, a corollary to the Not Invented Here syndrome that might be called Not Funded Here. Explains HongJiang Zhang, "As long as the money comes from Research, the product groups say, 'Yeah, I'll take it [the technology being transferred].' But then they can cut it, because they haven't put any money in." Requiring Microsoft's businesses to ante up for any project they believed the new technology development center should take on would give the product groups a bigger stake in making it work—increasing the odds of success.

On the issue of staffing, one point Rashid made was that by the time an innovation made it to the center, it should be pretty much assured of becoming part of a commercial product. Therefore, unlike in Research, where projects were inherently more risky and size limits helped contain the risk, it didn't make sense to arbitrarily cap its size. As long as the product groups were willing to pay for the work, the center should be free to hire as many people as it took to get the jobs done.

Another consideration was that although Microsoft had tradition-ally been a headcount-driven organization—a set number of person-nel assigned to a project or organization—the very definition of headcount was different in an emerging nation like China. "Head-count is not really comparable between England or India or China," says Rashid. "It's not a currency, it's not equivalent." That is, it doesn't necessarily take the same number of people to get a job done in each place, because so many additional factors come into play. In China, one of those factors was training. Although there were many talented engineers available, very few had experience in western R&D organizations. Additional personnel might be needed to train them; and, because of the inexperienced workforce, more engineers than usual might have to be hired to complete a given job. Taking into account both these considerations, Rashid decided it would be much more effective to assess the dollar cost of the center rather than the number of personnel it needed.

On its surface, this Advanced Technology Center, or ATC, as it came to be called, was not unique. Literally hundreds of similarly named organizations exist at universities and companies around the world, including Microsoft competitors such as IBM and Sony. With-out studying the workings of each organization, it is impossible to say for certain how different they are from what Ya-Qin Zhang envi-sioned. But the coupling of such an organization directly to a research lab in a foreign country clearly put it on rarified ground.

The change in the funding scheme—requiring the business divi-sions to pay for most of the work—was not as unusual. Firms world-wide have found that requiring all parties in a tech transfer to have a stake in the effort—both in how it is funded and responsibility for its outcome—can greatly raise the odds of success. The change still marked an astute move, however, because Microsoft Research remains one of the few such organizations to get virtually all its funding from a central corporate pool, giving the business units little say in what researchers work on.* So changing the funding paradigm for the new center marked an awareness that even though it was an offshoot of the Beijing lab, it should not be run like a research lab.

All this happened in March and early April 2003. Microsoft works on a fiscal year that begins July 1, with the budget for the coming year approved each May. Sometime within a few weeks of the e-mail to Rashid, Bin Lin was in the Seattle area, on vacation with his family (Beijing lab members often bring their families to Redmond with them, for working vacations). He stopped by the Microsoft campus, where both Ya-Qin and HongJiang were on yet another of their frequent headquarters visits. Says Lin, "Ya-Qin had a one-on-one with Rick, came out of the meeting and he told me and HongJiang, 'I just got Rick's okay.'"

The next five months were spent in a flurry of recruiting, planning, and *guanxi*-building reminiscent of the lab's early days. That fall, Ya-Qin hosted a roundtable meeting of about fifteen or so "opinion leaders." Most were leading academics, including some from the Chinese Academy of Sciences. A great strength of the Beijing lab—a key selling point to some of these same officials—was its focus on fundamental research, about which China had a lot to learn and from which it

---

* Microsoft Research's funding system has its own rewards and pitfalls. Most firms today finance central research labs largely through contracts with their own business divisions. This helps ensure that what Research is working on is of great relevance to the business units. However, it runs the risk of tying research projects to the short-term, often unimaginative goals of the product divisions, reducing the chances of a game-changing idea or breakthrough. As Rashid notes, "You want to do things that product groups don't think is a good idea, because you want to be ready when the world changes." Like Bell Labs before it, Microsoft has chosen a central funding scheme, largely to ensure that its labs can think independently and pursue high-risk, high-reward studies. Only there is an interesting twist to how Microsoft handles funding for Microsoft Research. Rather than drawing on general corporate coffers, the Research organization's budget comes directly from a special fund controlled by Microsoft chairman Bill Gates. "Bill himself has a cost center," explains Rashid. "We sit within Bill's cost center." With the founding chairman personally committed to an independent research organization, this is about as good as it gets for a research director.

could expect to benefit down the road. Zhang was worried that creating an Advanced Technology Center would be seen as selling that mission short, maybe even as a new way to hire cheap Chinese labor. So at the meeting he filled officials in on the company's motives for starting the center and stressed that its creation would free researchers from being distracted by the demands of product groups, allowing them more time for basic studies. Such consensus building is always important, he says, but it's especially critical in China. "You start something and you have to have support," he says.

A different kind of diplomacy was needed in Redmond, where Rashid assigned a staff member to be the center's full-time liaison to the product groups. The exact nature of the job would not be flushed out for several months. But the liaison, Dennis Adler, a veteran of many Microsoft technology transfers, would prove instrumental in the ATC's subsequent success—greatly easing communications between the center and the product groups thousands of miles away.

A network of similar liaisons already existed in Redmond to facilitate relationships between Microsoft Research and the various product groups—helping inform the business side of what was going on in the labs while also making sure that researchers knew what their product colleagues desired. While such liaison systems are not unusual in large corporate research organizations, the practice was something Bill Gates had insisted on almost since the creation of Microsoft Research in 1991. In particular, Gates worried that his lab would follow the path of Xerox's famous Palo Alto Research Center, which invented many hallmarks of modern computing—the graphical user interface, what-you-see-is-what-you-get word processing, and the Ethernet among them—but successfully commercialized almost none of them. "We wanted to make sure that we weren't just like Xerox . . ." Gates says. "We wanted to make sure we weren't just doing it for ego and general contribution, that it really helped our products to be better."

Back in Beijing, the ATC also had a new recruiting challenge on its hands. In the original technology transfer group, all of Bin Lin's existing twenty-five or so staffers had been developers. These engineers turned research prototypes into professional software code that served as a "raw algorithm," in Lin's words, for the product groups to further refine into a real product feature such as an improved text-to-speech converter or red-eye correction for digital photos. The Redmond teams would then integrate that feature into an existing Microsoft application such as Office or Media Center.

Now, though, the new center planned to develop innovations almost end-to-end—completing full features itself rather than merely transferring a piece of technology that would be transformed into a product feature. That meant understanding product group requirements, specifying capabilities, setting project and coding milestones, and doing the test engineering to evaluate the product's performance. And instead of a team's disbanding after a technology was transferred and moving on to the next task, the ATC would have to assemble more permanent teams that would continue to maintain and improve the original innovation. In business parlance, they would "own" it.

A far more comprehensive effort was needed for this job—probably at least nine people per technology team instead of the two to five they currently put together. And instead of one job classification, there were three. Developers, known inside Microsoft as software design engineers, still formed the backbone of the enterprise, and a lot more needed to be hired. The new organization also called for software test engineers—often less experienced engineers who would put the code through its paces. Finally, program managers were needed to assemble and oversee the teams and make sure a professional product, fully integrated into Internet Explorer, Outlook, or some other application, was turned over to the Redmond business groups.

The program managers—PMs in Microsoft-speak—had to be experienced in Microsoft operations. A few veteran personnel were also required to lead employees in the other two areas. These experienced hands almost assuredly had to be recruited from Redmond. Virtually all the rest, though, were to come from China. It was critical to catch the next hiring season that fall, when top college students were lining up jobs for when they graduated the following summer.

"I was the main recruiter," says Lin. "Back in July or August, [it was] the very first thing I started thinking about, before we had any formal announcement. I would say 95 percent of my time was spent on recruiting." Taking the lead with him were Hong Jiang Zhang and Eric "90210" Chang, the Taiwan-born head of the lab's speech group who had spent much of his youth in Beverly Hills.

The three made several trips to Seattle to try to lure some of Microsoft's 2,000-odd Chinese employees there to Beijing. Inside China, they visited all the top computer-science and engineering schools—spreading the word about the new organization. They were helped by the Microsoft China business arm's human resources department, which hired recruiting consultants and placed ads in professional magazines.

Although they successfully recruited a core of experienced developers and program managers from Redmond, it was the reaction inside China that blew everyone away. Thousands of résumés poured into the lab. To screen applicants, Lin's team began administering written tests in eleven cities around the country—and from those they selected about 250 to bring in for personal interviews. All this to hire 50 to 70 new staffers.

Interest in the new center was so intense that job candidates began posting their experiences on a popular computer bulletin board maintained by Tsinghua University students. Some shared interview tips, others discussed strategies or just passed on their impressions about the hiring process. One guy from Beihang University in Beijing stole the show, however. He wanted the job so badly, he reported, that he had changed his dog's name from Lucky to Offer.

"Every morning when I get up," he wrote, "I call to him, 'Offer come!'"

Microsoft formally announced its newly christened Advanced Technology Center that November in another grand ceremony at the St. Regis Hotel in downtown Beijing—as part of the research lab's five-year anniversary celebration. The new center and the "old" lab complemented each other beautifully, staff members felt. In Mandarin, they loved to relate, the characters that form the name Microsoft Research Asia translate literally as Microsoft Academy of Sciences. The term Advanced Technology Center translates as Academy of Engineering. Its very name signified the lab's emergence from a source of basic investigation and idea creation to an organization also dedicated to the implementation of those ideas into tangible products. And perhaps even more importantly, the Chinese names of MSRA and ATC intentionally corresponded to the names of two homegrown institutions: the Chinese Academy of Sciences, set up in 1949 with the Communist takeover, and the Chinese Academy of Engineering, which was founded in 1994. This homage would not go unnoticed. Jian Song, the former state councilor who also served as president of the engineering academy, once complimented company officials about their choice of names: "I see you Microsoft people also learned something from China!"

HongJiang Zhang was sitting in his office a few weeks after the opening ceremony when Ya-Qin walked in. HongJiang often came across as more down-to-earth and less corporate than some of the lab's other senior staff members. He had grown up chiefly in agriculture-rich Henan province near the middle of the country—sort of the Kansas of China. And unlike Ya-Qin, Kai-Fu Lee, or Harry Shum, he had not attended a top university or been a youthful over-achiever. Instead, he had received his bachelor's degree in electrical engineering from Zhengzhou University, which he called a "third-tier" school, near his hometown of Yexian. His choice of college was partly strategic. The Cultural Revolution was just ending when he was finishing high school in 1976—and HongJiang was part of the first national college entrance exam offered in China in ten years. The backlog of applicants was huge, and he figured competition would be incredibly tough at the top schools. As it was, HongJiang and his older brother were two of only six from Yexian county who passed the entrance exam.

Although he excelled in electrical engineering at Zhengzhou, he again took a different path from some of his future Microsoft colleagues. Rather than moving to the U.S. for graduate studies at a place like MIT or Carnegie Mellon, HongJiang took a Chinese government scholarship that paid for his Ph.D. at the Technical University of Denmark. He later joined the faculty of the Institute of Systems Science at the National University of Singapore, and then in the mid-1990s moved to HP Labs in Palo Alto, where he had spent four years as a research manager until being lured to Microsoft in early 1999.

But from his modest background, a star had been born. Now, in late 2003, HongJiang found himself at a pretty great time in his career. On his wall hung plaques from the ten U.S. patents he had been awarded to date. A stack of Microsoft-awarded "patent cubes," signifying additional patents pending, sat on a bookshelf: each of these mementos of intellectual property was inscribed with his name, the title of his invention, and the date the application was filed. In addition, HongJiang had authored or co-authored some 300 peer-reviewed papers. He headed important research efforts in search and information retrieval that were key to Microsoft's growing war with Google—as well as another in home entertainment. Indeed, three of his projects were "charter members" of the ATC, moving toward commercialization. To cap it all, just a few weeks earlier, he had been named a Fellow of the Institute of Electrical and Electronics Engineers back in the United States (an honor Kai-Fu Lee and Ya-Qin Zhang had also received). It had been an incredibly busy four years. But now he was ready to ramp down. "It was time to start playing with my kids," he says.

Looking up from his desk, HongJiang watched as Ya-Qin sat down across from him. A while back Ya-Qin had told him there was a 10 percent chance he was going to be tapped to go back to Redmond to run a product group, like Kai-Fu Lee. Now, his friend reminded HongJiang of the conversation and jokingly related, "Oh, by the way, that 10 percent chance has become 100 percent."

HongJiang's first reaction was sadness that his comrade of more than four years was leaving. His sadness turned to something closer to shock when Ya-Qin said he should take over the Advanced Technology Center. "I said, 'Why?'" HongJiang relates. "He said, look at how many projects are in the ATC—half of them are actually from you." More to the point, though, HongJiang was one of the most senior and respected people Microsoft had in Beijing, experienced in both research and technology transfer, the latter from his days at Hewlett-Packard. Who better to guide the new venture?

Rick Rashid also supported the move. "This is a tough job, but we are confident you will be able to do it," he told HongJiang in a conference call a few days later. After that, HongJiang felt he couldn't say no. There went his plans for free time. "My feeling was here comes another start-up," he remembers. A headhunter had just tried to get him to start a Beijing lab for HP—he had turned him down. "I didn't want to go. I didn't want to have another start-up."

HongJiang Zhang stood confidently at the front of the large meeting room on the sixth floor of MSRA. It was November 10, 2004, less than a year after his unwitting recruitment as head of the Advanced Technology Center. Scattered around the room before him were various staffers and members of the Beijing lab's Technical Advisory Board, in town for the lab's annual Faculty Summit, as well as the 21st Century Computing tour that had begun the day before at Tsinghua University and would continue in Chengdu the following afternoon.

The occasion also marked the ATC's first anniversary. To help commemorate the event, HongJiang introduced a few key personnel, including Bin Lin and Eric Chang, both of whom had been so instrumental in recruiting: Lin had signed on as the ATC's director of engineering, while Chang had become its assistant managing director. Then Zhang went briefly through the ATC's history and mission. "We consider ourselves an extension of the business groups in Redmond," he told the advisory board. "Everything we deliver has to be fully tested. Rick made it very clear to us that we needed 100 percent customer satisfaction." Only then, HongJiang continued, could the ATC get projects funded and build Microsoft's pipeline to Asia and beyond.

Now, at the close of the ATC's first year, he enthusiastically reported, the center had exceeded all expectations. Privately, HongJiang admitted things had been "chaotic" earlier in the year, as hiring continued at breakneck pace. He had also lost many hours of sleep fretting over whether the product groups would really get behind the ATC. He had made several trips back to Redmond to meet with the vice presidents and their key managers, explaining the new organization. Ya-Qin Zhang had helped make key introductions, and both his group and Kai-Fu Lee's had given the center early support by funding projects not part of the original ATC charter.

But all that was behind him now. The center had just hired its 101st and 102nd employees, to go with thirty or so outside contractors who helped with some testing. Eleven of the hires were senior personnel plucked from various Microsoft groups in Redmond. Almost all the rest came from Chinese universities. All told, HongJiang and his colleagues had gone on more than twenty campus recruiting trips. In its first year the ATC had received some 30,000 applications, including 10,000 in the last six weeks. Some thirty candidates were still visiting the lab every week for interviews. "Every employee is spending two afternoons interviewing people," he said.

This was the cream of China's crop. A significant percentage had master's degrees. Virtually all came from the top fifteen Chinese universities (one hailed from Harvard), and almost half ranked in the top 5 percent of their class: 90 percent were in the top 20 percent of their class. Many of the new ATC employees, HongJiang told the Technical Advisory Board members, had won programming Olympiads and other contests: they averaged 1.4 awards per person. "If you look at the source of talent," he said, "you would really be overwhelmed by the talent pool here in China."

Starting a new organization and bringing in this many fresh recruits was not easy, HongJiang admitted. As with the research side of the lab, senior managers spent a lot of time familiarizing junior staff on Microsoft processes and mentoring future managers—but now, rather than teaching them about independence of thought and initiative, they had to show them about product teamwork and development cycles. "How do you follow up, how do you work with a team that is 16 hours time zone away, following through on all the deliverables?" he explained.

But so far, so good, he continued. The ATC was fully engaged with a wellspring of efforts for virtually all Microsoft's business groups and was set to double in size by the middle of 2005. The original seven projects had swelled to sixteen, each encompassing a series of features or pieces of technology conceived in the Beijing research lab.

One of the original seven projects—a computer simulation tool for testing wireless networking technology—had already been transferred to the Windows product group and was being adapted for use on the CE platform, the version of Windows for portable and consumer electronic devices. The first technology to actually make it from the center into a commercially shipped product would be a video editing feature that made it easy to summarize sports and news highlights, compacting an hour of video to five minutes or so. The software had been handed over to Redmond and would soon become standard in Moviemaker version 2.1, part of the Windows XP operating system. And the Windows XP Media Center Edition 2005, a version of Windows XP designed to make Microsoft a bigger player in home entertainment, would also contain technologies created by the Beijing research lab and productized by the ATC. These included automatic image processing for digital photos, as well as a function that automatically located the center of attention in a photograph and highlighted the most promising area to crop.

None of these technologies would rock the world—but so much of software development was about creating cool additional features that kept mainstay applications competitive. And besides, bigger things were on the way that targeted major new growth areas for the company. The ATC, HongJiang reported, was developing a suite of technologies bound for "Magneto," the codename for the next release of the Windows Mobile operating system being developed by Ya-Qin Zhang's group in Redmond. The wireless market was the company's fastest-growing business arena, and Microsoft was aggressively pushing its operating systems to compete in PDAs and cell phones—taking on Palm and Nokia, respectively. Meanwhile, Kai-Fu Lee had dramatically upped the ante on text-to-speech funding, as the ATC was now developing the technology for French, Japanese, and a host of other languages beyond Mandarin and English—increasingly critical for making Microsoft's products truly global. And the new graphics engine, one of the original seven projects, was looking good for the all-important release of Vista, less than two years away.

If all this weren't enough, Hong Jiang told the advisory board that the Advanced Technology Center employed fifty people devoted to search technology for MSN. This was a special area of pride for the center director, who had launched the research lab's search and information retrieval efforts. He then introduced lead developer Baogang Yao and research manager Wei-Ying Ma, who gave detailed briefings on the search-related projects under way.

One last project, code-named Windsor, had advanced along the ATC pipeline from the beginning, even though it wasn't listed in the original seven. It involved a novel pen interface for doing computing—melding the analog and digital worlds in a way a keyboard couldn't. Bill Gates himself had thrown his support behind it.

The jury would still be out on Windsor some two years later. In the meantime it would spawn several offshoots, including one central to Microsoft's Tablet PC effort. More importantly, Jian Wang, the brilliant inventor behind it, embodied what the lab was all about—a future where the best companies would reach deep inside any country on the planet to nurture the talent lying latent there.

Talent that might otherwise be unknown to the rest of the world.

8

The Curious Inventions
of Jian Wang

September 1999–June 2005

> *I realized this is the place to be if you want your invention to*
> *be used by millions of people instead of just a couple.*
>
> —JIAN WANG

I f Jian Wang had his way, everything would be digital. "I hate printers—they turn digital things into analog," he laughs, wading through a sea of cubicles on the research side of Microsoft's Beijing outpost. Fortyish and lanky, Wang is the engineering psychologist and virtual reality specialist from Zhejiang University who ignored Kai-Fu Lee's initial recruiting efforts and then signed on as the lab's first visiting researcher before finally joining the staff. With a unique way of looking at just about everything Microsoft does, he quickly established himself as a star recruit—perhaps the brightest of them all. At the Beijing lab, he has focused on developing new interfaces to let people interact with computers more freely and easily and "close the loop," he says, between the analog and digital worlds. As if to facilitate that, his personal interface is a denim shirt, wide smile, and easygoing manner.

Wang's office sits tucked away in an alcove on the fifth floor of the Sigma building. He jokes that his office space possesses the best *feng shui* in the building. Translated literally, the phrase means "wind and water"—and Wang is being ironic. An industrial fan from the kitchen five floors below blows exhaust fumes up through his open window, so Wang can tell what's for lunch every day; and the pipe behind his office wall leaks water from time to time, requiring frequent maintenance.

Himalayan stacks of papers line Wang's desk, despite his proclaimed distaste for printouts. And other traces of the analog world (how computer types often refer to the real world) abound. Toy soldiers, antiaircraft guns, and army vehicles lie scattered about—Wang is a military history buff, particularly World War II. His favorite movie is *Nan Zhen Bei Zhang,* the war film that the former state councilor Jian Song referred to in his "Brother, give me your hand" speech at Ya-Qin Zhang's farewell party. That was one of a handful of films that people of Wang's generation grew up watching, he explains. Wang is also an avid player of computer war games such as Sudden Strike. "If not for games, interaction with PCs would be much different," he observes. The books on his shelves span titles from *A Companion to Cognitive Science* and *Human-Computer Interaction* to *Windows Interface Guidelines for Software Design.* Bill Gates's *The Road Ahead* and several dense rows of Chinese literature and textbooks round out his expansive collection.

But what is most intriguing about Wang is his growing impact on Microsoft's business—and what that says about the importance of mining global talent. On a shelf behind his desk lie thirty-five "patent cubes" stacked pyramid-style. His pace of more than five patents filed per year is extraordinary, ranking Wang among the most prolific inventors anywhere at Microsoft (though he admits only that his output is "definitely above average"). On a small table in front of his desk rests a silver plaque with a Microsoft logo that reads, "Every time a product ships, it takes us one step closer to the vision: empowering people through great software—any time, any place, and on any level. Thanks for the lasting contributions you have made to Microsoft history." The signatures of Bill Gates and Steve Ballmer are engraved below the text. The plaque was awarded to Wang and his team for developing handwriting technologies for "digital ink" software that enables users to take notes and draw diagrams freehand on Tablet PCs. Not bad for a research manager from the ivory tower of academia who only a few years ago was unknown to virtually everyone at the company.

Today, Wang is fast becoming a Microsoft legend known for his work on handwriting interfaces, which include digital ink and a newer technology dubbed the "universal pen." For the past several years, that project has been one of the Beijing lab's top demos, trotted out for domestic and foreign press, developers, students, and academic leaders. The universal pen embodies Wang's mantra of fusing the real and digital worlds. The basic vision is a pen that captures your handwriting on paper digitally and automatically incorporates it into any document or application you're running on your computer—word processing, e-mail, spreadsheets. So an executive could mark up a hard copy of a document or presentation on a plane and later transfer the changes to his or her computer files automatically. Extrapolating years ahead, people might use such a pen to edit and store files, send e-mails, and get information about the world around them, in essence turning any writing surface into a computer interface—and fulfilling Wang's dream of converting mounds of analog paper back into digital files.

The universal pen was the mysterious eighth project, code-named Windsor, in the newly formed Advanced Technology Center—not on the official list because it was further from commercialization than the others. As of late 2005, its future as a new hardware offering from the software powerhouse was still unclear. But Wang's contributions also go far beyond handwriting technologies. The story of the Chinese scientist and his inventions provides a perfect window into Microsoft's strategy of tapping both global markets and global talents—perhaps first and foremost with China. "I look at him as a rising star, someone who has a great trajectory in the research field, and an example of the kind of talent we're nurturing in the lab," says Rick Rashid.

Wang has watched the Beijing lab grow from its infancy, and he has grown with it. To explain the history of his projects, he retreats to a nearby closet outside his office and pulls out a series of digital writing implements, placing them in a row on a small table. The gizmos come in different shapes and sizes; some look small and sleek like a ballpoint pen, others fat and clunky like an oversized metallic cigar. Behind this parade of pens, a collection of other computing devices lies scattered about Wang's desk: two large Dell monitors sharing one keyboard, a Tablet PC, a cell phone, a personal digital assistant.

It's a snapshot of today's different user interfaces and current notions of computing, he explains. But in this setup, Wang also sees a new, more integrated model of personal computing—and he hopes to take Microsoft there. To understand what that means, you must look at all the different pieces and the software that binds them together.

For each of these devices, Jian Wang has a story to tell.

Wang's meteoric rise seems unlikely, given that he almost didn't make it to Microsoft in the first place. When the Beijing lab was formed, Wang was at the height of a remarkably successful academic career. At age thirty-seven, he had been a tenured professor and chair of the psychology department at Zhejiang University for five years— the youngest chair in the department's history. He had lived his whole life in Hangzhou, a scenic subtropical city about a hundred miles southwest of Shanghai. He was married to a professor of developmental psychology, and they had a young daughter. Life was very comfortable.

In the early 1990s, as a young professor, Wang had made his name winning a prestigious grant from China's "863" program, a national high-tech initiative that supported research on everything from magnetic levitation trains to cloning. His project involved designing novel human-computer interfaces—"the first one in this area where the principal investigator was a psychology major," says Wang. In 1995, he co-wrote a proposal that secured $1 million in funding over three years, about ten times the going rate for Chinese research projects. The idea involved "multimodal" user interfaces: combining speech, computer vision, and 3-D virtual reality techniques to create richer ways to interact with computers. "Before, people thought user interface is just design work, to improve what's already there. I tried to convince them there is a different level," he says.

But while Wang published dozens of papers and gained wide academic recognition, largely within China, he felt frustrated by the slow pace of getting his technologies into the hands of everyday users. "I was happy with the vision, but not happy with the approach," he explains.

So in 1998 when Kai-Fu Lee and Microsoft came calling, Wang was primed to listen, though he did so reluctantly at first. After months of phone and e-mail tag (and his conspicuous no-show at the lab's opening ceremony), Wang finally proposed working in the Beijing lab for six months as a visiting researcher. He arrived in March 1999 and joined a project to develop a system for inputting Chinese characters into a computer—including the "wheel" interface to correct errors that Gates had liked at the lab's first Bill G. review. He also had discussions with Lee about the future of computing, and the lab's managing director implored him to join the staff. Wang had never considered working full-time for a company, let alone a foreign company. But the lab's core leadership won him over. "Kai-Fu appreciated what a psychologist can do for computer science," says Wang. "I realized this is the place to be if you want your invention to be used by millions of people instead of just a couple." In September 1999, Wang left academia and officially joined Microsoft.

His colleagues at Zhejiang University wondered why he would give up such a prestigious and secure position to take a chance at this foreign company's lab, which was barely established at the time. "Nobody thought I made the right decision," he says. And Wang had to uproot his family and adjust to the hustle and bustle of Beijing. His wife pounded the pavement for academic jobs, eventually landing an associate professorship at Beijing Normal University. Their daughter was just starting first grade, so she had to adapt to a new school. But in characteristic fashion, Wang dove in head-first, taking on Beijing's fearsome traffic by riding his bicycle to work every day.

Wang's first solo project at the lab was to develop a new kind of handwriting interface. The research was inspired in part by his desire to enable computers to better handle Asian languages, which remained difficult to input through keyboards. It added another dimension to the lab's efforts to make easier-to-use interfaces for global users, complementing the research in speech recognition and keyboard-based systems for typing Asian-language characters that had existed since day one. For Asian users especially, Wang believed, handwriting could be a more natural and convenient way to interact with computers.

Over the years, a handful of companies had developed "pen computing" technologies to digitize handwriting. But they were unwieldy and plagued by a series of technical constraints, including the fact that handwriting was not easily integrated with the files and software that people needed for their jobs and everyday tasks. That made life difficult for users. Consequently, none of these digital pens had taken off commercially, and none had been designed from an Asian-language perspective.

Wang set out to change all that. However, his initial efforts to make a digital pen more flexible—able to write text in any direction on a screen, for instance—made him realize that he was on track just to improve what researchers before him had already developed. He wanted instead to invent a new way to interact with computers via a pen. "We wanted to make a breakthrough, not improvements," Wang says. So he, Lee, and Harry Shum, who was Wang's manager, began daily brainstorming sessions to iron out the high-level goals of a new handwriting interface. Pen computing should not strive to replace the keyboard and mouse, they decided, but rather complement it by enabling people to do things they couldn't do on PCs—take notes on the run, sketch diagrams, fill out paper forms—thereby extending the range of computing. "The pen is so pervasive, so expressive, and one of the best inventions," says Wang. "So I think the pen could be a very good computing device for the future."

The first step was to develop the digital ink software that made sense of almost any kind of handwriting on a computer display, and enabled the user to work with it. This took about two years to work out. The trick, Wang explains, was getting a computer to recognize different types of writing and drawings—to distinguish between a box, a sentence, and a doodle—and store them as such for later reference or incorporation into a digital document. Wang and his team of a dozen students and researchers developed pattern-recognition algorithms that classified sequences of marks as words, diagrams, or shapes based on distinguishing features like spacing and line angles. If it was text (either cursive or printing), the user could leave it as handwritten notes or else use existing optical character recognition software—already quite advanced, thanks to years of research at Microsoft and elsewhere—to turn it into typed text. Similarly, if it was a diagram, the user could leave it as drawn, or turn it into a formatted box, a flow chart, or a limited number of shapes by selecting a tool from a pop-up menu.

But Wang's longer-term vision centered on the second aspect of his work: building the hardware and additional software needed to make a pen that would write on paper (not just a display screen), transfer handwriting to the digital domain, and integrate it with existing documents, not just create new ones. He called it the "universal pen" because, in theory, it could work anywhere and on any kind of file. It would capture handwriting on paper—in real ink—but in such a way that a computer could also understand the writing and, just as important, the context of any file the user was working on. In addition to enabling users to import handwritten text, tables, and charts directly into a digital file, says Wang, such a pen could do things like allow multiple collaborators to make comments on separate printouts of a document; the computer could then integrate them all into the same document, in the intended locations.

Wang's group got to work designing the device—one of the few pieces of hardware being designed at the Beijing lab, or anywhere in Microsoft Research. The first problem was how to capture the user's handwriting in a way a computer could comprehend. An initial prototype was designed in early 2000 in collaboration with researcher Lyndsay Williams from Microsoft's Cambridge lab. (Williams, also well known as an inventor, had built a similar digital pen in her garage before joining Microsoft.) The pen she and Wang came up with was small and sleek—exhibit A in the array of pens laid out on his table. The only sensor in it was an accelerometer; an onboard microprocessor tried to deduce what the user was writing based solely on the motions it registered of the pen's tip. While the theory was elegant, the approach had practical drawbacks. Even after training the system to work with a person's particular style of holding the implement, small errors in tracking the pen's movements made it imprecise. Also, the pen had no way of keeping track of what part of a page it was writing on—or even whether it was writing on a page.

So the next prototype, built in late 2000, carried five measurement devices: the original accelerometer, a small digital camera, a gyroscope to gauge the pen's orientation, a pressure sensor, and a magnetic sensor. This contraption (exhibit B), was clunky, shaped like a fat submarine the size of a stapler, and held together with clear plastic tape; you could see the messy wiring and circuit boards on one side. The researchers wouldn't keep all those sensors in the final pen. But Wang's team wanted to test what kinds of information could be extracted about what the user was writing—and on what surface—from the various sensors, both individually and in different combinations.

But whatever sensors worked best to capture handwriting, Wang began to realize that the software behind the pen was even more important. The sensors would only provide raw signal readings: the pen's orientation, acceleration of its tip, and so forth. Software had to translate these signals into reliable code that the computer could understand and the user could work with. "Most of the pen technologies on the market today are hardware-centric solutions," says Wang. "We really figured out that we should build a pen where the software is the power for the pen." That was the real opportunity for Microsoft—to make handwriting interfaces fully compatible with its dominant software packages. Integrating with Word, PowerPoint, and Excel would eventually mean doing almost anything you wanted by pen as easily as by keyboard.

By early 2001, things were coming together. Digital ink was working well, able to handle text written in any direction, hand-drawn flowcharts, and the like: the user had to write with a stylus on a special display. Pursuing his original goals for joining Microsoft, Wang initiated discussions with the company's Tablet PC product group in Redmond, which was interested in making handwriting recognition a core part of its user interface. The universal pen was still fairly crude, but initial tests of the multisensored prototype showed that using the digital camera to capture photos of handwriting was a promising approach. Kai-Fu Lee had already gone to Redmond, but Ya-Qin Zhang, the lab's new managing director, was just as enthusiastic and decided to take the projects to the next level.

It was time to show Bill Gates.

On a pleasant morning in Redmond that April, Wang felt relaxed and confident. During the week before the lab's fourth Bill G. review—this one dedicated to handwriting interfaces, Internet graphics, and speech synthesis—his team had still been fixing bugs in the universal pen. Now he was ready for showtime. The initial feeling of awe had dissipated—this was Wang's third meeting with Gates—but it was his first formal presentation to the chairman. As the half-dozen members of the Beijing team gathered in the small conference room outside Gates's office in Building 8, Wang focused on collecting his thoughts; he barely heard the questions directed to Harry Shum, who was finishing up his discussion of Internet graphics.

When it was Wang's turn, Gates smiled at him, which helped him relax even more. Wang began his presentation with a demo of the digital ink technology. He used a stylus to write on a tablet screen connected to a PC, with a monitor in the middle of the table so everyone could see what he was writing. In a clever touch, he sketched a flowchart that explained how digital ink worked. The chart, with handwritten text inside boxes, could be stored in its original, freehand state until the user wanted to format it into typed text and rendered graphics, Wang explained. Already adept at Microsoft's penchant for marketing catchphrases, he enthused: "People should be able to think in ink."

Gates liked what he saw. He turned to Alex Loeb, then the vice president in charge of the Tablet PC effort. "Can you ship this?" he asked. Although Wang had already conducted some talks with the product group, those simple words from the chairman effectively fast-tracked the technology for transfer to the Tablet PC product team, which was gearing up to release its new operating system the next year. Loeb would later send a company-wide e-mail to thank the Beijing lab after the product shipped. "I was deeply moved," says Wang.

In the last ten minutes of his talk, Wang introduced the universal pen, almost as a teaser, stressing that some of the principles behind digital ink could be applied to a more general kind of pen technology—one that worked in the world of paper and not just computer screens. While he spoke, Gates held the bulky pen prototype in his hands for a few minutes, turning it over, intrigued by this new piece of hardware. In fact, it didn't really work yet, and Wang ended up not doing any writing with it.

After the session, Gates sat with Wang's team and discussed the concept further, running overtime by fifteen minutes. "How do you do the absolute position calibration?" he asked. This was a fundamental question. Unlike a mouse, which only needs to keep track of "relative coordinates"—whether the user wants the cursor to move up or down, for example, relative to where it was before—the pen needed to know exactly where it was on the page at all times; only then could handwriting be incorporated into the right places in a digital document. Next, Gates asked, how do you deal with a blank sheet of paper, where there are no visual landmarks?

Those technical details, Wang confessed, remained to be worked out. But some high-level ideas emerged from the meeting. In particular, Gates helped them frame what they were doing in a way they hadn't thought of before. The key new insight was that a document could potentially be modified digitally even in its printed form. "When we talked with Bill," says Wang, "we realized we're creating a new kind of document, not just a pen."

Digital ink would make its debut in two key Microsoft products. First launched as part of the Tablet PC operating system in 2002, it also came standard with the 2003 release of OneNote, a note-taking program that synchronizes audio recordings with handwritten or typed text. Buoyed by the success of getting its technology into the product pipeline, Wang's team returned to Beijing and stepped up efforts on the universal pen. Wang added more full-time researchers to his group, bringing it to twenty strong. That gave him more access to the skills in programming and hardware he needed to design a more streamlined, working prototype of the pen.

The new version of the hardware was no-frills: the ink cartridge was made of bamboo from a chopstick. When the user began writing, a pressure sensor in the pen's tip triggered a tiny embedded camera, which snapped pictures of the handwriting 120 times a second. The images were stored on a memory chip like those found in digital cameras. From there, the photos could be transmitted to a PC that used digital ink algorithms and optical character recognition to make sense of what was written. For the time being, the pen had a long cable coming out of the top to connect it to a computer—it wasn't wireless yet. "This is actually the most ugly one," Wang laughs, picking up exhibit C in his parade of pen models. "Software was really the king this time."

The pen's software worked with regular paper—sort of. Unlike existing digital pens that required special forms to let them track where they were on a page, Wang's made use of software that embedded a background pattern, like a watermark, on standard copy paper as a document was being printed. That enabled the universal pen to figure out not only exactly where it was in any printed document but also which document was being hand-edited, since each file was given a unique code. And although what the camera saw from sample to sample depended on the orientation of the pen, the software was smart enough to adjust for a range of pen angles.

By the spring of 2002, Wang's team was ready to present a live, working demo of the universal pen to Gates. The setting for that Bill G. review was the larger boardroom near Gates's new office in Building 34, north of the old location in Building 8. This time Wang sat right next to Gates at the center table. Harry Shum, Ya-Qin Zhang,

Dan Ling, Rick Rashid, and Kai-Fu Lee joined them at the table. Lee was curious to see how the project had progressed since he had left the lab. About a dozen other researchers and guests perched nearby.

Wang picked up a sheet of paper and doodled on it with the pen. Ironically (and intentionally so), the paper was from a fifty-page internal document from Microsoft's Office team detailing how and why users print out hard copies of documents. A few seconds later, Wang's doodle showed up on his laptop screen—in the same spot on the document as he had written it on the printed page. Next, he scribbled some notes in the body of the document, inserting phrases here and there. The words again showed up handwritten on the screen in the correct places. Wang then explained how the pen could eventually save users from retyping their handwritten notes into digital documents. Gates seemed pleased and wanted to hear more about the technical details.

One of the big concerns with research demos is that they tend to work only in idealized lab conditions. "Because the hardware looked very shaky, we really wanted to show Bill how robust our software was," says Wang. They were discussing exactly that point when Shum jumped in with a bit of showmanship. He got up from his chair, picked up the piece of paper Wang was writing on, and crumpled it into a ball. Then he asked, "Will it still work?"

Most of Wang's team was shocked—they had never tested the pen under this condition. But it was important to show how it would perform in the real world of crumpled or folded papers pulled out of pockets and briefcases. Wang calmly flattened the paper out a bit and then wrote a note on the wrinkled sheet. There was a pause as those in the room held their breath.

The words appeared on the screen like clockwork, unsmudged and perfect.

Gates was impressed. Out of that meeting came the go-ahead to refine the universal pen and explore how it might extend personal computing to places that PCs and existing mobile devices could not go. "After that, we moved the whole project faster than ever," says Wang.

Wang's team spent the next year streamlining and testing the sensors, circuitry, and software. They made the pen wireless using a Bluetooth connection and a small antenna installed on top of the pen. When brought within a few meters of a PC or laptop that had the compatible software installed, the pen transmitted its images wirelessly. By early 2003, less than two years after first discussing the raw concept with Gates, Wang was deep in discussions with a hardware team in Redmond to transfer the technology and launch Microsoft into an entirely new arena that hadn't even been on its radar screen.

In March 2003, Wang had a special visitor at TechFest, where he had set up a universal-pen booth. Stopping by unannounced to see his demo was group vice president Jeff Raikes—a member of Microsoft's senior leadership team who oversees all the Office product groups and guides the company's strategy together with Gates and Ballmer. After some friendly chitchat, Raikes tried out the pen on a piece of paper. Wang's team waited eagerly for a few seconds as his handwriting registered in the computer. Then the words Raikes had written appeared on the laptop screen:

"When can I have this?"

Twice a year, Bill Gates abandons the day-to-day affairs of his software empire. The chairman retreats to a secret location in the Pacific Northwest with a view of the mountains and sequesters himself for seven days; he seldom sees visitors, not even family or Microsoft staff. He lives on Diet Orange Crush, Diet Coke, and two meals a day delivered by a caretaker. There he takes the time to refresh, recharge, brainstorm, jot down ideas, and, most of all, read—technical papers, memos, books. He works up to eighteen hours a day, typically going through more than 100 papers during the week, allowing himself an occasional break to solve an online bridge problem or take a short walk.

The papers are handpicked by Gates's top technical assistant, Alex Gounares, who was formerly a general manager of the Tablet PC product group. Most are internal Microsoft reports and memos suggested by employees. Some recent topics: new methods for software

1

2

Kai-Fu Lee (above left) "fit every single bill" to head Microsoft's new Beijing lab in 1998, says Nathan Myhrvold (right), the company's visionary former chief technology officer. A top early recruit was multimedia whiz Jin Li (below, left foreground), shown in a famous photo taken in 1984, when Chinese leader Deng Xiaoping (center) visited a Shanghai science fair and proclaimed youth like Li the future of China.

3

4

The lab's first anniversary gala, on November 5, 1999, included Peking opera, dinner for 200, and a group sing led by PR manager Sheila Shang. Kai-Fu Lee stands at back, hands folded. Shang is flanked in the front row by Eric Chang, left, and Ya-Qin Zhang, far right.

5

6

Only months after joining the Beijing lab staff, engineering psychologist Jian Wang (left) makes a point with Bill Gates at TechFest 2000, as Ya-Qin Zhang (hand on chin) looks on. At right, Wang demonstrates "digital ink" technology, now standard on Tablet PCs.

7

Lee passes the baton to new lab director Ya-Qin Zhang at Lee's goodbye party in July 2000. That September, Microsoft CEO Steve Ballmer, introducing the company's .NET initiative, drew 2,000 students at Tsinghua University in Beijing (below). He was accompanied by then-university president Dazhong Wang.

8

9

In February 2003, Bill Gates visited Beijing and met with then-President Jiang Zemin (above), good-naturedly calling the Chinese leader a "real capitalist." Gates also took part in the Dean Summit (below), co-hosted by Microsoft and the Ministry of Education. Flanking Gates are (from left) Ya-Qin Zhang; director general of higher education Yaoxue Zhang; vice minister of education Xingsheng Zhang; and Kai-Fu Lee.

10

11

While Gates was in China, Beijing lab staffers traveled to Microsoft head-quarters for TechFest 2003, showing off research projects for product group colleagues. Internet media group leader Shipeng Li (right) and Bin Zhu (second from right) demonstrate video streaming technologies.

12

13

Ya-Qin Zhang and Microsoft senior vice president Rick Rashid cut the cake at the lab's fifth anniversary celebration in November 2003 (at left is vice president of research Dan Ling). In tandem with the celebration, HongJiang Zhang (right) announced the creation of the Advanced Technology Center.

At the Conference on Computing in the 21st Century, held at Tsinghua University in November 2004, lab director Harry Shum (top, at right) relaxes in the VIP lounge with Nobel laureate Chen Ning Yang before introducing the all-star lineup of presenters (below).

14

15

16

The Beijing lab motto is "work hard, play harder." In June 2005, on a visit to China's capital, basketball lover Ballmer partook in some hoops action with students and staff from Microsoft Research Asia.

17

In a Microsoft executive suite at Key Arena in Seattle, March 2005, Beijing staffers and guests take in a basketball game between the hometown Super-sonics and the Houston Rockets, led by Chinese superstar Yao Ming.

18 19

In 2005, Kai-Fu Lee left Microsoft and signed a $10 million deal to set up a China R&D lab for Google. In September, he spoke at the launch of his book, *Be Your Personal Best* (left). Microsoft quickly sent Ya-Qin Zhang (seated, in a 2004 photo) back to Beijing to head all China R&D operations—reuniting with HongJiang Zhang, center, head of the Advanced Technology Center, and research lab managing director Harry Shum.

20 21

Reinforcing the Microsoft lines are Silicon Graphics co-founder Kurt Akeley (left) and Hsiao-Wuen Hon (right). In fall 2005, Hon became director of Microsoft's new Beijing-based Search Technology Center.

security, the proliferation of Internet video, analyses of computer storage capacity and processing speed, and novel interfaces for foreign-language users. Gates takes copious notes and sends prolific and highly detailed comments to the authors and other concerned employees via e-mail.

"Think Week," as it is called, has been happening in some form since the 1980s—and the impact on Microsoft and the computer industry has been far-reaching. Positive comments from Gates during this week can green-light projects and open up new market avenues for Microsoft, or in some cases jump-start efforts to catch up to its competitors. One such week in 1995 helped lead Microsoft to develop an Internet browser to compete with Netscape. (Observers lambasted Microsoft for getting into the game so late, but its entry was still in time to eventually dominate the browser market.) And legend has it that the Tablet PC software platform and Microsoft's video-game business strategy were also inspired by Think Week papers.

Beginning in 2004, Jian Wang's Beijing team has provided the novel computer interface, called "Thought Explorer," that Gates uses to meet the task. While he also reads printouts of the papers—kept in orange folders and marked "Microsoft Confidential"—the bulk of his Think Week work is done online. Wang's team designed the interface so Gates could read and take notes, look up any supporting information he needed, and deliver action items to the right people inside his company—all in a highly intuitive way. "The best tool does not allow people to be aware they are using the tool," Wang says, sitting down in front of two computer monitors in his office to explain the workings of the interface.

In his hideaway, Gates works with two large monitors, arranged side by side, that let him access a database of hundreds of papers and supporting materials stored on a Redmond server. The monitor on the left displays a list of the papers to be read—sorted by technical category, title, or lead author's name. Clicking on a title brings up a brief summary of the paper and a rectangular tab representing the full paper. Clicking that tab opens the paper and lets him type annotated comments along one side as he reads. Reference material automatically pops up in different quadrants of the monitor on the right: information about the authors and names of related papers, definitions of technical terms, Web pages, and relevant e-mail threads in Gates's inbox.

The high-octane software running behind the scenes—Wang's invention—makes it all possible. It organizes the papers, Gates's comments, and the list of people who will receive his communiqués into clusters on the screens, so the information can all be kept straight. The software also scours the Microsoft database to come up with suggestions about which people are most relevant to the project and lists them on one side of the right screen.

There can be a lot to grasp across two screens. But the management of the icons and compartments of the screens puts some aspects of Microsoft Windows to shame. For instance, the user can change the content of all the windows to focus on a piece of information from a particular paper, bringing up Web pages, related e-mails, and other supporting material "with just one click," says Wang. No more having to close a bunch of old windows and open new ones sequentially to focus on one area of interest.

The interface is a striking example of Wang's ingenuity and breadth of contributions to the company. Neither of which seems to escape Gates's attention. One of Wang's recent meetings with his top boss—and customer—took place in March 2005, just two weeks after a Think Week retreat. The goal was to discuss this interface and possible improvements for the next version. In fact, Gates was not even scheduled to be there. The meeting, in the Redmond boardroom, was mainly between Wang's interface group and Gounares's technical support team. Gounares, an avid sailor, has growing influence at Microsoft and is often included in discussions with senior management. He has always had a good relationship with the Beijing lab, exhibiting a keen interest in its projects: he even takes Harry Shum and others out on his boat (which has an Xbox console installed) when their schedules allow it. Gounares once had a discussion with Wang about the Tablet PC that lasted from seven o'clock at night until two in the morning. Paying tribute to his energy and drive, Beijing researchers call him "Alex Go."

Gates dropped in for the last twenty minutes of the March meeting to give his personal feedback on the Think Week interface. His main criticism had to do with the feature in Wang's software that automatically identifies the relevant experts in the company for particular technical topics. Gates pointed out that the system either suggested exactly the right person or someone who was totally irrelevant to the problem. They discussed technical ways to make the algorithm more reliable.

But otherwise, Gates came to say that he was pleased with the efficiency of the interface and what it allowed him to do. In his highest praise, Gates commented that Thought Explorer should form the basis of tools that more people could employ when they search for information on the Web or work with large databases. In fact, it was already being used by other top executives at Microsoft, including Windows head Jim Allchin. But Gates thought people outside the company would also find it a useful interface for sifting through mounds of data for the essential nuggets of information that can make all the difference in business decisions. "We are data-overloaded, not information-overloaded," Gates emphasized.

"He definitely thinks it's not just his personal tool—it's a tool for everyone," says Wang, who adds that some of the ideas behind Thought Explorer may contribute soon to Microsoft's search and retrieval interfaces. "So what we are building right now is another paradigm for processing information."

A visit to Wang's office in the summer of 2005 finds him moving on to new and greater responsibilities. He has met with Gates three times in the past four months on a variety of topics. He drives himself to work these days and puts in hundred-hour weeks—though, he laughs, "A lot of it is on e-mail, I'm sorry to say." Although Wang is only loosely involved in handwriting projects now, he still occasionally fires up the universal pen. He's used to the routine: when he travels to universities and expos around Asia, he almost always shows the demo. It's like asking a magician to do his most famous trick, or a band to play its greatest hit. "The pen really helped us understand the company, and how to use other people's brains to help you," says Wang.

Drawing on these insights, the inventor has rapidly moved beyond handwriting interfaces. One example: Wang is working on a new camera interface that uses pen-related computer vision technology. "You can smell the power of the camera sensor," he says. "If cameras are pervasive, could we use a camera in a completely different way from today?" It's all part of his continuing vision to fuse the real and digital worlds. In addition to taking snapshots of family, friends, and scenery, people might use camera phones to get information about their surroundings—the name of an exotic flower, perhaps—by beaming a photo to a Web site or home PC that processes the picture and sends back the relevant information. The software could allow users to scan bar codes and pay for merchandise in stores without ever standing in line, record a new acquaintance's business card, or look up information on restaurants, attractions, or products just by photographing them.

It's also part of his newest and most ambitious role to date: heading up what is called the "incubation" team at the Beijing lab. Its Chinese name, *fu hua,* translates roughly as getting something from sitting on an egg, where the word "something" symbolizes new Microsoft products. This effort, which quickly grew to twenty researchers, matching the size of his universal pen group, was formed in late 2004 to boost the impact of research on the company's businesses. Its goal is to investigate new product areas by focusing more on what consumers want—not just what researchers find compelling. If successful, it could become a new model for product development, in which a team based in research directly drives new applications and product lines. Wang was the clear choice to lead that effort, because of his long-standing passion to get technologies into the hands of users, says the lab's current managing director, Harry Shum. "Nobody has a more appropriate mentality than Jian."

Wang's incubation team is already paying dividends to Microsoft.

Its first project, a type of "data-driven software," originated from a discussion between Wang and Steven Sinofsky, senior vice president of Microsoft Office, when the Redmond executive visited Beijing in 2003. Sinofsky suggested that Wang's team apply its expertise on user behavior to help his product groups track how people use software to do everyday tasks. But because the project would be focused on customers and not basic research, Wang felt a separate team was needed. The idea was to study the nuts and bolts of user behavior by analyzing "billions and billions of clicks," says Wang. A central question: do customers use software the way it was designed? The answer is often, no. The study showed, for instance, that users needed an average of more than ten adjustments, or nudge commands, just to insert a photo into a PowerPoint slide. And certain combinations of clicks, previously unknown to testers, were found to crash various applications. That kind of knowledge can help software engineers develop more useful and reliable applications and features and streamline what consumers don't use as much.

Wang and Shum presented this work at yet another successful Bill G. review in January 2005. The Beijing lab's analysis software was deployed that summer to Microsoft Office teams as they made final tweaks to their next release. Longer term, the data-driven approach could transform the way the company's software is developed, by using huge amounts of customer data to improve reliability and security—which Gates announced in 2005 had become the company's top priority.

For Wang, all of this fits into a grander framework of "aggregate computing." The ideas behind this overarching goal first developed out of another long conversation with Alex "Go" Gounares, in which they discussed how people could most efficiently harness the computing power and hardware in the vast array of electronic devices now available to them. Because the proliferation of mobile computer power meant desktop PCs were no longer the dominant interface, they concluded, new software needed to be built to unify all the different platforms.

Looking around at Wang's workspace, the myriad gadgets and

piles of papers aren't going anywhere soon. For the foreseeable future, says Wang, people will use a handful of different computers: a desktop, laptop, cell phone, media player, and so on. "That means two keyboards and two or three screens. But humans have only two hands, two eyes," he explains. So there is a lot of redundancy in all this digital equipment. The question is, how do you make these machines work together like a single, intuitive device? "Think about a chair—there are so many different designs," says Wang. "But you don't need to think about how to sit on a chair. Not like computer interfaces today!"

Half a dozen members of Wang's team are developing software that allows you to do things like type text messages for the cell phone on your laptop keyboard, use your phone to run your presentation, and unify the storage and computing power of your laptop and desktop PC. "Right now to do this is basically hardwired," Wang says; the user must actively synchronize his or her devices just to transfer data, for example. The goal of aggregate computing is to make sharing between devices completely automatic and invisible to the user. It's also about aggregating different kinds of data—e-mail, Web sites, contacts—so you don't have to. Your phone should be compatible with your laptop and PC, for instance, allowing you to keep your latest calendar, contact information, and important files and links handy on any device, wherever you go.

If Wang's effort is successful, it could redefine the very notion of personal computing—and, of course, further establish Microsoft's dominance in software platforms. But to accomplish that will probably require a fundamentally different platform, not tweaks to existing operating systems like the various incarnations of Windows. So, will that mean tearing down his company in order to save it?

Wang won't go quite that far. "We should build a new computer system that's different from anything we have today," he vows, matter-of-factly. "That's what our lab should do."

9

Search War

March 2003–March 2005

We have no place to go but to stand up and fight with Google.

—HARRY SHUM

O ne gloomy morning in March 2003, still more than six months before he would take over the Advanced Technology Center, HongJiang Zhang arrived at his Beijing office to find an e-mail from Bill Gates waiting for him. The message had gone out overnight to some of the company's vice presidents and to senior managers within Microsoft Research. It was one page long, with several short paragraphs comprising one or two sentences each—the typical style of the chairman's communications. But the content of the e-mail was anything but typical. In it, Gates identified the Internet search company Google as a major threat to Microsoft and challenged his executives to devise a strategy to combat it. He also admonished his deputies for failing to appreciate the importance of Web search as a business opportunity. "Bill was very pissed," said one senior manager.

It wasn't as if Microsoft was out of the game—but it had fallen far behind. Back in the States, everyone was talking about search. Google was no longer just a Web site that people used to find documents online. Its annual revenue had skyrocketed to $348 million in 2002, on its way to a staggering $3.2 billion when the company went public in 2004. The source of most of this cash was paid Web advertising—a business model that many had believed would never take off. Meanwhile, Yahoo was in the process of buying the search engine start-up Inktomi for $235 million and was positioning itself to acquire the Internet advertising firm Overture in a $1.6 billion deal that would go down that July. At the time, Inktomi supplied the search engine for Microsoft's MSN Web portal, while Overture supplied its paid advertising system, which was doing only modest business. While licensing technologies had worked well enough to this point, the search stakes had grown too high. Microsoft needed to develop its own technologies and integrate them into its products to catch up.

The situation was reminiscent of the threat from Netscape's Web browser in the mid-1990s—and it demonstrated Microsoft's continuing slowness to embrace certain business realities of the Web. In an exploding online economy, search represented a fundamentally new kind of platform for managing information that went far beyond what Windows and Web browsers could do. Technologically, it was richer, more complex, and ultimately more of a threat to Microsoft's business. What's more, Google had a four-year head start on developing the technology and had become *the* hot place for computer-science talent in the field—something that must have irritated Gates. At the next two meetings of the World Economic Forum in Davos, Switzerland, Gates would be widely quoted in the press as saying, "Google kicked our butts," and "We were stupid as hell."

As he read the chairman's e-mail again, Zhang thought, "We have to do something." The Beijing lab's assistant managing director paced around for a bit before picking up the phone to call his longtime colleague, Wei-Ying Ma, manager of the lab's media management group. Ma's fields of expertise, information retrieval and data mining, encompassed algorithms for extracting hidden patterns from large digital databases—the very building blocks of search. A minute later, Ma poked his head into Zhang's office. Zhang motioned for him to come closer and showed him Gates's e-mail on the computer. Ma, a rather reserved fellow with a polished look about him, took a moment to digest the serious tone of the message. The researchers then shared a look.

"Can you make this an opportunity?" asked Zhang. "Can you own this?"

Ma nodded emphatically.

"Go full speed. Do everything you can," Zhang directed.

The search war had been declared in Beijing. But in fact, the back story began four years earlier in 1999. Unknown to most outsiders—and even to many within Microsoft—one of Zhang's groups had been working on fundamental algorithms for data mining and Web document retrieval all along. By mid-2000, the group had grown to a dozen staff members. But its growth coincided with the start of the dot-com bust, and with online ads and paid content generating little revenue, people grew wary of devoting resources to the Web. "We were told there were too many people working on data mining," recalls Zhang. "It's a sad story." So he had to cut the group down to six. "Even today, senior executives would admit that at the time, we didn't figure it out," Zhang says. "We didn't believe online advertising would sustain business."

Still, the small group had kept plugging away, under the guise of doing multimedia research. (Disguising research to pursue bootleg ideas is a time-honored tradition in research labs—if you can get away with it.) In early 2001, Zhang had recruited Ma to join the Beijing lab. He knew Ma well. While at HP Labs in Palo Alto, Zhang had plucked the young researcher straight out of graduate school from the University of California, Santa Barbara, where he had specialized in systems for retrieving images from databases. Reunited in Beijing, Zhang put Ma in charge of the media management group, one of three research groups he led at the time. Over the next two years, Ma's team did standout research on image and video retrieval but kept a relatively low profile in the company.

Gates's e-mail changed all that. Ma quickly took inventory of the lab's search-related projects. "In Microsoft, no group had yet done a large-scale search effort. We realized there was no expertise," he explains. That went for everyone—in product development, testing, marketing—not just in Research. But Research was in a unique position to contribute. Although Ma's group had recently focused on multimedia search—algorithms for finding photos, video, and music online—the same principles could be applied to text-based Web searches. So Ma began to identify areas in which his team could make a splash quickly.

Later that month, on the first day of spring, the Beijing lab's senior managers flew south to Suzhou for another management offsite. A city of 5 million just west of Shanghai, Suzhou was famous for its silk production and its intricate network of canals and curved bridges that earned it the nickname "the Venice of China." Just west of the city lay the Grand Canal, the largest manmade waterway on Earth. At its height in the 13th century, the canal reputedly stretched some 1,100 miles from Hangzhou all the way to Beijing, connecting the Yangzi River and the Huang River and providing the dominant mode of transportation for the burgeoning silk trade.

Suzhou was a fitting locale to discuss the technology of Web search, with its own intricately woven network of page links and connections to navigate. Zhang, Ma, and the others took a stroll through one of the city's scenic parks and enjoyed a classical music performance. It had been a long, cold winter in Beijing, and the researchers reveled in Suzhou's warm breeze. They also found time for karaoke. Little did they know that this would be the last time any of them would travel for several months. The SARS epidemic was about to hit China, striking first in the southern provinces before spreading to Beijing and all but shutting down the city.

At the offsite meeting, which was held in a conference room in the researchers' hotel, the number one topic of discussion was Gates's e-mail. With Microsoft well behind in search, how could the Beijing lab best contribute? Where were its areas of expertise? What new resources were needed? From that encounter, Ma's mandate was to hire new researchers and double the size of his media management team, which would be renamed the Web search and mining group.

Within six months, it would grow to 15 full-time staff and become a major contributor to the company's ramp-up in search.

Microsoft was mobilizing for what would potentially be its stiffest challenge to date. It was late to the search party, no question—Yahoo and especially Google were far out in front. But Microsoft had been late before, and once it woke up and got organized, it would have the size, speed, and talent to catch up quickly. Previously, it had reinvented the Web browser. Now it meant to reinvent the search industry.

The Beijing lab would be its secret weapon.

By that summer, it was time to go to camp. Search camp, that is. Microsoft's researchers and developers needed some basic training to prepare for their all-out assault on Google and Yahoo. To that end, the research lab in Redmond launched the inaugural MSR Search Summer Camp by serving up six weeks of intensive meetings, group projects, and weekly guest speakers. Some 40 participants—mostly researchers but also a few key developers from MSN and other product groups—were required to commit a significant percentage of their time to the camp. The goal was to kick start the effort to put Microsoft out ahead in the search war. As a first step, the camp would promote discussions among researchers and MSN engineers about how to implement the company's new search engine, which needed to be built from scratch—no small task.

The camp's main organizer was Eric Brill, a senior researcher in Redmond and head of the newly formed text mining, search, and navigation group. Rick Rashid and Dan Ling had also recognized the importance of Research in winning the search war and had tapped Brill to coordinate researchers from the company's labs in Redmond, Mountain View, England, and China. A former professor at Johns Hopkins University, Brill was known for his contributions to natural-language processing—in particular, the "Brill Tagger," an algorithm that automatically labeled words and grammar in a text so a computer could learn to understand the meaning of sentences.

Wei-Ying Ma coordinated the Beijing contingent of the camp. His knowledge of data mining meshed nicely with Brill's natural-language expertise, and the two worked well together. "We had just started to understand the technical issues in Web search," Ma explains. "Through the event we learned a lot and also got people to know each other. It really kicked off the major research effort within the company."

Half a dozen researchers from Ma's group also made the trip. It was July 2003, and the World Health Organization had just lifted the SARS travel advisory across China. "Some of the U.S. researchers were a little afraid to meet with us," joked one member of Ma's team. To the Beijing crew, the forests surrounding the Redmond campus had never looked greener or more radiant. Ma in particular enjoyed the temperate climate of the Pacific Northwest, especially compared to the heat and humidity of the Beijing summer. (He had been spoiled, perhaps, by the weather in Santa Barbara.)

The camp's participants divided into four groups, each of which would yield its own line of research projects. The "relevance ranking" group worked on generating a list of results—links to relevant Web pages—that was meaningful to the user's query; this was the fundamental challenge in search. The "user interface" group worked on designing the query page and presenting results in a more useful way than the long lists of pages that Google and other search engines returned. The "query log analysis" team tackled the problem of how to analyze data on users' tendencies—what they searched for and which links they clicked on—to improve the search algorithms. Lastly, the "multimedia" team developed specialized search methods for Web content such as photos and music. Brill, Ma, and other senior researchers floated among the four groups, helping to unify technical approaches and making sure each team understood the overall context of the work. Each group reported regularly back to the whole camp and put together a demo as part of a small closing ceremony.

Unknown to many in the States, though, the Beijing contingent also coordinated its own summer camp, which overlapped with the one in Redmond. Earlier that spring, computer-science departments around China received a poster in the mail from the Beijing lab.

Emblazoned with the four-color Microsoft logo, it read, "We are look-ing for the twenty best students in all of China to work on Web search at Microsoft Research Asia."

And it had worked like a charm. With word of the Microsoft lab having spread throughout Chinese academia by now, the Beijing "Search Summer Campus" attracted a wide variety of fresh talent from across the country. Ma's twenty top recruits came from Tsinghua and Peking universities locally, but also from Shanghai Jiao-tong, Hong Kong University of Science and Technology, and other schools. Most of these students had never set foot in the lab before—many had never even been to Beijing. But now they were to spend three months in the Microsoft lab on a modest stipend. (The lab also picked up housing costs for out-of-towners.)

The start of camp was delayed because of the SARS outbreak. But by July, as the Redmond search camp was getting under way, life in Beijing was returning to normal. Stores, theaters, and other establish-ments opened again after being shut down for the better part of two months. As the city emerged from its shell, students began arriving for camp. At the same time, MSRA welcomed back all of its student interns who had been sent home during the epidemic, though many of them would long for the days of relaxing on their respective cam-puses without having homework or classes.

Ma was touched by the dedication of his charges. The students he selected were the cream of the crop, but even some who didn't cut it right away surprised him. One student from Peking University, a young woman named Feng-Ping Zeng, didn't do particularly well in her interview and didn't receive an offer. But she sent an e-mail back to Ma and offered to work for free—she just wanted an opportunity to attend the camp. Ma was impressed with her drive, so he gave her a shot as an unpaid attendee. Zeng went on to excel at the camp, writing some of the best code for categorizing and ranking Web pages, and later earned a position as a lab associate researcher. "Through that program, we actually identified some very, very moti-vated students," Ma recalls. "They showed me this kind of passion and commitment, so I decided to give them a try."

While in Redmond that summer, Ma and a few members of his team did double duty, spending all day at their own search camp and then working late into the night to overcome the time difference with Beijing and supervise the students they had recruited there. "You basically got two jobs," he says. To keep the Chinese students engaged, Ma and his team gave daily feedback and encouragement by e-mail or phone and held trans-Pacific videoconferences at least once a week.

Ma would repeat the Beijing camp the next two summers, each time with tighter connections to the search product groups and better equipment so students could "do much faster experiments and try out ideas fast," he relates.* The camps offered another way to accelerate what the Beijing lab was all about: reaching out to a new part of the world to find the best talent possible to help Microsoft compete. "Through these camps, we grow the students in Beijing to tackle the search problem," explains Ma. By the time he came back from Redmond that first summer of 2003, Ma was convinced his group could make major contributions to Microsoft's search business—and do it quickly. For starters, his team got four papers accepted in the next year's SIGIR, one of the most prestigious international conferences on data mining and information retrieval.

At around the same time, the MSN product group was starting to see results from its massively ramped-up search effort. Christopher Payne, a Kentucky native and vice president of MSN who was fresh from a stint at Amazon, was charged with leading a team to develop the company's homegrown search engine. The first major challenge had been to build a Web crawler—a software program that went out and collected Web pages so they could be catalogued and analyzed by the search engine. By mid-2003, Microsoft's crawler had successfully

---

* The 2005 camp, named "Best Rank," focused on improving relevance ranking by training the software to match human decisions. This time, Ma held weekly competitions to see whose code worked best to perform certain tasks like categorizing Web pages by topic; the weekly winners then competed in a code-writing tournament that ultimately crowned an overall champion. Ma planned to fly the winning team to Redmond in 2006 for a special visit with MSN Search.

indexed 500 million Web pages. It was a good start, but Google already had several *billion* pages indexed and ready to go. Payne knew his team had a long road ahead to catch up to its competitors, who were not exactly standing still. That summer, as Ma was growing his group in Beijing, Payne came up with a codename for the MSN search engine that epitomized the scrappiness of his own team: Underdog.

Beginning with the search camps in the summer of 2003, the Beijing lab moved three major technologies to the front lines of the search war. Each was based on fundamental algorithms of data mining and information retrieval. Each had roots in research with an eye toward products. And, most important, each would make it into the MSN Search pipeline within two years, on the way to commercial debut in 2006 or 2007.

The most fundamental of these technologies was called "block-based link analysis." It sounds technically complex, but the idea behind it is simple. The analysis has to do with the relevance ranking—how Web pages are ranked in importance—which determines the order of page links that come up when the user types in a search query. Google's scheme, the state-of-the-art technique known as PageRank, works by ranking Web pages by how popular and connected they are to other pages. The method treats each Web page as a node in a network and uses mathematical algorithms to compute the rank of each page relative to others. A Web site about Apple computers that is connected to 50 other sites will tend to be ranked higher than one linked to only a few. The mathematics are tricky—each page has something like 20,000 parameters to consider—but that is the essence of the scheme, and it works pretty well.

The problem is that being popular doesn't guarantee that the sites are actually more relevant to the user's query. Two young Beijing researchers, Ji-Rong Wen and Deng Cai, a visiting student from Tsinghua University, noticed that some queries (on Google and other search engines) returned pages that weren't relevant because the topics they were looking for appeared in advertisements or other sections away from the main thrust of the page. That gave the computer scientists an idea for a method to rank pages in a finer, more detailed way.

Building on research their boss, Wei-Ying Ma, had begun years earlier, Wen and Cai developed a method to account for different parts of a Web page that they called "blocks." Using computer vision techniques—a major strength of the lab that the researchers were able to tap—the software examined each page and partitioned it into distinct blocks, or regions, based on features like horizontal and vertical divider lines, background shading, colors, density of text, and images. A news site like the CNN home page would be divided into headlines, banners, photos, ads, and links to stories by topic. For each page, the blocks were ranked in importance. Next, the algorithm used the block information to compute an overall ranking for the page by analyzing the network of links between individual blocks and other Web pages. It was, in effect, a refined PageRank algorithm in which the fundamental unit was a block rather than a whole page—which resulted in a more finely tuned score for each page.

In two SIGIR papers published in 2004, the Beijing team showed that block-based analysis led to improvements over conventional PageRank methodology that were both statistically significant and lauded by a small pool of test users. The researchers showed this by running experiments to pull up the top fifteen Web pages for various search queries such as "science" and comparing the relevance of the pages with and without block analysis. The results were good enough to convince Microsoft to build block analysis into the new search engine it was erecting for its MSN Shopping Web site. The new engine was being specialized for finding things to buy online and was slated for release in 2006. More broadly, says Ma, block analysis underlies several algorithms being tested by MSN Search that could be incorporated into the company's general search engine by 2007.

The second salvo of the search war was launched by one of the Beijing lab's most compelling success stories. Zheng Chen was a standout Ph.D. graduate from Tsinghua University who was hired in 1999 and two years later was promoted to full researcher. To get a sense of Chen's value to the company, just ask his boss. "Very few people can be a top-level success from elementary school to research," gushes Harry Shum, who once took Chen on a tour of Singapore and introduced him to numerous university presidents. "Number one student from his province. Number one student from Tsinghua University. Almost number one at MSRA. I say almost, because I don't want to offend my other guys," laughs Shum. "If I had ten Zhengs, I could just sleep every day."

One of Chen's projects, done in Ma's group with help from mathematicians at Peking University, had to do with a critical feature of search—the user interface for browsing results. Normally when you do a search on any standard site, the result is a long list of links—pages and pages of them. You have to go through them one at a time and read a few lines of context to see whether it's the type of result you're looking for. If any of your search terms have more than one meaning, the problem is exacerbated. Chen's technique of "clustering" results aimed to solve this problem of ambiguous queries.

Just sitting in his office, Chen spouts energy and expertise without so much as a trace of grandeur. "I talk fast, so just stop me if you need to," he says cheerfully. To explain the concept of clustering search results, he brings up a search demo on his desktop computer and types in "jaguar." Such a query could mean the user is interested in finding Web sites about the animal, the car, or the Apple operating system of the same name. On a conventional search engine, that might mean scrolling far down the list of results before seeing what he or she is looking for.

Clustering changes all that. On the left side of Chen's screen pops up a list of a half-dozen different clusters, or categories, of links, including: "jaguar cars," "big cats," and "Mac OS." The user can identify which type of result he or she is seeking and bring up only the links from that category. It's not an entirely new concept—other Web sites like Clusty offer similar features—but it all depends on how accurate and useful the cluster categories are, and whether they make sense. The trick lies in extracting meaningful phrases within the Web pages listed and evaluating whether they are useful cluster names. Chen and his colleagues used statistical machine learning techniques—another lab strength, like computer vision—to train the software on results from human workers. By learning which phrases humans judged as useful (and not useful) cluster names for a given set of Web sites, the software extracts patterns that allow it to categorize new sites.

One interesting application of clustering is to help people track networks of professional and social relationships. This could be useful, for example, in searching for experts within certain companies or technical areas. In his demo, Chen would enter "Ya-Qin Zhang" and "Kai-Fu Lee" together as a query and watch as cluster categories popped up on the left side of the screen: MSRA managing director, Microsoft employee, vice president of Microsoft, and various technical societies and conferences. These were all things that Zhang and Lee had in common, which might be useful to know before approaching them, for instance. If Chen then added "Harry Shum" to the query, the vice president category would vanish from the screen. "No more VP!" laughs Chen. It was a popular joke in the Beijing lab trenches, much to Shum's chagrin.

Before being transferred to the MSN Search group, Chen's clustering technology also yielded a paper in SIGIR 2004. The conference was held in Sheffield, England, a gritty steel town perhaps best known for giving the world *The Full Monty*. Besides being a forum for exchanging scientific ideas, the conference had become a fertile recruiting ground for research positions at Google, Microsoft, and other top companies involved in search and digital media. That year, the conference featured dueling banquets from various companies (including Microsoft) to attract job hunters—and other, more subtle maneuvers. "At that time, the NEC China lab director was busy with approaching our team members," remembers Chen. "And every time, Wei-Ying Ma would run to the right position and stand there to monitor what happens."

After the conference, the Beijing team took a train to Cambridge to visit the Microsoft lab there, before flying out of London. It had been a successful trip, and the researchers looked forward to relaxing a bit and then following up on their new contacts and the feedback they had received at the conference. Shortly after boarding their train at Sheffield, Chen and a few others noticed they seemed to be bound for Bristol, in the southwest of the country, instead of Cambridge. They got up to tell their boss, but he wasn't having any of it. "Wei-Ying was maybe too tired from preventing people from being hunted by other companies. He just looked at us with 'Hmm . . .' We had to go back to our seat," Chen relays. "But after a few minutes, there was an extreme yell from Wei-Ying: 'We take the wrong train!'"

In the end, the research thrust most immediately relevant to Microsoft's search business would not be found in any academic paper or conference. Its origins dated back to a chance meeting at Redmond headquarters in the spring of 2003. At TechFest, Microsoft's annual research fair, Ma gave a lecture on advanced techniques in text mining and statistical algorithms that could enable computers to learn to associate certain groups of words with their semantic meanings, another idea that promised more accurate Web searches. Sitting in the audience was Ying Li, director of iDSS, the MSN product group in charge of online advertising. (The cryptic name stood for Intelligent Decision Support System; the group evolved from MSN's business intelligence team.)

An expert in multimedia and data mining herself, Li had made her name at Microsoft in studies of users' click-through patterns on Web sites. She had developed a method to map out what percentage of users clicked through to various levels and branches of the MSN site, providing insights into how well structured the site was for users and advertisers alike. As she listened to Ma's talk, Li grasped immediately how his text-mining techniques might be used to help her product team streamline facets of its advertising system. The two spoke briefly and then followed up at a SIGIR conference in Toronto a few months later, agreeing to collaborate on a top-secret project already in the works, codenamed Moonshot—Microsoft's homegrown ad platform that was being groomed to take the place of Overture's system on MSN.

That summer, wunderkind Zheng Chen from Ma's team followed up with Li in Redmond. In the course of his research on clustering, Chen was working on Web page categorization, a set of techniques that allows software to sort huge numbers of Web sites by their meaning and content. Li asked Chen whether he knew how to automatically judge how related any given word or phrase was to a Web site's content, a feature that could allow MSN to sell ads more effectively. Sensing a golden opportunity to contribute to the business, Chen said yes—and boldly promised a prototype within a month. "We realized to optimize revenue for MSN and advertisers is really a mathematics and computer-science problem. More users, more traffic, means more money," he explains. Chen and his colleagues worked night and day to deliver the software on time.

They were attacking a fundamental problem in paid search called "relevance verification," which was a twist on the relevance ranking used in search. Companies that wanted to advertise with MSN, or sponsor links to their site, had to bid on certain keywords. If a user included a particular word or phrase in his or her search query, an ad for the company or a link to its Web site would appear on the top, bottom, or right side of the results screen under the heading "paid ads" or "sponsored sites." The bid represented how much money the company had agreed to pay Microsoft per user click—though no money changed hands until a user clicked through to the advertiser's site. The higher the bid, the more prominent the link's position on the page.

But some companies would buy keywords that had nothing to do with their own business, just to maximize their exposure. In an extreme example, says Chen, an automated bidding system might lead a computer company to buy the term "running shoe." For a search engine selling ads, this was bad for two reasons. First, it was unlikely that users would click on a computer ad if they were searching for shoes, so little money would be made. Second, if the problem persisted, users might get annoyed and stop using the search engine, which was even worse. Relevance verification was a method that automatically checked whether a keyword was relevant to a particular Web site. It was like search (and relevance ranking) in reverse, in that you knew the Web page, but you had to evaluate how closely related a given word was to that page.

Pulling off this feat wasn't simply a matter of determining whether the query words appeared on the Web page, because the page could be about the topic without containing those exact words. (An ad for a cookbook triggered by the query "Julia Child," for example, could link to a page of her recipes that didn't mention her name.) Microsoft closely guarded the specific details of its technology. But the gist is that Chen's algorithm combined Web page categorization, machine learning, and natural-language processing to train software to understand the semantic meaning of a Web site and compare *that* to the keywords to see how well they matched. The researchers then tested these ratings against how humans scored the same combinations of keywords and Web sites and adjusted the mathematical settings of the algorithm accordingly. The final prototype was fully automatic and very quick—making reasonable decisions on relevance within milliseconds.

In the fall of 2003, the Beijing lab's technology package for Moonshot was successfully transferred to the newly announced Advanced Technology Center as one of its original seven projects. "That was a telling moment, when we got that project," beams HongJiang Zhang, the center's managing director. The Moonshot package included relevance verification and a related algorithm for checking the relevance of "contextual ads" on any Web page. The latter technology had to do with the rapidly growing search-engine business of matching customer advertisements to specific content on any given Web site.

Barely six months after Gates's infamous e-mail, the Beijing outpost was poised to make its mark on Microsoft's burgeoning search business—and hopefully turn the tide of the search war. Other search companies like Google and Yahoo reportedly had large teams of editors who checked the relevance of sponsored links and contextual ads manually. That took a lot of time and manpower. Chen's and Ma's relevance verification system would do the job automatically, seemingly giving MSN a clear edge in the advertising space. "Automating the process," Ma said pointedly, "is our competitive advantage over Google."

Heading into 2004, much of the Beijing search effort was still under wraps to the outside world. In the meantime, the management upheaval sparked by Ya-Qin Zhang's promotion to vice president was taking center stage. With the former managing director leaving for Redmond that January, Harry Shum took over the reins of the research lab, while HongJiang Zhang moved over to lead the Advanced Technology Center's product development efforts. Together they would become the key forces spearheading Microsoft's search technology strategy in China. To be successful and move quickly, the research lab and ATC had to cement their bonds and learn to blend research and development efficiently. "Harry will be my deputy, and I will be his deputy," explained Zhang.

But on the research side, Shum found he had big shoes to fill. "I'm actually not in a very good position," he admits thinking. "Kai-Fu was so successful, Ya-Qin was so successful. My goodness, there's nothing else but going down!" As if to compensate, Shum came across as a tougher and more demanding boss than either of his predecessors, at least on the surface. One result: no more playing computer games in the lab. If he came upon a student gaming, Shum would stand behind the student silently until he or she quit the game and got back to work. At the same time, he was more outwardly social, cracking more jokes than either of his predecessors and starting regular basketball games with students at Tsinghua University. While no match for Ya-Qin at karaoke (few were), Shum could hold his liquor—especially Chinese rice liquor—better than almost anyone. "Harry's a partier," says HongJiang Zhang.

With the larger and more mature lab Shum inherited came even greater expectations for it to contribute to Microsoft's bottom line.

"Contrary to my appearance, I'm pretty conservative," Shum says, meaning that he has taken more pains than his predecessors to make sure research projects were relevant to the company's main line of business. "We understand the company a lot better now . . . But since we are a remote research lab, we can't just have lunch with product people," he explains. "So we have to try twice as hard, three times as hard. We have to be more focused on projects. When we have the opportunity, we think, 'Let's make a big contribution.'"

Shum focused his lab on all aspects of the company's business, from Xbox to Windows to wireless. But never was his philosophy more evident than in search. In July 2004, with the company's search war rapidly becoming his top priority, Shum finally spoke publicly about the lab's search effort. At a press conference in Beijing attended by about fifty Chinese reporters and a few academic officials, he announced the official launch of a new, fifth research focus area for the lab—called "information search and mining"—to go along with user interfaces, multimedia, wireless networking, and graphics and entertainment. "Search will be a major emphasis of the lab," he stated. By then, the announcement was hardly surprising to observers, but it emphasized the prominence of the Beijing lab in the company's search strategy.

This was the same event at which Shum announced the arrival of two new assistant managing directors. The first was Hsiao-Wuen "Dark Side" Hon, the Redmond veteran who had worked closely with the lab from its beginning. Hon would later be tapped to lead a key part of Microsoft's search effort in China. The second was Kurt Akeley, the first non-Chinese researcher to ascend to the ranks of Beijing lab management. At the press conference, Shum welcomed Akeley's arrival with typical flair, making a quip about his marriage to a Chinese woman. "Ladies and gentlemen," he said, "may I introduce to you the famous graphics researcher and member of the National Academy of Engineering of the United States—and most importantly, Chinese son-in-law—Dr. Kurt Akeley."

The arrival of Hon and Akeley could be seen as a sign of the Beijing lab's emergence as a desirable outpost, a stepping-stone to greater heights at Microsoft. Both men also had extensive product development experience, and their presence underscored the research lab's greater awareness of Microsoft's business needs—and probably increased the synergy between it and the ATC.

By late summer, Shum's and Zhang's teams in research and the ATC seemed to be firing on all cylinders, successfully working with MSN product teams and moving various search technologies into the product pipeline. Block-based analysis software from Wei-Ying Ma's research group had been transferred to MSN Search. Zheng Chen's clustering interface was not far behind. At the same time, Redmond developers were getting the MSN Search platform ready for its beta launch, which would go live that November. On the ATC side, a forty-person team led by engineer Baogang Yao had spent the last year refining and testing the code for relevance verification of keywords. The software was ready to be integrated into the Moonshot ad platform, officially called MSN adCenter, which was slated for beta release in late 2005, first in Singapore and France; Microsoft would stagger the global release points to transition smoothly out of the old Overture ad system.

The work in search, especially, earned the Beijing outpost a growing fan club in the Redmond product groups. One glowing endorsement came from Yusuf Mehdi, the MSN vice president who oversaw the entire search business and would soon be promoted to senior vice president. Mehdi had previously led the marketing of Internet Explorer, Microsoft's Web browser that had crushed Netscape. After approving the next fiscal year's budget, which called for increased funding of search projects in Beijing from MSN product groups, Mehdi sent an e-mail message to both Zhang and Shum. "I am a big fan of what MSRA and the ATC can do to improve our critical Moonshot/Ad platform efforts," he wrote. "The implications for us funding and working more closely have my full support."

For Shum and Zhang, the praise only reinforced the importance of research to Microsoft's search war. In early 2005, upon hearing the astounding news that twelve of the Beijing lab's papers had been accepted at SIGIR—the entire conference would have only 74 papers—Shum treated his researchers to a lavish dinner at a local restaurant and paid for sixteen bottles of wine.* During the dinner, he proposed a toast: if the researchers could beat that number of papers at next year's conference, he would personally charter a seaplane in Seattle and fly them all to wherever they wanted for a special celebration. "I am always really paranoid about next year," Shum explained. He sounded proud.

TechFest 2005 was a sight to behold, as a quintessentially rainy Seattle morning gave way to a sunny, breezy afternoon. In Building 33, the large convention center on the north side of the main Redmond campus, researchers and technical assistants scurried to make final adjustments to their demo booths. In all, 150 research demos and 2,000 feet of blue curtain for booths filled the first-floor showrooms, which were all named after local mountains (Rainier, Hood, St. Helens, McKinley). Access to the showroom floor was tightly restricted. Employees flashed badges to security personnel before entering the demo rooms. Public relations escorts stayed close to the few reporters allowed inside and made sure they spent time at the booths they were scheduled for—and only those booths. The glossy brochures read, "All material presented/shown at TechFest is Microsoft Confidential. Please refrain from using cameras or other recording devices."

The fifth annual TechFest was also the biggest to date. By the end of the two-day event, roughly 6,000 product people would pass through its doors, including many senior executives—and Bill Gates himself. Although it was an internal event, the importance of doing

---

* As an Area Chair for the SIGIR 2005 Conference Technical Committee, HongJiang Zhang attended a meeting at the University of North Carolina in spring 2005. The committee evaluated papers that had passed the first round of reviews and were short-listed for the conference. Each time an MSRA paper came up for discussion, Zhang was asked to leave the room to avoid any conflict of interest. The next day, he was in Redmond, meeting with Rick Rashid. Zhang related that he had been asked to leave the meeting nine times, meaning the odds were good that many Beijing lab papers would be accepted. He was surprised when twelve got in. "Apparently, I miscounted," he quips.

global research and tapping talent pools could not have been clearer. Just six weeks earlier, the company had announced the opening of Microsoft Research India in Bangalore. The half-dozen members of the new lab, headed by P. (Padmanabhan) Anandan, a renowned computer vision researcher who had spent years in Redmond, joined colleagues from Beijing, Cambridge (England), San Francisco, and Mountain View in contributing demos to the show. In all, some 400 researchers based on three continents attended. "What's interesting is the diversity," said Rick Rashid, the head of this growing empire. "Research is a truly global enterprise. It always was, but it used to be that people around the world would do it in the U.S."

Because the global landscape had changed so dramatically, Tech-Fest was also about deepening the understanding of foreign technology markets and cultures. "There is the danger of being mindlessly global," warned Kevin Schofield, general manager of strategy and communications at Microsoft Research, and one of the main organizers of the event. Schofield, whose polo shirt read "TechFest 5.0," acts as a liaison between research and product groups worldwide. "If you're designing products for different parts of the world, you better have people from those countries working on them," he stated.

The Beijing contingent contributed 39 demos, including three from ATC, which had its own booth. About half of the dozen demos related to search technologies were from Beijing, including a booth on text mining techniques that could be applied to contextual Web ads. And already, some of the data mining techniques used in search—statistical algorithms for extracting underlying patterns in data, like finding a needle in a digital haystack—were being applied to other areas as far-ranging as health care and software security. (Key demos included a search for an HIV vaccine and an effort to track patterns in hacker activity by monitoring chat rooms—both based loosely on search algorithms.) But by most accounts, the most popular search demo was the Beijing booth on clustering, which featured Zheng Chen's "jaguar" query project. Several vice presidents, including Dan Ling, stopped by and gave feedback to Shum and Ma.

Beyond its booths and demos, TechFest also featured invited talks on subjects officially classified as of "strategic importance." On the first day, Ma gave a lecture entitled "Toward Next Generation Web Information Retrieval." Two years earlier, he had spoken about text mining; now his expertise in search was gaining wide recognition. Some 400 people packed the auditorium adjacent to the booth areas. In his talk, Ma laid out his vision for how Microsoft could define what he called the third generation of search—after Alta Vista, the pioneering search engine built by Digital Equipment Corporation researchers in 1995, and after Google. "Search is in its infancy," said Ma, matter-of-factly.

To provide a taste of what he meant, Ma showed a demo of an academic search engine called Libra. This system made it easy to map out professors' social networks and rank their impact level—a subjective measure of importance in their field—based on their papers and connections to others. The demo represented a first step toward the next level of search, where anything and everything could become searchable. Looking further out, Ma spoke about developing a search engine that could understand users' search queries typed in as natural language, such as "Where can I buy a new coat?" or "What's the score of the Seahawks game?" Finally, he gave a quick preview of technologies his group was developing to facilitate mobile search on handheld computers and cell phones. "Eventually," he said, "we want to be able to search anywhere, anytime, and on any device."

After the talk, the lead architects of MSN Search came up to congratulate Ma on the technologies his team was exploring and discuss further collaborations. By all accounts, Microsoft's battle for search was coming to a head. The MSN Search beta—Underdog—had launched on the MSN home page just a few months earlier; MSN teams were busy gathering user data from query logs to make improvements. The next month, the beta version of the Beijing team's clustering interface would launch on Sandbox, MSN's Web page for showcasing new features and prototypes. And final preparations were being made in Redmond and Beijing for the launch of MSN's adCenter platform. All of these were scheduled for commercial release by the end of 2005.

But something even more far-reaching was brewing. In the days immediately following TechFest, senior managers of the Beijing outpost held closed-door meetings with MSN vice presidents Yusuf Mehdi and Christopher Payne. The executives were putting the finishing touches on plans to build what seemed certain to become the largest collaboration to date between MSN and Microsoft Research. The effort would be headquartered not in Redmond or Silicon Valley, but across the Pacific in Beijing, the burgeoning capital of the search war.

10

The Further Adventures of One-Handed Jordan and Mr. Magneto

March–May 2005

> *We are training a new generation of leaders to ensure Microsoft has a future.*
>
> —HARRY SHUM

> *Microsoft is a global company. We need to access global talent and the global market.*
>
> —YA-QIN ZHANG

On a picture-perfect evening in downtown Seattle, the 17,000-seat Key Arena was packed and buzzing with anticipation. It was March 8, 2005, just a week after TechFest, and Chinese basketball superstar Yao Ming and the Houston Rockets were in town to play the Seattle Supersonics. The teams were in the midst of a tight National Basketball Association playoff race, with Seattle leading the Northwest Division (the team enjoyed the league's best record at the time) and Houston battling for a spot in the Southwest.

Up in a Microsoft executive suite, high above the court, Harry Shum and the Beijing team soaked it all in. A huge basketball fan, Shum (who had earned the nickname "One-Handed Jordan" playing pickup hoops in the U.S., for his tendency to use only his right hand to dribble and shoot) had bartered for access to the suite with Microsoft's Executive Briefing staff, the group in charge of organizing product presentations to customers and partners. In exchange for giving a special presentation to Microsoft VIP partners in Shanghai the previous year, Shum was able to invite a group of friends and colleagues to witness the Yao Ming phenomenon firsthand. Yao, a 7-foot-5 center from Shanghai in his third year in the league, was perhaps the most popular figure in China. His games were televised in his home country and drew tens of millions of viewers who otherwise wouldn't watch the NBA.

Shum's guest list included former Beijing lab director Ya-Qin Zhang and his wife Jenny; Hsiao-Wuen Hon, one of the lab's two assistant managing directors; Jian Wang, the user interface guru; Qian Zhang, research manager of the Beijing wireless networking group; Lei He, Shum's assistant; and Ming-Ting Sun, an expert in image processing at the University of Washington. To accommodate six members of Wang's "universal pen" team who had come to Redmond for TechFest but for whom there wasn't room in the executive box, Shum paid for separate tickets out of his own pocket; the team members sat in the arena's upper deck, within waving distance of the box.

The suite guests enjoyed an array of catered food and drinks—standard stadium fare like chicken fingers, nachos, spring rolls, popcorn, and bottled beer. Early on, someone in the Microsoft suite got excited, thinking he had spotted CEO Steve Ballmer sitting on the floor near midcourt. That wouldn't be surprising, since Ballmer was also a big basketball fan and was intrigued by Yao as a global marketing icon. But the Beijing crew later said it was not Ballmer—just a lookalike in a black shirt and khakis.

The Beijing team was feeling good about TechFest, which everyone declared a great success. Before the game started, Shum played the jovial host, greeting guests with handshakes and hearty laughter. "Have you seen my nephew, Yao Ming?" he joked. "He's a little taller than me, but otherwise . . ." Shum felt energized as well by his recent meetings with product groups in Redmond, particularly MSN Search.

He even acknowledged that the Beijing lab could provide a decisive edge in the search war. But beyond his joviality lurked a trace of nervous energy: he had a meeting with the real Ballmer the next morning, as well as his annual review with Rick Rashid.

As Yao was introduced to the capacity crowd, the Beijing contingent erupted in applause. Shum announced that he would cheer for Yao's team until the game's final two minutes, at which point he would switch allegiances and root for the home team. True to form, he cheered boisterously for the underdog Rockets for most of the game, providing a steady stream of clapping, shouting, and even some dancing over particularly good plays. But down the stretch—when the game was on the line—he pulled for the Sonics to win, though he still applauded every good Yao Ming play and rooted for his countryman individually.

It all came down to the last minute. Yao, who had been relatively quiet for the first three and a half quarters, made a key basket and two free throws, and then blocked a Seattle shot to secure the victory—a huge defensive play. The final tally: Houston 97, Seattle 95. Score one for the Chinese juggernaut. Yao ended up with 22 points, 4 rebounds, 3 steals, and 2 blocks. Not a monster game, but impressive nonetheless.

As the game unfolded, it was not too much of a stretch to see the scene as symbolizing how the Beijing crew viewed its role with China and Microsoft—two powers that were sometimes at odds but which had enough common interests that it was possible to root for both simultaneously. While the lab's staffers wore their company hat proudly, they were also committed to supporting Chinese science and education—and the advancement of China's global competitiveness.

That win-win mentality was a hallmark of the two Microsoft leaders present that night, Ya-Qin Zhang and Harry Shum. They had different personal styles: Zhang appeared the more conservative, buttoned-down executive; Shum was the gregarious, risk-taking researcher (though he called himself conservative in the sense that he believed research needed to be tied to products). While Shum had cheered and hooted and danced, Zhang had been far more reserved, spending most of the time sitting quietly next to his wife and only occasionally getting up to chat with colleagues or grab a bite to eat. Yet both men exhibited incredible passion for both Microsoft and China and wanted to see their company succeed in their native country, while also helping lift the nation up.

In many ways, Shum and Zhang were like twins in the Microsoft system. They were about the same age, both born in 1966. They had both been child prodigies in China, going to college ridiculously young and becoming stars in their fields of research in the States. They had even joined Microsoft Research China (the lab's original name) on the same day, meeting at the Tokyo airport and drinking sake all the way to Beijing. Now, the slightly older Zhang had passed the managing director's torch to Shum—and with it the never-ending job of building relationships in China while also leading the lab's research efforts. As a Redmond vice president, Zhang oversaw product development for Microsoft's fastest-growing business area: software for mobile and handheld devices. His division had its eye squarely on the exploding wireless market in Asia. His chief project—seeing the forthcoming Windows Mobile 5.0 operating system for cell phones and PDAs through to release—was codenamed Magneto. This earned Zhang the moniker "Mr. Magneto" in the trade press.

At the end of the night, it was time for a group picture. The Beijing crew posed together in the executive suite, standing in a row with their backs to the court, the Jumbotron scoreboard with the Sonics logo lit up behind them. In the photo, Zhang stands in the center, ever the calm and composed leader, flanked by his former Beijing colleagues. A smiling Shum, looking relaxed and confident, stands just to Ya-Qin's right. "Dark Side" Hon, on Ya-Qin's left, is laughing mischievously and making rabbit ears behind Lei He's head. Jian Wang stands off to the side, looking like he hasn't seen a bed in weeks.

It's a snapshot of a critical juncture in Microsoft's global plans. The lab's two China-born prodigies, Shum and Zhang, were growing up fast. With one in Beijing and the other in Redmond, they seemed to be following separate paths. But One-Handed Jordan and Mr. Magneto were really pursuing different aspects of the same all-out effort to develop talent and products around the globe—like Kai-Fu Lee before them, climbing toward the highest levels of decision-making at Microsoft.

It was shaping up to be a busy spring for Harry Shum. At the time of the basketball game, he presided over the best-kept secret at Microsoft Research Asia. It involved a series of projects with the Xbox video-game group in Redmond. "Whoever knows about this needs to be killed," was the tongue-in-cheek mantra from headquarters. "It's something very significant, graphics-related, for the upcoming Xbox 360," was all Shum would reveal.

Indeed, the Beijing lab's managing director's area of expertise, computer vision and graphics, was becoming more and more crucial to the company's business. (He liked to quip that researchers in his field could be broadly successful because they had vision.) Slated for release in November 2005, the Xbox 360 would be Microsoft's second-generation game console—and critical to the company's efforts to beat out Sony's upcoming PlayStation 3 and other competitors. "One thing we are so confident about is that Sony is in trouble," Shum said later. "Sony keeps making mistakes—it's almost sad to see. Everyone from Bill Gates to [Xbox head] Robbie Bach to us, everyone in the company is very confident now about 360."

Like his predecessors Lee and Zhang, Shum wore many hats in China. And as the lab continued to gain prominence in Microsoft's strategy in entertainment, search, and other fields, another aspect of the job began to take more of his time in the early months of 2005. Attending to *guanxi*—especially relationships with Chinese students and academic officials—would be ever more crucial as the company strived to maintain its advantage over rivals like Google, Sony, and Nokia in recruiting top local talent. Activities like the annual search camps brought fresh batches of students to the lab every summer and helped spread the word about MSRA. In the meantime, Shum had also stepped up his lecture circuit at universities around Asia. For his efforts, he had earned several honorary appointments, including guest professorships at Tsinghua, Shanghai Jiaotong, and the Hong Kong University of Science and Technology. And that February, around Chinese New Year, he had received a medal of achievement from the Ministry of Education of China. (Ya-Qin Zhang had garnered a similar award before he left the previous year.)

Around the same time, Shum was also preparing to host the tenth IEEE International Conference on Computer Vision, which would be held the following October in Beijing. He was a general co-chair of the conference, along with Songde Ma, one of several Chinese vice ministers of science and technology, who helped set the government's research and development budget and made funding decisions. Over the years, Shum had cultivated a friendship with Ma, a world authority on image processing and pattern recognition who was widely regarded as a progressive official—a strong promoter of commercializing Chinese technology. The two had originally met at the same conference back in 1995, when it was held at MIT and Shum was finishing his Ph.D. at Carnegie Mellon. Besides image processing and other technical topics, they enjoyed discussing the finer points of culture and food.

One day, at an outdoor barbecue at Shum's house, they had wondered why barbecue wasn't popular in Beijing. Shum decided it was because not enough people owned a grill. Soon thereafter, Ma threw a party at his family's home outside of the city, not far from a section of the Great Wall of China. Shum and his wife were invited and presented Ma with a barbecue grill as a housewarming gift. "Only ten bucks, but it looks pretty big and can cook a lot of meat," says Shum. Ma used the grill to entertain colleagues from academia and government at a Chinese New Year bash that February. Barbecue became a hit—at least in science and technology circles.

But Shum's commitment to Chinese research and education shone through most strongly in his attitudes about publishing research results. Shortly after the Yao Ming basketball game, Shum learned that SIGGRAPH had accepted nine of the Beijing lab's papers out of a total of 98—an unprecedented number for a single institution at the prestigious conference. Shum recognized what that meant, not only for his lab, but also for the state of Chinese research as a whole. "Chinese institutions can be at least as successful as MSRA," enthuses Shum. "Each institution has more money, more talent, more everything. If MSRA has nine SIGGRAPH papers, then Tsinghua University could have nine, Peking University could have nine . . . Half the SIGGRAPH papers could be from China. It's all possible."

In April, the next month, Shum's outreach took him to a more remote (but still familiar) part of the country. He was hosting a special visit from Craig Mundie, the Microsoft senior vice president and chief technology officer. Shum had nurtured a strong relationship with Mundie, who was a great supporter of Microsoft Research Asia. While in Beijing, Mundie performed a formal review of the Beijing lab, complete with evaluating demos of the latest research. He also took time out to meet with Chen Ning Yang, the Nobel Prize–winning physicist at Tsinghua University.

Shum and Mundie next planned to take a short family vacation together. They would fly southwest to Chengdu, in Sichuan province, with Tim Chen, Microsoft's Greater China CEO, and their wives. It would be Shum's second trip to Chengdu in half a year, after the Computing in the 21st Century conference tour took him there the previous November. But during their so-called "vacation," Shum and his colleagues ended up working every day to build bridges to local government and industry. Mundie gave a keynote speech at a software developers conference. The group also visited the Panda Breeding and Research Center just outside Chengdu for a photo opportunity. Parts of the trip played out like a media circus, with photographers' flashbulbs going off and newspaper and television reporters hovering nearby.

The first night, at a predinner meeting with Xuezhong Zhang, the party secretary of Sichuan province (similar to the governor of a state), the group got to talking about the local software industry. To Chinese officials, Microsoft's presence in Chengdu indicated a desire to partner with regional companies for mutual benefit. Mundie then quipped, "I'm sure today our wives' contributions to the local economy will be more than ours."

During the meeting, Secretary Zhang mentioned that a month earlier, he had taken a trip to Europe. On the airplane, he had read a magazine article about Microsoft's universal pen project. "I heard Microsoft invented something called the digital electronic pen," said Zhang. "I think it would be a really great idea if Microsoft let [consumer electronics maker] Changhong manufacture the pen. It would be a great partnership." Headquartered in Sichuan province, Changhong was one of the largest enterprises in all of China.

The Microsoft team was pleased to have Zhang's recognition—but careful in how they proceeded, for they didn't want to promise any specific partnership. "Well, Mr. Secretary," replied Mundie, "I actually have with me Dr. Harry Shum. The technology is from his lab."

"Mr. Secretary, if you're interested, we would be very happy to set up a private demo for you," said Shum.

Apparently the reporters following them around took some leeway in interpreting the conversation, which they must have overheard. The next day, a local newspaper headline read, "Microsoft Agrees to Partner with Changhong to Manufacture Digital Pen." The Microsoft contingent was taken aback—and now had to deal with a public relations snafu. "I was just glad Craig was there," says Shum. "So it's not my problem!"

It was a strong reminder of the cultural mismatches and communication gaps that could still occur. For Shum, the end of the trip held one more reminder—of the price he paid for running himself ragged. On the last morning, he woke up in his Chengdu hotel room feeling like death. Overnight he had become violently ill from something he ate. "Too much spicy food," he claims. Sichuan province was famous for its fiery hot cuisine, served up in popular dishes like *ma po tofu* (spicy bean curd) and *shui zhu yu* (fish in hotpot); prepared locally, they were nothing like what you'd find in a Chinese restaurant in the

States. "Normally I enjoy spicy food, but I must have been very weak, very tired," Shum explains.

It was just a few minutes before the Microsoft group had to leave for a meeting with the mayor of Chengdu, Honglin Ge. (Shum had met Ge the previous November during the 21st Century computing conference.) But Shum made a last-ditch effort to get ready, dressing in his suit and hurrying down to the lobby to meet the others. He hadn't slept much, and his face was as pale as a ghost. Mundie took one look at him and said, "You're crazy! Go back to your room and get some rest." As Shum relates, he was barely even able to make it onto the plane back to Beijing later that day. "I had to say, 'Please give my regards to the mayor.'"

About forty miles northwest of Beijing, just off the Badaling Expressway, the Great Wall at Shuiguan (Water Gate) rises from the shadows of the late afternoon sun. The wall winds its way along the tops of the surrounding terrain through lush green hills and valleys, its stately watchtowers spaced every few hundred yards. Not far away, but out of view from the main road and the busloads of tourists, lie portions of the "wild wall," unrestored ruins that date back to the 14th century, when invading Mongols clashed with Han soldiers at the start of the Ming Dynasty. In these parts, the wall is constructed of stone and brick with a tamped earth and rubble interior and averages about twenty feet in height and width. Crumbling and overgrown with vegetation, portions of the ruins are steep and jagged enough to require climbing on all fours. On rainy days, local workers discourage travelers from trying to hike the slippery trail, and tour group leaders make guests sign insurance waivers.

Down the hill from these ruins is a stunning architectural exhibit of ultramodern homes that contrasts with the wall's antiquity—yet somehow fits. Spread across three square miles of remote valley, the Commune by the Great Wall doubles as a high-end resort. Opened in 2002 by Chinese real estate entrepreneur Xin Zhang, the Commune displays eleven villas with unusual and descriptive names like Cantilever House, Furniture House, Distorted Courtyard, Bamboo Wall, and The Twins. Their designers include renowned Asian architects such as Rocco Yim from Hong Kong, Cui Kai from China, Shigeru Ban from Japan, and South Korea's Seung H. Sang. Affluent companies like Audi and Porsche hold events here, and Western celebrities occasionally pass through. (The actress Renée Zellweger was rumored to have been a guest.)

In May 2005, this was the site of a historic meeting between Microsoft Research Asia and the Chinese Ministry of Education, as they prepared to renew their joint venture, the Great Wall Plan, for three more years. Originally started in 2002 under Ya-Qin Zhang, "Phase One" of the Great Wall Plan had contributed to developing curricula and training professors and developers at thirty-five software colleges around China. Besides the Great Wall connection, the setting at the Commune might have also symbolized the meeting of the traditional Chinese establishment with the new Microsoft. For the latter, the main goal of the event was to build stronger relationships with Chinese officials—the essence of *guanxi* in Microsoft's plan to work with its host nation to improve education.

The two-day event began on a Friday afternoon. The Microsoft contingent consisted of Harry Shum, Hsiao-Wuen Hon, Sheila Shang, the heads of a few business teams from Microsoft China, and Lolan Song, the lab's university relations director, who organized the meeting. Their principal guests from the Ministry of Education were Yaoxue Zhang, the director general of higher education, who had spoken at Microsoft's Faculty Summit in Beijing the previous fall; Daokai Ge, the deputy director general; Chaozi Lei, vice director of science and technology; Zhanshan Liu, vice director of vocational education; Xuzhong Lu, deputy director of normal (K–12) education; Guoxing Chao, director of international affairs; and Ming Xu, counselor of international affairs, who had become a personal friend to both Shum and Ya-Qin Zhang. To Song's knowledge, it was the first time that a foreign company had hosted representatives from every major division of the ministry.

The main meeting took place at the Commune's Bamboo Wall

house, which included a Zenlike meditation chamber made of bamboo set over burbling water. To reach the chamber, you had to step on a series of stones to cross over a narrow stream. One side of the room opened out onto the surrounding hills, with a view of the Great Wall. After milling around the chamber, the twenty or so participants filed into the living quarters to get down to business. A large picture window looked out over the hills. Along the back wall, two blue-and-yellow banners hung down, each emblazoned with Chinese characters representing Microsoft and the Ministry of Education. Typical of such gatherings, the principals took a few minutes to organize where people should sit, everyone deferring to the most senior attendees. In the end, the chairs were arranged in a large square, with the senior staff sitting along one side of the square and the most senior, Yaoxue Zhang and Shum, sitting next to each other in the middle of that side. All business was conducted in Mandarin.

After some pleasantries, Shum introduced his people one by one. They stood up when their names were called. "Dr. Hsiao-Wuen Hon has been in Beijing for almost a year," he announced. "If he knew how nice it was at the Commune, he would have moved here much earlier." Yaoxue Zhang did the same for his people and explained their various backgrounds. Zhang, who had done his Ph.D. at Tohoku University in Japan, was a professor of computer science at Tsinghua University. His group conducted research on computer networking and Internet routers. At the ministry, Zhang had worked under Yu Wei, the former vice minister of education who had spoken at the Microsoft lab's opening ceremony. He had gotten to know Shum over the past two years, as they had worked together to implement the Great Wall Plan.

Sheila Shang said later that the start of the meeting felt a little tense, but this was not apparent to an outside observer. To break the ice, Lolan Song went over the agenda for the two-day gathering. She referred to her clipboard, which held a full schedule of activities. "The first order of business is, how many people are going hiking tomorrow morning?" she asked. Most of the men raised their hands, and then there were a few jokes and laughter all around. During the next few hours, they would review Phase One and rough out a direction for "Phase Two" of the Great Wall Plan, covering the next three years. The plan committed Microsoft to further investment in software colleges and new programs for elementary and high school education. Included in all this was a proposal to launch a talent development center to train students, faculty, and software developers. The center would be run jointly by Microsoft and the Ministry of Education.

The centerpiece of the meeting was a fifteen-minute speech given by Yaoxue Zhang. In it, he summarized the state of Chinese higher education and how he believed Microsoft could work with the Ministry of Education to improve it. The ministry's threefold focus now was on upgrading rural education, making Chinese universities world-class, and expanding vocational schools, he explained. All of this was crucial to preparing the 240 million Chinese students currently in primary or middle school—almost the entire population of the United States—to lead the nation in the 21st century. "China is a developing country. Investment in our education is strategic. It is unwise to rely only on government to do this. Consensus needs to be reached among government, industry, and society," Zhang stated. "I want to express my thanks to MSRA and Microsoft for supporting China's education through programs like the Great Wall Plan."

After the meeting it was dinnertime, and everyone made the short walk down the hill from the Bamboo Wall to the Commune's expansive clubhouse, as resort workers hovered along the path wearing black uniforms with red stars on their chests. The clubhouse was a study in decadence, from the animal furs and peacock feathers adorning the walls to the purple velvet chairs to the vast wooden hall that recalled the kung-fu training scene in *The Matrix*. The center also boasted an outdoor reflecting pool, an Olympic-size indoor swimming pool, a private cinema, and restrooms as ornately decorated as a boudoir (and about as far removed from the squalid toilets of Chengdu as one could imagine).

The resort's menu advertised the finest in Beijing, Sichuan, and Cantonese cuisine, with "Western desserts"—and dinner did not disappoint. The buffet showcased succulent Peking duck, meat kebabs, fresh tofu, noodles, fried rice, red wine, and an assortment of cakes for dessert. Guests sat at three round tables. Every few minutes, glasses clinked as the officials performed informal toasts. The rules of Chinese toasting dictate that you should always toast one-to-one, not a group; toast throughout the meal, even if your glass is empty; and hold your glass lower than that of the person you are toasting, as a sign of respect. The latter custom sometimes leads to funny displays in which two people keep trying to go lower until they both hit the table.

After dinner, Shum, Yaoxue Zhang, and a few others retreated up the hill to the Bamboo Wall meditation chamber. It was dark outside by now, with just a sliver of a moon overhead. A gentle breeze blew through the open room. Candles were lit so you could just see people's faces. Sitting on the floor on pillows, the men took turns telling stories about their recent travels. With drinks being refilled by an attentive server, the conversation spanned everything from the discomforts of flying Indian Airlines to whether the first emperor of China, Qin Shi Huangdi (259–210 B.C.), might have been gay. Shum laughed out loud frequently, while Zhang was more reserved.

Then it was time for cards and karaoke. The more senior people seemed to stay away from the karaoke—perhaps they didn't know each other well enough yet. But in the game room, set up next to the Bamboo Wall's meditation chamber, everyone played cards and mahjongg, the traditional Chinese game using domino-size tiles. "I must say, I am very, very good," Shum boasted. "Anyone whose family is from Shanghai must be good." He backed up his talk by winning more than his share of games.

And the drinks kept flowing. Late in the evening, one meeting attendee who was getting particularly tipsy wandered off by himself. A minute later, there was a cry for help. Everyone rushed into the meditation chamber, which was pitch dark. Splashing was heard, and more shouts. It turned out the man had fallen into the water and needed help getting out. He was soaked and a little shaken up but not seriously hurt—just a few scrapes and bruises. A few minutes later he emerged from his room sporting a bandage on his cheek and a warm bathrobe. With that, he sat down to play mah-jongg. Nobody gave him a hard time. Apparently, this was par for the course in such a get-together.

Shum and his team would make no obvious missteps on this trip. They made sure things went smoothly and everyone was taken care of. The next morning, after a Western breakfast, the whole group headed back to Beijing for a visit to an exclusive country club, where polo shirts sold for more than a hundred dollars. After exploring the grounds, everyone sat down to lunch. The ministry officials wore Titleist caps. Over a light meal of noodles, peanuts, watermelon, strawberries, chicken—and beef intestines—Shum and Yaoxue Zhang talked about their experiences as graduate students outside of China and then reflected some more on their partnership.

Zhang said he believed Chinese industry needed better midlevel managers—and that multinational companies could help them fill that void. "We need to train students to manage in industry and understand the whole system and structure," he said. "Foreign companies like Microsoft, yes, they help train students to learn their approach and bring in creative ideas."

In turn, he continued, foreign companies needed to understand Chinese cultural issues in order to succeed in the Middle Kingdom. And that seemed to be the crux of what the Beijing lab had accomplished in its years of reaching out to local academe and government ministries—something that had been lacking in the company's China presence for much of the 1990s. "I didn't know much about Microsoft before I met Kai-Fu," Zhang related. That kind of personal contact was crucial. "If you try to develop software and products and don't know the language and culture, you can do nothing."

By helping cement those bonds, the Microsoft event seemed to be a success—but as usual, it was only a beginning. After lunch, Shum and Hon spent half an hour saying goodbye to their guests and thanking them for their cooperation with Microsoft and the Beijing lab. Director General Zhang and his team seemed gracious as well, looking forward to the next phase of their collaboration. But Shum was hardly done with his workday yet. That afternoon, a Saturday, he hopped on a plane to Dalian, a scenic and bustling port city northeast of Beijing, where he gave a lecture on his research to students and faculty at the Dalian University of Technology. When it came to building relationships, the lab director's work was never done.

While Shum reached out to build relationships in China, Ya-Qin Zhang was focusing inward on the company's core mission of developing software products, in part *for* China. At the time of the Yao Ming basketball game, Zhang had settled into his role in Redmond for a little more than a year. He was well over the bit of culture shock he had felt back in January 2004, when he had arrived in Redmond as a newly minted corporate vice president. Besides the obvious logistical changes and the dearth of great Chinese food in the area, there had been some minor cultural issues. From Beijing, he had brought back several receipts from a Sichuan-style restaurant whose English name was South Beauty. Zhang told his Beijing colleagues that he hesitated in filing the receipts for reimbursement in Redmond. "My secretary will think, what kind of place is that?" he joked. And at headquarters, Zhang's outgoing voicemail message was an automated female voice that curtly pronounced his name "Yakkin' Sang." He never bothered to change it.

His family seemed happy to be back in the U.S., however. They had grown to enjoy Beijing, but life was just more comfortable in the States. Besides, now that Zhang worked "only" ten hours a day, instead of fifteen, they could expect him to be home for dinner at least three times a week. He reported to senior vice president Pieter Knook, who headed up Microsoft's Mobile and Embedded Devices and Communications division—one of the seven business units within Microsoft at the time. (Knook had previously spent several years as president of Microsoft Asia, overseeing sales and marketing in China, India, Korea, Japan, and Southeast Asia.) The division encompassed Windows software for all devices other than desktop and laptop PCs. That meant handheld computers, PDAs, cell phones, printers, and even TVs and other "smart" appliances.

Zhang led a 600-strong engineering team that ballooned to 800 during his first year on the job. It was all part of a reorganization of two major product divisions—Windows Mobile and Windows CE—which Zhang was brought in to help unify into one entity. Previously, certain devices like PDAs ran on the Windows CE operating system, while others like Pocket PCs ran on Windows Mobile. But the entire mobile-device business had been doing poorly, losing money for three years running. In terms of revenue, it was the smallest division in the company, though even with its stumbles it was the fastest growing. Zhang's goal was to make his product division more agile, more flexible, and more efficient—crucial for the fast-paced world of mobile devices, which Bill Gates once called "a big growth area and probably the hottest area of innovation."

During the spring of 2005, in the same general time frame as the basketball game, Zhang's group was gearing up for a major product release aimed to put Microsoft on the mobile-device map for good. Specifically, he was in charge of shipping the next (fifth) generation of Windows Mobile, also known as Magneto. The operating system represented the great hope of Microsoft's mobile software business. It was designed to run stably and reliably on all types of mobile devices, acting first and foremost to support voice and data communication. It would also provide specialized services like e-mail on handhelds and "smart phones"—cell phones that doubled as organizers and could run software for Web browsing and TV viewing, among other features. Unlike most of its competitors, Magneto allowed software developers and handset manufacturers to add their own features. It could handle next-generation graphics, Web browsing, and multimedia such as photos, music, and video. Moreover, it claimed to do all this for a lower price than any of its individual competitors.

Unlike the previous releases of Windows Mobile, Magneto was designed to provide a unified operating system for all handheld mobile devices, running on different networks such as Wi-Fi and next-generation (3G) cellular systems. But Microsoft, a relative newcomer to the mobile market, faced serious competition from the heavy hitters of the industry: Nokia, the world's largest maker of mobile phones and a part-owner of Symbian, a major producer of cell-phone software; Palm, the manufacturer of the Palm Pilot and Treo digital organizers, which used their own proprietary operating systems; and Research in Motion (RIM), the maker of the famed BlackBerry mobile-messaging device that as of mid-2005 boasted three million users (among them celebrities like Oprah Winfrey and Al Gore). In terms of software market share for mobile devices, Microsoft trailed far behind Nokia-Symbian in cell phone operating systems, as well as RIM in mobile messaging. But it was highly competitive with Palm in operating systems for PDAs.

Zhang seemed like the right choice to bring Microsoft's mobile technology up to speed. Although his group was larger and more spread out than his previous teams at MSRA and Sarnoff, his ability to communicate effectively through the ranks shone through. A few months before the basketball game, in December 2004, he had held a team rally in a Redmond auditorium for some 500 members of the Magneto team. "This was the meeting to make sure people deliver on quality, and make sure we don't slip the date," he related later that day, dressed neatly all in black. Group members from around the world tuned in to the meeting via a Web conference hookup. When Zhang announced that Windows CE had just passed Palm in PDA software market share, cheers erupted across three continents. Afterward, at around six o'clock in the evening, he finally took a break to wolf down a sandwich—"lunch," he explained, implying that his workday was only half done. He still had to prepare for a one-on-one meeting with Gates the next day.*

Once the trade press caught wind of Magneto, Zhang reluctantly found himself in the limelight, receiving floods of requests for inter-

---

* In contrast to his generally pleasant and encouraging demeanor during research reviews, product reviews with Gates could be brutal. The chairman was known for ripping apart incomplete arguments or weak technical approaches. "He's very direct— more than direct," says Zhang. It was not uncommon for Gates to criticize product prototypes as working poorly, not being innovative enough, or, worse, taking a totally wrong approach.

views and business partnerships. It was around this time that articles in the press dubbed him "Mr. Magneto" and "BlackBerry Killer." Zhang seemed to have moved on completely from the research world; even his manner of speech had changed. He casually dropped jargon about "APIs" (application programming interfaces that make it easy for third parties to add software), "OEMs" (original equipment manufacturers), and "AKUs" (adaptation kit units, or software updates to the operating system), and weaved businessspeak like "synergy," "leveraging," and "engaged" into daily conversation.

For a guy obsessed with the mobile market, Zhang himself was almost never reachable on his cell phones. He typically kept two at a time, both of which already ran on Magneto, and he traded them in for new models frequently. He'd use one for his e-mail and calendar and the other for calls—but very sparingly. "I make about two calls a day to my wife," he says, "and maybe make two others and receive a couple."

From time to time, he sought out Kai-Fu Lee's thoughts and advice on the business side of things. Lee was practically a Redmond veteran by now, having been a vice president for almost four years. For Zhang, it was nice to have an old friend in the company who could relate to many of the corporate experiences he was going through— and, of course, who shared his passion for China. The two were appointed to the company's China-Redmond Advisory Board, a committee that reviews Microsoft's plans for the China market. Co-chaired by chief technology officer Craig Mundie and Kevin Johnson, group vice president of Microsoft's worldwide sales, marketing, and services, the highly confidential "CRAB" committee meets quarterly to discuss critical issues like investments and staffing decisions in China. Because of his busy travel calendar, though, Zhang had a hard time with scheduling. "I never attended any of the meetings," he quips. "Every time I was somewhere else."

More often than not, that somewhere else was China. In the battle for mobile supremacy, Zhang held an important trump card: his ties to the Beijing lab and knowledge of the Chinese market. In the Middle Kingdom—which in mid-2005 boasted nearly 400 million cell-phone users, tops in the world—phones are like fashion. "Some people in China say your phone should be like your lover—it knows your secrets," says Eric Chang, the lab's former speech research manager who became the Advanced Technology Center's assistant director and wireless group leader. "Others say it should be like your mom." Once, on a trip to Beijing, a hotel concierge even recognized Zhang and asked him whether he could get a discount on a new phone with Magneto. That reinforced the notion that with its citizens' exploding interest in online text messaging, Internet gaming, and photo and music sharing, China is the heart of the action.

Seizing on that reality, Zhang stayed close to the wireless networking and multimedia research groups at MSRA and the Advanced Technology Center's development teams. "That's my native area," says Zhang. "I still know all the bits and bytes." In fact, fully one-third of the ATC's first batch of projects was sponsored by Zhang's group in Redmond.

To get those collaborations going, the various teams had needed to meet face to face. In the spring of 2004, Microsoft had held a two-day "MindSwap" meeting in the Shanghai Westin Hotel. MindSwaps are a Microsoft tradition that bring together product teams, researchers, and Microsoft partners to brainstorm around a specific theme. This one was devoted to the Chinese wireless market. Ya-Qin wasn't there, but some of his key people attended, joined by other senior staff from Redmond, including Dan Ling and Alex "Go" Gounares. The Beijing contingent included Shum, Shipeng Li, and Qian Zhang from Research, and HongJiang Zhang and Eric Chang from the Advanced Technology Center.

After a long dinner of sharing ideas and strategies, one of Ya-Qin's general managers, Chee Chew, stood up and told HongJiang, "I have a project for you." It was to develop a Beijing lab technology that used photos taken by cell-phone cameras as the interface for contact lists on cell phones and Outlook: in one use of the technology, you might get a phone call from a Bill Smith or George Chen and the software would match the phone number to a face, so you know which Bill Smith or George Chen is calling. A year later, the technology would make it into Magneto. "The first project from Ya-Qin's organization was not from Ya-Qin," quips HongJiang. (Even as the ATC worked to implement the current generation of mobile software, MSRA was already working on technologies for the *next* release of Windows Mobile after Magneto, codenamed "Photon." One major project in the works was "seamless roaming," which would enable users to automatically receive multimedia content or any kind of data on their phone, laptop, or other device as they moved across different wireless networks. This had been one of the demos wheeled out for the lab's Technical Advisory Board visit in November 2004.)

If Zhang's first priority was developing global products, his second priority was creating partnerships to sell them. Around a month after the Yao Ming game, as Magneto was being put through its final stages of testing, Zhang was off spreading the word of its impending release across the U.S., Europe, and Asia. In April 2005, a month before the launch, Zhang was in Shenzhen visiting a few companies, including Huawei, the "Cisco of China." Late one night he came back to his hotel to find someone waiting for him in the lobby. The mystery man said he was going to lead a major mobile device company in China. He wanted to talk to Zhang about partnering with Microsoft so his company's handset could run on Magneto. So he invited Zhang to dinner the following evening. The Microsoft executive was noncommittal but agreed to meet. The next night, at a fancy restaurant in the downtown high-tech zone of Shenzhen, Zhang was greeted by a team of fifteen people and a PowerPoint presentation. Dinner was served in a private room with a TV and sofas, and the presentation was made via laptop, with Mr. Magneto sitting close to the screen and asking many questions. A few months later, he still couldn't reveal the company's name or whether a deal had been reached—but, at the least, he was intrigued.

It's a telling example of the often informal and personal way in which technology partnerships are initiated in today's China—and how the global wireless market for software could eventually be won. Whether the deal worked out or not, China was increasingly where the action was in mobile devices. As Bill Gates remarked at a recent

Beijing appearance: "The Chinese market is not only the biggest, but in many ways the most innovative as well. And so we are doing more and more of our development and our partnerships in this area here in China."

Gates had continued on this thread, laying out what amounted to a global strategy for winning the mobile software war—starting with the Middle Kingdom and Mr. Magneto. "We will have a mix: development going on in the United States and development going on here. And Ya-Qin is in a great place to coordinate that. The mobile market here really is quite phenomenal, and his background and the learnings [sic] from this market and some of the surrounding market will be key for us getting it right. That is an area where the United States is not a leader, and so it is particularly important for us to look around the world."

The Mandalay Bay Resort and Casino rises majestically out of the Mohave Desert, its curved, gold-hued tower shimmering in the early morning sun. One of the flashiest hotels on the Las Vegas Strip, the structure looks like a beacon for lost gamblers. Its tropical, South Seas theme encompasses some 3,300 guestrooms, 24 restaurants and bars, a saltwater aquarium with sharks and crocodiles, and an 11-acre sand beach, complete with manmade waves. Across the street from the hotel, the one-million-square-foot Mandalay Bay Convention Center is the fifth-largest meeting hall in the United States and a popular spot for telecommunications and electronics expos.

This was the setting for Microsoft's Mobile and Embedded Developers Conference, or DevCon 2005—where Magneto, or Windows Mobile 5.0, would be formally launched. On the morning of May 9, 2005, a crowd of more than 2,000—mostly developers and handset manufacturers—waited in the auditorium with great anticipation. There had been a fair amount of media coverage about Magneto, but the mainstream press did not know exactly what to make of it. To most observers, it seemed like just another product launch—in an area in which Microsoft was not even a leader. One trade-news Web site had doctored a picture of Gates, dressing him in the helmet worn by the villain Magneto in the *X-Men* movies.

At nine o'clock, the auditorium hushed and Gates took the stage to polite applause. In his ninety-minute address, the Microsoft chairman was all business and hardly cracked a smile. "In the past five years, there's been a profound shift in the kind of data and services people access on their mobile devices—from multimedia to business applications," said Gates. "Windows Mobile 5.0 enables our industry partners to develop exciting new hardware designs and solutions that will revolutionize how customers use mobile devices."

Gates backed up his business-speak with concrete examples. One demo showed how a user could automatically exchange documents between a desktop PC and a handheld Pocket PC. The mobile device, running Windows Mobile 5.0, could display a PowerPoint presentation on its small screen and also hook up to a digital projector. Another demo showed how a smart phone could be used to take pictures and organize them via camera-interface software. Gates also talked about storing a thousand songs on a cell phone. It sounded like a thinly veiled threat to Apple's iPod and other portable music players. Toward the end of his speech, Gates emphasized the importance of research for creating the future of mobile computing.

Zhang could not have agreed more with his top boss. He sat in the front row, filled with pride as he watched members of his team run the demos for Gates, including the camera-user interface developed by the Advanced Technology Center in Beijing. Zhang would spend the day talking to customers and developers, answering questions about what kinds of features could be supported now and in the future. "In three years, cell phones will be the primary device for playing music and taking pictures," he predicts.

That night, Zhang hosted a special awards dinner at the Mandalay Bay hotel for what he called "MVPs" (most valuable professionals)—top software hackers whom he wanted to recruit to help Microsoft get a leg up on its wireless multimedia competitors. During dinner, they joked with Zhang about his recent profile in *The New York Times,* an article that called attention to his Go skills and work habits, among other personal details. The next morning, while waiting for the shuttle bus to take him to the airport, Zhang tried his luck at a low-stakes blackjack table. He played for ten minutes and won fifteen dollars.

From the desert glitz of Las Vegas, Zhang would fly to Silicon Valley for a series of secret meetings with Palm. Behind the scenes, his team had been working with Palm executives on a key partnership that would cause a stir in the mobile industry. The two former competitors were planning to join forces to produce a Treo handheld computer (cell phone and organizer) that ran on Windows Mobile 5.0 and was slated to hit store shelves in 2006. The Treo already had a million users and would provide an anchor for Microsoft's software in the market—something it did not have to this point. Within the year, Magneto would also be released on handheld devices from Motorola, Hewlett-Packard, Samsung, and HTC in Taiwan. Furthermore, just a month after the Las Vegas launch, Steve Ballmer would announce a new mobile e-mail service that would finally allow Microsoft to compete more strongly with RIM's BlackBerry.

After years of floundering, Microsoft's mobile business finally seemed ready to take off. "The outlook is pretty bright," said Pieter Knook, speaking at a Microsoft financial analyst meeting in the summer of 2005. He too emphasized the importance of the mobile market in East Asia and India, adding, "We have worked with many other local manufacturers in the Chinese market, too. So you can expect further geographical expansion."

The competition to control the business of mobile software was shaping up to be a legitimate three-way slugfest between Microsoft and Palm, Nokia and Symbian, and RIM. But as Zhang saw it, knowledge of the Pacific Rim—especially the China market and how to do product development there—would be the key to winning the war. By the end of the summer, China would become Microsoft's number-one market for mobile device software, with a factor-of-ten increase in sales in just two years. And China Mobile, the country's leading wireless provider, would enter into a new partnership with Microsoft to subsidize users who bought cell phones running on Magneto. All these signs pointed to the Redmond powerhouse using its China experience as a proving ground to approach the rest of the mobile market. "I'm very, very confident we will be a major player," says Zhang.

He didn't realize it yet, but his expertise in global product development and markets—and especially his *guanxi* in China—was about to become more valuable than he had ever imagined.

11
Battle Over
Kai-Fu Lee

August 2000–September 2005

*I would like my legacy to be really two things. One is having
made a difference in the two great countries and two great
peoples. The second is making very complex, challenging
technologies usable by everyone.*

—KAI-FU LEE

Kai-Fu Lee waited serenely at Todai, an upscale all-you-can-eat
Japanese sushi and seafood buffet in Redmond town center.
Traffic had been a mess and his two dinner companions—
one of the authors and Ya-Qin Zhang—were a bit behind schedule.
The writer got there next. Lee, perched against a big glass window
near the door, explained the setup at the cavernous eatery—pointing
out the vast seafood island with forty varieties of sushi, the hot entrée
counter, salad bar, and dessert station, bejeweled with cakes and
fruits. It's all pretty good, he explained.

Lee and his guest were about to give up on Mr. Magneto when he
strode through the door, scanning the tables for his dinner mates.
Everyone dispersed to fill their trays, mixing sushi with hot dishes
heaped with fish or pork—and shedding the road stress by the time
they returned to the table. Lee and Zhang sat comfortably side by
side. They had become even closer friends since Zhang had moved to
Redmond. A few weeks earlier, just before Magneto's launch, they

had spent a brief vacation together with their families (both had two school-age children), up in Vancouver, British Columbia. It was something they did regularly—make the two-and-a-half hour drive north for a day or two of mouthwatering Chinese food (better than Seattle, a bit better than San Francisco, and even surpassing much of China, they agreed), shopping, and family movies. On this trip, they had seen *The Incredibles*. Later, the grownups sat down to play pushing pig. "Kai-Fu won't like it that I say this, but he gets most of the pigs," Zhang once laughed. "His wife gets the least amount." Lee, though, was undisputed master of their dining excursions. A true connoisseur, he kept stacks of notes on his favorite restaurants—analyzing not just the establishments but what dishes were best. He always ordered for the table.

It was May 31, 2005. The founding director of the Beijing lab had not been able to attend the Seattle Supersonics basketball game a few months earlier, so a main goal of the dinner interview was to catch up on his work and general life, but in a setting outside the office. He had a lot to say (it soon became apparent there was even more he *didn't* say). Sitting in the noisy restaurant, Lee spoke quietly but passionately about two of his favorite subjects: China and Chinese students. Although he had been born in Taiwan, he had never forgotten his father's dream of unification—and helping China and its people was always on his mind. When most people are transferred back from an overseas assignment, they stay in touch with friends and colleagues still abroad. Lee had worked hard to stay in touch with an entire country.

Much of Lee's passion arose from his insights into the Chinese education system that had spurred so much discussion at the Dragon Villa retreat years earlier and prompted his open letter to students. Since becoming a Microsoft vice president in August 2000, Lee had returned to China three or four times a year—giving several university lectures each trip. He had even created his own Web site, www.kaifulee.com, to stay in contact with Chinese students and better convey his thoughts about education and work. Everything on the site was in Mandarin, except the top of the home page, which read: Kai-Fu's Student Network. "I go there daily to answer questions," he related. "[It has] more potential. But even now it's gratifying."

Out of Lee's passion and writings for Chinese students had come a book project. Written in Mandarin for the Chinese market, the book went beyond his views on education and careers and amounted to a philosophy of life. In large part, it was about incorporating what he considered the best attributes of the United States and the Middle Kingdom—blending the Western tradition of being proactive, direct, and confident with Asian virtues of humility and perseverance—to live the most meaningful life possible. "I think what it is going to take for success in the 21st century is a combination of both," Lee says.

Another big theme of the book was that people should not have a singular view of success, but multiple views. "It's not money or the size of your organization or fanciness of job title," says Lee. "It's really being the best you can be, doing the things that you love and really creating a legacy for yourself." To do this, he adds, people must know their dream or vision and pursue it with discipline, passion, and integrity, while also striving for teamwork and good communication with others. "These are the various elements that I think need to be weaved together to realize one's potential." The book, which included a DVD of some of Lee's talks in China, was due out that September. Loosely translated, it was called *Be Your Personal Best.*

Lee laid most of this out at Todai and in a follow-up telephone call on July 1, 2005. He looked a bit tired at the dinner, and revealed he was planning a twelve-week sabbatical that would start in mid-June and continue until mid-September, about the time his book came out. It was to be his first lengthy vacation in years.

Kai-Fu Lee was still only forty-three. Already he had been on an incredible journey, leaving his native Taiwan at age eleven and becoming a renowned speech researcher and key figure in some of the legendary computer companies of the day—Apple, Silicon Graphics, and Microsoft.

Now, however, after nearly five years in Redmond, he was entering a new era. Far beyond his specific technological accomplishments in research and product development, his growing ties to Chinese academe and an increasing presence in Microsoft's strategic decisions had enhanced Lee's ability to bridge West and East. In the process, he had become an icon for innovation in the age of global competition.

Arriving in Washington state in the summer of 2000 had offered a study in contrast for Lee. Teeming Beijing suffered oppressive summers and severe winters, seeming to move perpetually from hot and humid to frigid and snowy, and all under a haze of gray pollution. The Seattle area could be famously wet and its roadways equally crowded, but its relatively mild temperatures, greenery, and breathtaking views of Mount Rainier made it seem far more livable. In Beijing, Lee had a car and driver. In Washington, he drove himself between work and his Bellevue house: it was harder to make phone calls and impossible to read or fire off e-mails when he was the driver. But the biggest contrast might have been the nature of the jobs. Risk-taking was rewarded in research, but it was a pariah in development, where bringing products to market as smoothly and efficiently as possible was paramount. Jokes Lee, "In research, people remember you by your most glorious project. In product groups, they remember you by your most glorious failure."

Still, Lee had been eager to justify the faith Rick Rashid, Steve Ballmer, and ultimately, Bill Gates had placed in him. He continued to believe that speech was the computer interface of the future. Given the proliferation of mobile devices, eliminating the need for clumsy keyboards or keypads had taken on even more allure in recent years. Redmond was the perfect place to make the transformation happen—offering the opportunity to bring cutting-edge technology to millions of people.

Lee's job was to unite Microsoft's efforts in speech and natural-language processing—previously split between several groups—into a new business unit that came to be called the Natural Interactive Services Division (pronounced "Nisdy" in Microsoft-speak), a key part of Microsoft's Servers and Tools business.* He reported to newly named senior vice president Eric Rudder, the technical strategist who had sat in on Lee's last Bill G. review as head of Microsoft Research China. Nearly 400 Microsoft employees—roughly eight times the size of the Beijing lab at the time—reported to Lee. Rather than develop code for one specific product or suite of products, Lee's charges would supply core technologies for applications that cut across all of Microsoft's businesses. At the most basic level, the task spanned language identi-fication, word-breaking (in Chinese, for instance, there are no spaces between written words, so the system must learn to recognize indi-vidual words), parsing, derivational morphology, determining parts of speech, and semantic understanding. From the consumer point of view, these elements formed the underpinnings of features like Help, text-to-speech, speech recognition, grammar and spell-checking, and Web and desktop search, which were essential to every aspect of per-sonal computing—and almost every piece of software Microsoft made.

Microsoft had worked in all these areas for years. In fact, when the Research lab was formed in 1991, its first employees were three speech recognition and natural-language experts lured from IBM. When he arrived in Redmond, Lee set about methodically reorganiz-ing all of Microsoft's product efforts in speech and natural-language processing—delegating much of the job to his old colleagues X. D. Huang, then general manager of the speech product group, and Hsiao-Wuen Hon, who at the time oversaw statistical learning tech-nologies for "Nisdy."

From the start, Lee turned to Research—the Beijing lab in partic-ular—to get a leg up on Microsoft's next generation of speech and natural-language products. Nowhere was the synergy between the Beijing lab and its founding director more powerful than in text-to-

---

* Lee ran a somewhat convoluted route to get to this, his main position in Redmond. He first was assigned to the User Interface Technology Division. Roughly nine months later, he took over a team named MSN Search, at a time when Microsoft still licensed core search engine technology. After about a year in that job, he moved to NISD.

speech. The ability to translate text into spoken language was critical for enterprises such as call centers, which relied on vast text databases to answer queries on everything from bank balances to flight schedules. It could also be extremely useful for visually impaired people who had trouble reading screens, or drivers who needed to keep their eyes on the road. But because bandwidth, display size, memory, and processing power varied widely in different types of devices, the system behind it had to be developed somewhat differently for desktop PCs, landline telephones, and mobile phones and PDAs.

The basic technology for these efforts had come from Microsoft's speech R&D group in Redmond. Lee, however, had launched the Beijing lab's original program in Mandarin text-to-speech. And within a few years, the outpost was given prime responsibility for *all* Microsoft text-to-speech research and development in the core languages that together represented about 90 percent of the company's customer base. Once the Advanced Technology Center got going in late 2003, it became the focal point for transferring this technology to Lee's product organization. The lab's former director funded a variety of efforts there.

The MSRA-designed text-to-speech technology—for English and Chinese—was set to debut in Windows Vista in 2006. The plan was to bring the Microsoft version of other core languages—including French, German, Italian, and Spanish—into commercial use later in the decade. All these systems initially targeted people with visual disabilities or severe carpal tunnel syndrome who absolutely needed documents or files read aloud—a small market. But by deploying its own proprietary technology, the company reduced the need to pay licensing fees and cut its dependence on outside suppliers.

Two other aspects of Lee's work—computer search and Help— were aimed for mainstream customers. Lee's work in search dated back to 2001. For roughly a year between then and 2002, he had been put in charge of Microsoft's Internet search team, before the company deployed the proprietary technology it now uses. A couple of years later, in the spring of 2004, a bootleg project in "desktop search" was started by a few members of Lee's group. The effort was meant to compete with Google Desktop Search, which was then only in beta form but already striking fear in Microsoft's executive ranks.

The main idea of desktop search was to instantly find information anywhere on a PC hard drive—a task that has frustrated every computer user—and present it in an efficient and friendly manner. Lee once noted that when Google's desktop application searches a hard drive, it often brings back a list of items much like those returned in Web searches. Microsoft, he said, wanted to do something much more powerful. Part of the solution involved "summarization" technology developed by Lee's group in consultation with researchers in Beijing and Redmond. The software indexes documents and pares them down to their essentials, creating a brief abstract by which you can easily tell if it has what you want. Say you know that Bill Gates and other Microsoft executives wrote e-mails about speech recognition but you can't remember when they were written, or even who wrote them. You could simply write a query like "Find every e-mail about speech recognition," and the technology would bring them back almost instantly. Only instead of simply a list of documents, you would see a brief caption that described the contents of each item, making it easier to find exactly what you are looking for.

Lee was hoping for big things from the project. When his workers told him about the bootleg venture a couple months after they had kicked it off, he approved it as an officially funded effort. A few weeks later, though, the project was transferred en masse to MSN. Lee would not comment on the decision, but a close colleague says he was not happy.

Work on Help features, by contrast, remained one of the pillars of Lee's job. In many ways, it wasn't much different from search. After all, finding the right Help documents was increasingly about matching keywords and natural-language phrases to a user's query, much like searching on the Internet: a box labeled "search" even appears when you call up the Help or Office Assistant features of Word. You type in your query, such as "print address labels." The software scours the Help database, giving a relevance score to any files it turns up matching those terms—and you then have to figure out which one to read to get your answer. The way the keywords are indexed and ranked is also a lot like an Internet search engine, but with a couple of key differences. First, the engine scans a limited set of prescribed answers, not the essentially limitless corpus of documents found on the Internet. Second, the database can be readily optimized. That is, if it doesn't hold what people want, Microsoft can add to it. Explains Lee, "With the Internet, the content is the content. With Help, you can actually say the answer's not there, but enough people are looking for it that we have to write it."

Lee wanted to standardize the Help interface across all of Microsoft's products and make it far more intuitive. As with the text-to-speech technology, an early indication of Lee's efforts in Help was set to appear in Windows Vista. But Lee's eyes were always on the prize years down the road, when a speech-enabled interface would completely blur the lines between search and help, to the point people wouldn't even think of them as separate applications. Suppose you still needed help printing those address labels, he explains. You should be able to simply say that to a computer instead of typing in keywords. And one glorious day years ahead, you might not even ask for help. You might just command: "Print these address labels," and the computer will figure out what to do. "Whatever the problem you have, it's phrased in natural language, it has to be," says Lee. "We want to basically take over the entry point of Help and gradually make it more and more natural."

Lee had arrived in Redmond with guns blazing, but he had forgotten how slow the pace of product development could be. "If there's one thing I'm not used to in a product group, it's that things take a long time," he notes. His first year was largely spent completing the product cycle already under way when he arrived. It would take close to three years beyond that for many of the initiatives he set in motion to begin to make their presence felt in products. "You have to look at backward compatibility, legacy, make tradeoffs, synchronize with other product team schedules—you add all this up and it pretty much becomes three years," he says. Even then, much of his work would not appear until the debut of Vista.

But if the outward manifestations of his contributions were minimal, Lee's influence rose steadily in Redmond. Bill Gates, for one, shared his vision that speech represented the computer interface of the future and loved to imagine the day when people could converse with their PCs. As the work Lee oversaw moved closer to market—and his group swelled to some 460 workers—Microsoft showed its appreciation: in 2004, his compensation surpassed $1 million.

At least as valuable as the technology he brought to the table was Lee's keen understanding of China. That, coupled to his unique ability to bridge Chinese and American cultures, had made him a natural choice to accompany Bill Gates on his February 2003 visit to Beijing, where they would meet with President Jiang Zemin, among others.

In the meeting with Jiang, Lee had listened as Gates and the Chinese leader covered the requisites—doing their duty, as he put it. They spoke about the software industry and the need to create an open, collaborative environment and build local partnerships that would benefit both parties. But things had quickly loosened up, as the men engaged in a genuinely friendly conversation that had culminated with the discussion about the stock market, which Gates had capped by quipping:

"You know, Mr. Jiang, you are a real capitalist!"

Lee would marvel over that conversation for years. "Ten years ago, it would not have been okay—it would have been a horrible thing to say," he notes. "But pretty much people in China, as far as the economy goes, it's more capitalist and a little bit of socialism."

It wasn't just the Chinese that had come a long way, either. When Lee had first arrived in Beijing to start the research lab in mid-1998, Microsoft was struggling mightily to improve its image in China. First had come the Venus project debacle, then Juliet Wu's Microsoft-bashing book, both public embarrassments. But Lee had reveled in the obvious comfort level between Jiang and Gates. He liked to tell people, too, how Jiang's first question had been about the success of Microsoft Research—and how it compared to Bell Labs. Witnessing the two dynamic leaders getting along so famously—and speaking passionately about a subject so close to his heart—Lee must have felt that all the relationship-building done over the four years leading up to the meeting was paying off.

But there had remained a lot to do, and Lee had grown even more important to Microsoft's China view since coming to Redmond. For one thing, he was named to the company's China-Redmond Advisory Board. Lee also routinely advised Ballmer and Gates on China strategy and policy, serving as a key headquarters liaison to the Beijing lab and later the Advanced Technology Center—and in some cases as a *guanxi* "fixer." Perhaps the most notable examples came in late 2003, when Lee was asked to help salvage a commitment Microsoft had made the previous year to outsource $100 million worth of software testing and development work to China over a three-year period, while also investing $20 million in local companies. As Lee explained the situation, when it became clear that the company was hopelessly behind on that commitment, Ballmer traveled to China and negotiated a new deal that called for $55 million in outsourcing over the next four years, coupled to a $65 million investment in local firms. Ballmer then asked Lee to ensure the new pledge was fulfilled. "That project consisted of identifying jobs that were then being performed in Redmond, or which were slated to be performed in Redmond over the coming months, and convincing managers in Redmond to move that work to China, to be performed by Chinese contract workers," Lee noted. He claimed that by mid-2005 the company "was on track to outsource over one thousand jobs a year to China."

Lee had fired off an e-mail complaining to the Microsoft hierarchy about the outsourcing situation—and apparently Microsoft's business practices as well—sometime in 2003. In it, he bluntly reported that he was "deeply disappointed at our incompetence in China—that we have wasted so many years in China with so little to show for it." Later in the year, he followed this up with a confidential memo titled "Making It in China: Strategic Recommendations for Microsoft." Lee called the document "a basic 'primer' on how to behave (and, equally important, how not to behave) as a multinational company trying to do business in China."

The document circulated to the company's highest levels, and Gates and company took heed—probably one reason the chairman once called Lee "one of the top two influential people in what we did [in China]." Late in 2003, possibly at least partly in response to Lee's warnings, the company hired a new head of its Greater China region, to which all sales groups in China, Hong Kong, and Taiwan reported. He was Tim Chen, a native of Taiwan who had worked nine years at AT&T Bell Labs before joining Motorola and becoming president of its China subsidiary. Soon thereafter, Chen took over the Microsoft China business, in addition to his regional duties.

Chen's appointment was notable in part because he was named a corporate vice president, marking the first time Microsoft had assigned a person of that rank to China. That was a key indicator of how important Gates and company viewed the country, and of Microsoft's awareness that it needed to work harder to build relations there before it could hope to earn a bigger share of the software market down the road. The move had Kai-Fu Lee written all over it.*

Still, a sense that he had even more important things to contribute, both in terms of helping Microsoft understand China and in assisting the country itself, seemed to consume Lee. Even as he skillfully handled an intense job in Redmond, he was drawn increasingly back to the Middle Kingdom. He didn't think there was one right way to thrive in the modern world—namely, pure capitalism—and he felt that a nation like China, with thousands of years of history, had a right to do things its own way. At the same time, the country had been mired in economic isolation until a few decades ago, and still had a long way to go in order to realize its true potential. Finding ways to

---

* Chen, who was still on the job as this book went to press, seems to have brought some stability to the business side. He is the third head of Microsoft China since Juliet Wu left in the summer of 1999. First came Jack Gao, who served roughly two years, then Jun Tang, who resigned in early 2004, again after about two years, to become president of Shanda Interactive Entertainment, the Internet gaming start-up that went public that same year.

blend the best of East and West was the key to that, and vital to the future of innovation. Lee worked hard to carry that message to the Microsoft hierarchy, but he aimed it especially at Chinese students.

Lee's status as an adjunct professor at a host of Chinese universities provided a ready-made opportunity to return to the country to lecture every three or four months: he would later claim to have given 300 speeches at twenty Chinese universities between 1990 and 2005. Lee was careful in his talks not to pump his own company. As he explained, his lectures "never have to do with Microsoft technologies. They're about helping students be successful, grow their careers, find answers to tough technical issues . . . I talk to students about integrity, importance of teamwork, encourage them to be more outgoing, speak up for themselves, become more assertive, more direct instead of roundabout, have courage and do the difficult things . . . That's what they most want to listen to. I could go in and tell them how great Visual Studio or .NET is, and they'll say, 'Here comes another commercial, I'm not going to come to the talk.' But truly teaching them builds up credibility for me and Microsoft."

The revered computer scientist had also continued to write the occasional open letter to students in Chinese newspapers. With his third communiqué, published in *China Youth Daily* in June 2004, Lee's popularity really seemed to soar. His article "Success, Happiness, and Self-Confidence" was built around the case of a troubled student who—apparently because he felt he didn't measure up to expectations—had murdered four other students. As Lee relates, "I made suggestions on how to gain self-confidence, why happiness is important, and why success isn't just being the richest and most famous person." The paper increased its print run by 100,000 copies and still sold out, Lee says. People began e-mailing him, asking for electronic copies—spurring him to create his own Web site to make it readily available. The site went up in July 2004. By the time of the Todai dinner a year later, it was getting some 1,200 hits a day, several hundred thousand a year—mostly students in college or high school, but some teachers as well. The site had some 40,000 registered users, and Lee reported that he had answered 3,000 questions in the past year alone.

It was while honing his message to Chinese students that Lee had gotten his book idea. A central thesis is that achieving one's fullest potential will come through combining traditional Chinese values of duty and humility with often harder-charging, more confident Western ways—much the same message he was delivering to students. But the book goes deeper, describing three concentric circles—representing Value, Attitude, and Action—around which people should evaluate, plan, and live their lives.

The innermost ring, Value, contains the basic attributes of integrity, honesty, responsibility, and conscience that form the core around which everything else is built, says Lee. Attitude, or the approach people take as they strive to put their core values into action, is the theme of the second circle. It specifically addresses the need to balance the best of East and West to form the approach one takes in life. "How you adjust the humility with confidence, the perseverance with self-criticalness, the courage with the humility and the serenity," explains Lee. The third circle represents Action. It includes establishing a vision for your life, finding the passion to pursue it, laying out a plan for achieving the vision, and then learning how to communicate and work well with others so that your goals can be fulfilled.

These ideas, at least as Lee describes them, might seem clichéd or overly New Agey to many Westerners. But Chinese students, especially as they sought employment with multinational firms, seemed to be struggling to come to grips with Western views and lacking in role models. And Lee seemed consumed with a desire to help them, almost as if he were trying to drive devils from his soul. Was it his parents' experiences in China or his father's unfulfilled dream of reunification that inflamed him? In any event, it's hard to imagine how Lee found time to plan lectures, travel back and forth to China to deliver them, pen letters for Chinese newspapers, start an interactive Web site, and write a book—all while holding down an executive position that likely took fifty or sixty hours a week when things were slow. Not to mention he was a husband and father with two school-age children.

But Lee's whole life had been about achievement—some might

say overachievement. Heading into 2005, he wanted to accomplish even more. In particular, he became increasingly disturbed over what he saw as Microsoft's slow progress in some aspects of its China strategy. He felt there were still several changes that were urgently needed, steps that would smooth the company's way while helping it become a more attractive place for students to work. On the sixth floor of the Sigma building, the company employed about 100 developers who "localized" Microsoft products for the China market. In addition, software testing and development operations were scattered around the country. All these developers and engineers worked in separate teams that reported to the specific Redmond business group for whom they were working. There were good reasons for operating this way: namely, that the teams needed to report to whoever was funding them to ensure the right jobs were being done at the right pace. However, in Lee's view the lack of a centralized authority or director in China meant there was little cohesion between the groups and made Microsoft appear disjointed to Chinese authorities, and, perhaps, to students. As he once explained: ". . . each of the seven Business Groups has employees in China who report directly to it, rather than to MSRA or to ATC [the Advanced Technology Center]. This multiplicity of engineering groups in China has often created problems for Microsoft . . . I came to believe that all R&D efforts in China should be unified under one reporting structure."

Early in 2005, Lee proposed a meeting with Ballmer and other key parties to discuss unifying Microsoft's research and development activities in China. He immediately ran into internal objections. According to his account, the chief opponent was Steve Sinofsky, the senior vice president in charge of the Office business group, which probably did more localization work in China than any other business unit. Sinofsky, as Lee represented the situation, felt it was critical for the business groups to retain independent power and authority over the work they conducted in China.

Lee was severely put off by this view. He came back with a plan to establish an outward-facing head for China, for recruiting and relationship-building purposes. Even that proposal was watered down, in his mind, when Ballmer decided instead to create a head of human resources position that Lee felt was inadequate. It didn't much matter in any case. Sinofsky, says Lee, objected to this step as well, eschewing any position that would lessen the power of the product groups. Meanwhile, he added, Rick Rashid seemed concerned that the new human resources head would diminish the role of Microsoft Research Asia and the Advanced Technology Center, which reported to him.

Frustrated, Lee grew increasingly sour on the company where he had worked longer than any other. "Accordingly, I concluded that there was little chance of effecting any meaningful change in the organization of Microsoft's R&D activities in China," Lee summed up. ". . . I also concluded that the time had come for me to leave Microsoft."

On May 7, a disgruntled Kai-Fu Lee sent Google CEO Eric Schmidt the following note, copying company founders Sergey Brin and Larry Page:

Hi, Eric:

It's been over 10 years since we last met—hope you still remember me (we were discussing the Sun-Apple collaboration on Java + QuickTime). Congratulations on your success at Google.

I have heard that Google is starting an effort in China. I thought I'd let you know that if Google has great ambitions for China, I would be interested in having a discussion with you.

I am currently a Corporate VP at Microsoft, working on areas very related to Google.

http://www.microsoft.com/presspass/exec/kaifu/default.asp*

---

* This was a link to his Microsoft bio.

Before this job, I started Microsoft's research and R&D efforts in China. My efforts in China has led to what MIT Technology Review calls "the World's Hottest Computer Lab", and the group I established is now the most desirable place to work for top CS graduates in China.

http://www.technologyreview.com/articles/04/06/huang0604.asp ?p=1*

Please let me know if you would like to have a chat.

Thanks,
Kai-Fu Lee

While he clearly liked what he saw with the Beijing lab (as he bragged in his e-mail to Schmidt) and the Advanced Technology Center, Lee could not accept what he considered Microsoft's lack of progress on other research and development endeavors in China. Not long before he sent the note to Schmidt, he had read on the Sina.com Web site that Google wanted to establish a research and development presence in the country: increasingly attracted to the idea of returning to China, he had decided to throw his hat into the ring.†

The Google hierarchy was ecstatic. Lee was a prominent figure in Silicon Valley, and in computing circles in general. More importantly, his reputation and contacts in China were impeccable. A response quickly came back from Google's vice president of engineering, Alan Eustace: "We would love to talk to you. Please call me as soon as possible, 24 hours a day, on my cell phone . . ." Lee visited Google headquarters on May 27. The search company's executives were apparently so worried someone might recognize Lee and leak the information that they arranged to meet him in a remote build--

---

* This was a link to an article by one of this book's authors, assigned and edited in part by the other author, that inspired the idea for this book.

† Microsoft later charged that Lee had learned of Google's plans to establish a Chinese research and development center through a prospective hire he had interviewed the day before he contacted Schmidt. Lee insisted he had heard through Sina.

ing on the Google campus, bringing Lee in through a private entrance with no receptionist. The prize recruit then sat through eleven interviews, including forty-five minutes with Schmidt and a half-hour each with Brin and Page. Over the next several weeks, most if not all of it while he was on sabbatical, a whirlwind of negotiation took place that culminated in a formal job offer. At one point, Jonathan Rosenberg, Google's director of business development, e-mailed his colleagues: "I all but insist that we pull out all the stops and close him like wolves. He's an all star and will contribute in ways that go substantially beyond China."

As a deal became more likely, both Google and Lee expected trouble. Of key concern were the nondisclosure and noncompete clauses—part of Microsoft's standard executive employee agreement—Lee had signed just days after moving to Redmond as a vice president. The noncompete clause read in part: "While employed at Microsoft and for a period of one year thereafter, I will not (a) accept employment or engage in activities competitive with product, services or projects (including actual or demonstrably anticipated research and development) on which I worked or about which I learned confidential or proprietary information or trade secrets while employed at Microsoft."

Throughout the interviews, and, ultimately, the hiring process, Google directed him not to reveal any confidential or proprietary Microsoft information—a condition to which Lee stipulated. For his part, Lee negotiated a protection clause that required Google to pay his salary even if he had to sit out the year required in the clause. "Google agrees to provide the salary, bonus, benefits (including expatriate benefits), and, to the extent permitted, stock option vesting that Mr. Lee would have received if he were employed by Google under the terms of the Offer Letter . . ."

On July 5, 2005, Lee made his move at Microsoft. The Fourth of July weekend had just ended, but Lee was about to set off a different kind of fireworks. He went to see his boss, Eric Rudder, and told the Servers and Tools head that he didn't intend to return from his sabbatical, which had begun just a few weeks earlier. He was evaluating a few options, Lee told Rudder. Then he dropped the bomb: one option was joining Google.

Lee offered to spend a month or two helping transition his team to new leadership. After the meeting, he confirmed the conversation in an e-mail and assured Rudder he wouldn't access proprietary information, other than the employee reviews he still needed to complete. Rudder's response, according to Lee, was professional and even friendly. "You are an executive in the company. I trust you. But please talk to Bill and Steve, and give them a chance to talk you into staying." However, he also cautioned Lee that trouble might lie ahead. "I really don't think it is a big deal—Google, Oracle, IBM, or whatever company—these competitors come and go, but Bill and Steve won't feel this way."

Immediately, Microsoft went into overdrive to keep Lee—but it was a carrot-and-stick courtship. Over the next two weeks, a host of senior executives—from Rashid to Ballmer to Gates himself—tried to convince Lee to remain at the company. On Friday, July 8, Lee met with Ballmer to discuss what it might take to convince Lee to stay on. But Ballmer also warned, "If you leave, we would have to do something, and when we do something, please don't take it personally. We like you. Your contributions to Microsoft have been immense. It's not you we are after, it is Google."

Lee met that same day with Rashid, who had hired him in the first place. By Lee's account, the senior vice president related: "You should not go. Things will be very unpleasant for you if you go." Rashid would later speak only in general terms about the whole situation. However, he alluded to the dispute over how the company's China-based research and development activities organization should be run. "We've been running and organizing the same way in all our labs since the time I started the organization," Rashid said, referring to the six research labs the company operates worldwide, all of which are headed by a local director who reports to him. "We took that to Cambridge (England). We took that to Beijing—it's been incredibly successful there. It's the way we run down in the Silicon Valley area, and it's the way I want India to grow up. The reason we've been successful is that we are organized and run in the right way. Unless something happens and somebody decides to change that—I won't be here because I'm not going to change that."

Five days after the meeting with Rashid, a Tuesday, Lee was back with Ballmer, who presented him with an offer for "a new job, new title, and an improved compensation package," as Lee recounted. The details of this position were not released. However, Lee also related that during this period both Ballmer and Gates "discussed with me the possibility of creating for me a position in China that would direct all of the various Microsoft R&D activities in China." He questioned the two executives about the continued objections from Sinofsky, in particular, but got what he considered a vague response. In the end, Lee noted, "I concluded that no such position in China could be successfully created, in light of the strong opposition from Microsoft senior leadership in Redmond."

On Friday, July 15, Ballmer clarified some details of the job offer. Lee also met again with Gates, who by this time was apparently resigned to his leaving. "Kai-Fu, Steve is definitely going to sue you and Google over this," the Microsoft founder reportedly told him. "He has been looking for something just like this, someone at a VP level to go to Google. We need to do this to stop Google."

Lee determined to think about things some more that weekend—but quickly reaffirmed his decision to leave. That Sunday, he returned to the Microsoft campus and cleared out his office. "I retrieved only my personal belongs, including two paintings, pictures, books, food, medicine, tea, plaques, commercial electromagnetic frequency reducing plugs, gifts from my children, and other personal effects . . ." he asserted. "I did not access the Microsoft server. I did not take and do not have in my possession, custody or control any Microsoft confidential, proprietary, or trade secret information, or for that matter any non-public Microsoft information."

The next day was his last day of employment at Microsoft. At 4 P.M., he again met with Eric Rudder and tendered his resignation. Rudder told him: "Good luck at Google."

"What about the lawsuit?" Lee asked.

"You know, it's just going to be at worst some number of months you can't work," Rudder replied. "I know you'll be there sooner or later."

Microsoft had given up thinking Lee might stay. The legal staff had been busy preparing a lawsuit seeking to enforce the terms of the employment agreement—and make Google pay attorney's fees and compensatory damages. Immediately after the meeting with Rudder, a member of the legal department handed Lee a copy.

The day after he left Microsoft, Kai-Fu Lee was at Google headquarters in Mountain View, near the salt flats on the southern end of San Francisco Bay. He signed his employment agreement that day and took up California residence. The deal, later described as unprecedented for Google, gave Lee a $2.5 million signing bonus and promised another $1.5 million payment in one year. In addition, he received a base salary of $250,000 per year, with potential bonuses of up to one-quarter of that amount. He also received a housing allowance of $10,000 per month; a car allowance of $3,000 a month; a $2,000 monthly "hardship" allowance; and $1,500 per month in private tuition allowances for each of his two children. But the real treat was the promise of options for 10,000 shares of Google stock, plus a grant of 20,000 Google Stock Units—at the time worth more than $5 million. All told the package topped $10 million. News of Microsoft's lawsuit broke that night, and the story was immediately picked up by scores of outlets in the U.S., Europe, and Asia.

Less than a week later, Microsoft petitioned for a temporary restraining order to prevent Lee from joining its rival until the matter could be settled in court. The petition noted the fierce competition in search between Microsoft and Google and claimed that potentially grievous harm could be done to the company if Lee started right away. "By virtue of his leadership roles, Dr. Lee learned Microsoft's most sensitive technical and strategic business secrets about search technologies," the company stated. It also asserted that Lee had been a critical voice in Microsoft's strategic plans for China. As for its former employee's ambition to set up a Google R&D center in China, the Microsoft petition claimed, not unreasonably: "This places him in direct competition with Microsoft on two issues—search engines and China strategy—where Dr. Lee holds Microsoft's most propri- etary, confidential, and competitively sensitive information."

Predictably, Google fought the temporary restraining order. When it came to bombastic legalese that stretched the bounds of truth, the search engine juggernaut had the edge: "In a shocking display of hubris, Microsoft has rushed into court claiming the entire field of search as its own. In truth, Kai-Fu Lee's work for Microsoft had only the most tangential connection to search and no connection whatso- ever to Google's work in this space." On July 28, though, Washing- ton's King County Superior Court Judge Steven Gonzalez ruled for Microsoft, finding that there was "a well-grounded fear" that Lee's working for Google could harm the company. He set an expedited trial date of January 9, 2006. And he ordered Google and Lee back to court on September 6, 2005, to show cause why the temporary restraining order he had just imposed shouldn't stand until the trial was over and the verdict was in. Round One to Microsoft.

When the parties returned to court in Seattle right after Labor Day, the gloves came off. It was like a bad divorce, where things spi- ral out of control—and even turn gratuitously hurtful—no matter how much everyone intends to stay civil. A dozen attorneys crowded into the small courtroom, with each side bringing a half-dozen boxes of e-mails, depositions, and other documents—complete with spe- cialists to run their electronic displays.

Lee's new declaration and his testimony at the two-day hearing pulled no punches. He laid out his own failed efforts to unify R&D in China and generally lambasted the company's business operations, reportedly claiming there were many largely autonomous business groups operating with little cohesion. "After I ceased working for Microsoft in China, Microsoft executives, and its employees there, repeatedly angered and embarrassed various officials in the Chinese government," he wrote. Lee said these blunders "stemmed from Microsoft's failure to understand how productively and respectfully to approach the various levels of government in China." And he specifically named Microsoft's failure to live up to its $100 million outsourcing promise as an example.

Lee also shared his 2003 e-mail alleging "incompetence in China." He even recounted an episode when Bill Gates had reputedly yelled at him that the Chinese people and their government had "fucked" Microsoft (Gates vehemently denied making the remark). "It was a statement that my work had been in vain," Lee told the court. "I didn't know whether I should take it as a statement of ignorance or as an insult." He later described it as a low point in his years at Microsoft.

None of it seemed to bear on the issue of the hearing: would working for Google right away violate Lee's noncompete agreement? The nub of Google's claims in this regard was that Lee would not bring any confidential or proprietary Microsoft information with him—or that in any case Google would not act on it. It promised that Lee would not work in computer search, speech technology, or natural-language processing pending outcome of the trial—nor would he recruit Microsoft employees. However, the search engine giant argued, the court should not restrict Lee's general recruiting and management activities. Microsoft, it claimed, had no legal right "to prevent Dr. Lee from utilizing his charismatic, personal qualities and general skills to start up a facility and hire from China's universities, and from companies other than Microsoft."

Microsoft did a better job than Google of sticking to the issue at hand—though it wasn't exactly pretty. The company pored through Lee's schedule and e-mails and revealed instance after instance where its former employee had been privy to search plans, including a one-on-one session with Gates. It also showed how he had advised senior executives on China all the way into June 2005, after he had begun his courtship with Google.

And Microsoft could not refrain from getting personal, either. A videotaped deposition from a clearly rankled Gates hit Lee where it had to hurt—his honor. In one segment, Gates said simply: "When Dr. Lee was an employee at Microsoft, I—I thought of him as trustworthy. There's a lot of things around his leaving Microsoft that I wouldn't have expected. For example, if you had said to me, say, three or four months ago, 'Would Dr. Lee mislead us about his intentions relative to his sabbatical? Would he directly mislead us?' Or, 'Would Dr. Lee go and take a job in Google related to their China activities?' I would have said, 'Absolutely not.'"

Judge Gonzalez spent nearly a week deliberating. The moment of truth arrived on September 13, when he decreed that the noncompete agreement was valid, and at least until the trial (or any settlement), Lee would remain enjoined from working for Google in natural-language processing, speech technologies, or any branch of computer search—including Internet search, desktop search, or mobile search. Nor could he participate in setting budget or compensation levels for Google's new China research and development center—or take part in defining the scope of the work to be conducted there.

It was not all smiles for Microsoft, though. The judge also ruled that Lee should no longer be barred from using his deep knowledge of China or his extensive contacts in Chinese government and academia to establish and staff the Google center—so long as Lee didn't recruit from Microsoft. He wrote: "Google's use of Dr. Lee to engage in recruiting activities relating to Google's planned research and development facility in China pending trial, including establishing facilities, hiring engineering and administrative staff, interacting with public officials regarding the facilities and recruitment, meeting with university administrators and professors regarding recruitment, and offering general, non-technical advice to Google about doing business in China, does not violate the Agreement . . ."

In essence, Lee had a right to put his *guanxi* to work for Google by recruiting the best talent in the largest, most important emerging market on the planet. And ultimately that was the real prize in the fight: Round Two to Google. Kai-Fu Lee emerged from the courthouse victorious and raring to go. The ruling "allows me to do my job," he told reporters following the hearing. "Starting today, I have the green light to do what I wanted to do."

• • •

If Lee's departure felt like a bomb at Microsoft headquarters, a thermonuclear device might have gone off in the Beijing research lab. The lab's founder, and father figure, was no longer with Microsoft. Worse, he had overnight become its most formidable competitor—maybe even Public Enemy Number One. That put many of the senior Beijing staff in the uncomfortable position of being caught between their employer and their friend and mentor, whom they couldn't even speak to pending the trial. (In Redmond, Ya-Qin Zhang kept up on his friend's general spirits through his wife, Jenny, who stayed in touch with Lee's wife, Shen-Ling.)

Many Beijing researchers felt the new Google lab would be good for China overall—providing another world-class research and development center in a hot area of computer science and motivating another generation of students and young researchers to become leading innovators. But still, the personal jolt was to some even more upsetting than when Lee left Beijing for Redmond in 2000. Although no one wanted to come out and say it, there was a deep feeling of disappointment—even of betrayal.

"I used to regard Kai-Fu as a friend," said one staff member. "I really don't understand what he is doing . . . Kai-Fu has been teaching students to do things the right way. He basically is destroying that. The only benefit is to Google—they got huge PR here . . . Kai-Fu's lifetime friends are hurt from this lawsuit."

"It was a shock to us, definitely sad," remarked Hong Jiang Zhang, head of the Advanced Technology Center and the lab's original driving force in search research. "Harry [Shum] and I talked over the phone about this for an hour, right after I landed in Beijing, the night the news broke. I had been in Redmond. It's definitely going to be challenging. We're going to compete with an old friend."

The Advanced Technology Center leader felt that his organization would feel the brunt of the competition. "Definitely, Kai-Fu is going to compete head-to-head with me, ATC," he predicted. "Less with Research—he's not going to do much research." His biggest concern was what Lee's arrival would mean for Microsoft's recruiting efforts. "Last year, we offered 120 college hires, and only one person turned us down: she was afraid it was too intense," said Zhang. "But this year that situation will be more competitive. That's why Microsoft worries."

Shum, the research lab's managing director, also acknowledged the departure of Lee was a blow that had rocked his enterprise. "It's a huge loss. But at the same time, people in the lab are confident," he said. "If Google comes in and makes some ridiculous offers, then we should look at those things and think about, has the market really changed? What is the value of the people here? It's yet another new challenge for us."

Ever gracious, Shum even said that when the controversy settled down he would still greet Lee like the old friend he was. "When he gets back to Beijing, of course, I should buy him a welcome dinner to welcome him and his family back."

Lee clammed up to reporters once the case hit the courts. Just as this book went to press, Google and Microsoft settled their lawsuit, though neither side was talking in detail about the case. But in late July, before the temporary restraining order was issued, Lee surfaced briefly in Beijing—reportedly interviewing potential candidates for the Google center and possibly looking at prospective sites for the facility. According to one local account, he told reporters there that since he hadn't worked directly on search engine pursuits at Microsoft he didn't think he would violate his noncompete clause by setting up the center. But his comments to the Chinese press appear to mark the only time he spoke to journalists about the matter.

To understand Lee's deeper motivations, one had to visit his student Web site. In late July, he put up a somewhat syrupy article—at least in Western terms—explaining how Google had struck a special chord with him, a description that is sometimes translated as "shock" in English. Aimed at Chinese students, it was entitled: "I need to follow my heart."

"Microsoft is an outstanding company, and there are many things we can learn from it," Lee wrote. "But Google is a company that makes me feel a shock. The reason Google gives me a shock is the passion for creating a new generation of technology. I found treasures in Google everywhere. The technology and products are way beyond just the search."

He went on: "Google gives me lots of shocks. These shocks include technology of a new generation, desire for innovation, honesty, work for common people, emotional charm, freedom and transparency." The jolts, in turn, helped stimulate two fundamental ideas or revelations. One was an equation:

Youth + freedom + transparency + a new model of innovation + benefits for common people + honesty = miracle for Google

The other was more a dogma or tenet:

Google's culture and outstanding Chinese young people can make a great Google China!

Lee concluded the article by noting that he wanted to do influential things in his life—including helping youth—and that he had decided to go where his influence would be greatest.

In passionate terms, he explained: "No matter how difficult, if you don't follow your heart and insist on principles, how can you suggest other people to do it? Therefore I made a very important choice. I have the right to make my choice. I choose Google, I choose China."

12
How to Make It in China

Summer and Fall 2005

China is any company's largest opportunity for growth in the 21st century.

—KAI-FU LEE, "MAKING IT IN CHINA"

However the dispute between Google, Microsoft, and me is resolved, the ultimate winner will be Chinese young people— and China.

—KAI-FU LEE, POSTING ON HIS PERSONAL WEB SITE

I t was déjà Kai-Fu all over again. Following his own footsteps from 1998, when he set the location of the Microsoft lab, the new Google research and development center would be located in Beijing's frenzied Zhongguancun area, on the edge of the Tsinghua University campus. At least that's what the Microsoft Research Asia rumor mill was saying in the second half of 2005. The two enterprises would be fairly close to each other. But the Google lab's closer proximity to China's top engineering university—a symbolic issue more than one of physical distance—was not lost on a Microsoft crowd already leery of competing with its former leader.

Lee's trip to China that July had laid some of the groundwork for the new center—but his involvement in getting it off the ground was placed in limbo by the temporary restraining order preventing him from working for Google. When the restraining order was lifted on siting and recruiting that September, he dove back into the task with a vengeance. A January trial was still pending—so Lee continued to avoid making all but cursory public comments. Nevertheless, through his courtroom testimony and legal declarations, as well as his track record in creating the Microsoft lab, Lee revealed a good idea of what he wanted to do for Google—and how. More importantly, he left a primer for any company wanting to make it in the Middle Kingdom.

The original plan had been for Lee to spend two or three months at Google's Mountain View headquarters—going through corporate orientation, acquainting himself with senior management, and plotting the timetables for building and staffing the R&D center. Lee would pepper his orientation time with quick trips to China to oversee progress on the ground—and then he expected to move back to the country in late 2005 to oversee personnel recruitment and construction. Lee noted in court documents that he expected to receive as many as 20,000 job applications—mainly from students—and believed the interview process would continue throughout the year. The bulk of new hires wouldn't graduate until the end of the next academic term the following summer—and therefore he didn't expect the Google center to achieve "critical mass" until August or September of 2006. "Once the new center is ready to open, I will leave to take up permanent residency in China with my family as the president of the new Google China," he told the court.

The allure of China had proven irresistible to Lee on a personal level. It was irresistible as well to Microsoft, Google, and a host of multinational companies struggling to capitalize on the nation's vast potential. More than the market, the most forward thinking companies have come to realize the innovative power of a nation of 1.3 billion that reveres education and where high achievers abound. As the saying goes, "If you are one in a million in China, that means there are 1,300 others just like you." Talent in such numbers represents a prime recruiting opportunity for foreign firms, which could hope to lure the best China had to offer with top salaries, world-class training, and an unparalleled potential to work on products and technologies that would impact people around the globe—a package few Chinese firms could yet offer.

Navigating this capitalistic path through a communist forest has proven treacherous for many firms. However, it's ever more critical to find ways to succeed. The job market for the Chinese is moving upstream—from low-cost manufacturing to advanced technology development all the way to top-level research and global innovation. For multinational corporations, succeeding in China today presents a far more complicated challenge than in the past. It's not enough to simply bring jobs and capital. Companies must be willing to share their knowledge. They must invest in China's education system, provide managerial training, promote locals to top positions, and in short sow the seeds of future competition to get ahead. "Bring in new ideas and original thinking—don't just help the old system advance. Work on many levels—local government and central government," advises Yu Wei, the former vice minister of education who had attended the Microsoft lab's opening ceremony in 1998.

Nearly a decade ago, recognizing Microsoft's shortcomings in many of these areas and struggling with its Chinese business operations, Rick Rashid, Dan Ling, Nathan Myhrvold, and the Microsoft hierarchy had turned to Kai-Fu Lee for help. It had proven to be an extremely shrewd move. Lee had shown Microsoft the path to far greater success—and the company had seized the opportunity, building a world-class lab and ushering in a new generation of stars that included Ya-Qin Zhang, HongJiang Zhang, Harry Shum, Hsiao-Wuen Hon, and a few completely homegrown innovators like Jian Wang and Zheng Chen. Their accomplishments were greatly respected, not just in China, but around the world—and especially in Redmond. They were increasingly vital to Microsoft's future success: the plan had worked.

Now Google had tapped Lee to duplicate his Microsoft feat. There were some differences in his plans for the search giant, of course. Unlike Microsoft's Beijing lab, which was chartered to explore fundamental research five years or more from commercialization, the Google center would be oriented toward getting new technologies quickly into commercial use. "While I worked at Microsoft's China research center, the focus of its work was to conduct academic research and issue research publications," Lee said in a court declaration. "I anticipate the Google center will focus on product development, not academic publication . . ." Lee did not yet know what exactly that would entail—but his statement confirmed HongJiang Zhang's belief that his former boss would compete more against Microsoft's Advanced Technology Center than the research lab.

So how would he do it? Lee's track record in forming the Microsoft lab probably offered the best indication of how Google planned to go about building a viable research and development presence in China. Headquarter it in Beijing, close to government, top universities, and key ministries. Hire senior people from the U.S., preferably those born and raised in China or Taiwan who understand the culture and want to give back—and use them to mentor scores of university graduates hired as junior staff. Donate time and equipment to leading universities, and above all be sincere in making sure it isn't just Google that benefits, but Chinese education and industry.

But there were other clues as well. While employed at Microsoft and acting as a key member of its China advisory board, Lee produced a white paper that captured his philosophy on China. Although it largely summarized the strategy he had followed in creating the Beijing lab, he laced it with case studies and examples of successful practices and failures at Microsoft and other firms. Many management consultants and China scholars have produced similar papers and books on how to do business in the Middle Kingdom, and Lee even borrowed some of their examples for his own report. Few, though, have captured the critical issues as concisely as Lee—and backed up their words with real-life success. Microsoft viewed "Making It in China" as an important document. When it discovered that Lee had e-mailed a version of the report to Google CEO Eric Schmidt while still employed by Microsoft, it made the report part of the evidence against its former employee—using it to try to prove that Lee was already competing with Microsoft by giving the same advice to Google that he had given to Redmond's top executives, including Steve Ballmer and Bill Gates.

Lee told the authors he had prepared two main versions of his paper. The original document, written in late 2003, had the title "Making It in China: Strategic Recommendations for Microsoft." The second, completed around February 2004, was a generic version that he felt free to send to people outside the company. He removed the Microsoft Confidential stamp from its pages (he actually missed a few), stripped out two chapters of Microsoft-specific advice, and called it simply "Making It in China." Even without the recommendations for Microsoft, it was an impressive document—including an appendix of tables that detailed strengths and weaknesses of nine companies that had thrived in China, several of them Microsoft competitors.

On May 7, 2005, he e-mailed the generic version to Schmidt—later claiming in court that he sent it not to share secrets but to make sure Google agreed with his basic philosophy of doing business in China. That same day, he e-mailed a copy to the authors.

"With its booming economy, untapped talent base, and growing domestic markets, China offers massive business opportunities and great strategic importance for any company," Lee wrote to open the twenty-three-page report. "China is any company's largest opportunity for growth in the 21st century."

The nuts and bolts of Lee's carefully researched report were contained in six "challenges" he had identified of doing business in China—and his corresponding "formulas" for meeting those challenges that all foreign companies must practice "or they will be turned away." It was hardly brilliant prose: many of the challenges and formulas are repetitive, and sometimes the challenges read like formulas and the formulas like challenges. Still, it makes for fascinating reading and provides a clear blueprint for success in China. Following is a condensed and largely paraphrased version of the report. For ease of reading, unlike in the original, each challenge has been laid out alongside its corresponding formula for success, augmented by commentary from the authors.

CHALLENGE 1: UNIQUE PROTOCOLS AND RELATIONSHIPS

"China's culture is built on trust, relationships, and mutual respect," wrote Lee. "Trust takes a long time to build, but there are many ways to break trust: by showing disrespect, by failing to provide favors in exchange for favors received, by not following the protocols, by condescending, coercion, or by dwelling on controversial issues." Trust, he advised, is built by making and fulfilling promises. But it is much better, he added, not to make promises at all "than to over-commit and fall short."

(Written as it was in late 2003, it is hard not to see this as a pointed rebuke at Microsoft's 2002 promise to outsource $100 million in software development and testing to China—a commitment it was already hopelessly behind in fulfilling.)

Formula 1: Learn the Protocols and Forge Trusting Relationships

It is critical to build relationships with government at all levels from the start, Lee emphasized, even if it means seeking advice when advice isn't really needed. Finding ways to go beyond what other firms are doing is also crucial. Motorola signaled how much it valued relations with Beijing by sending its chief operating officer to China for high-level meetings at the apex of the SARS scare, dramatically bolstering its image, Lee noted. The company also came up with an innovative idea for going beyond the executive MBA programs being set up by Chinese universities for government officials—by offering "executive Ph.D." programs in partnership with a top Hong Kong university. Motorola parlayed this success by sending its own senior executives to the same classes offered to government officials, creating a unique opportunity for relationship-building. Because of such actions, Lee concluded, "Motorola remains the undisputed #1 company—most people in China would say they're 'almost a Chinese company.'"

CHALLENGE 2: CONTRIBUTE FIRST AND BENEFIT LATER

The Chinese look kindly on firms there to help China succeed, as opposed to simply trying to tap its vast potential market, Lee noted. Multinational corporations (MNCs) that demonstrate a long-term commitment to helping the country are often richly rewarded, both in terms of access to markets and human resources. "Friends will be given lucrative rewards, and others will wither into oblivion," he wrote.

For a firm to prove its commitment is serious might well entail taking a longer-term view toward success in China than is necessary in other parts of the world. However, the effort can be well worth it. "China is not hesitant to choose one 'friend' per industry and reward it richly," Lee stated. "For example, it is well known that the Chinese government favors Coke over Pepsi, Volkswagen over Toyota, Sony over Toshiba, Kodak over Fuji, and Motorola over Ericsson. Those who don't make long-term commitments will pay dearly for their myopic views."

Formula 2: Establish a Strategy for Long-Term Commitment

Access to technology is far more important to China than money. Originally, the Chinese were interested in obtaining capital through partnerships and joint ventures with overseas investors, Lee noted. "Now they are more interested in companies that are also willing to transfer technical and business knowledge." Companies must show their willingness to embrace this new era—and then wait patiently for their rewards.

Motorola was once again a poster child for how to do things right. The company, Lee advised, had established many Chinese joint ventures, including a research facility, and had donated regularly to local universities. By the time Lee's paper was written, he reported, the company earned 20 percent of its worldwide revenue in China. And other tech firms were also benefiting from a similar strategy. IBM opened an early research lab in China in 1995 and had contributed more than $100 million in hardware and software to the country's universities—benefiting in return by winning a large government customer base. Going back farther, Hewlett-Packard had established a U.S.-China joint venture in 1985, building it around strategic investments in technology and marketing knowledge, not low-cost manufacturing. Wrote Lee, "China HP is becoming the fastest growing branch of HP worldwide, as sales hit $1.2 billion in 2001."

CHALLENGE 3: HIRE SENIOR LEADERS AND NURTURE LOCAL PEOPLE

Part and parcel of winning favor and building lasting relationships in China is creating good leadership models that also develop Chinese citizens into leaders. Although it can be extremely difficult to entice senior executives to move to China, their presence as role models for training local talent is critical—and helps ensure that the government takes the company seriously. "MNCs that don't value and develop local talent are viewed as exploitative," wrote Lee.

Formula 3: Nurture Local Talent and Leadership

Ultimately, the Chinese government wants to see homegrown talent leading the local operations of foreign firms. It views such individuals as easier to deal with, more trustworthy, and indicative of the parent company's commitment to China. But while China's workforce is motivated, energetic, and smart, it is inexperienced in business processes and leadership skills. Therefore, Lee wrote, it is vital for foreign firms to provide in-depth training to their local employees.

Carrefour, the Paris-based supermarket and "hypermarket" giant that has become the world's second-largest retailer (next to Wal-Mart), hires Chinese employees and assigns them to assist French workers, promoting the trainees as soon as they acquire the desired skills. Over time, qualified local employees have filled virtually all of Carrefour's management positions, and the company has become the top MNC retailer in China. Similarly, the head of Coca-Cola in China was among the first Chinese nationals the beverage maker hired back in 1979, steadily working his way up to the chief executive spot, Lee noted. "He is now a member of the National Politburo as well as a national role model and a valuable asset for the company."

CHALLENGE 4: PLAY BY CHINA'S MARKET RULES

"The Chinese decide for their own reasons what rules to apply and who they would like to do business with . . ." observed Lee. The government feels no obligation to provide access to its vast and rapidly growing market simply because a foreign firm offers great products or possesses a sterling reputation. Moreover, he warned, China is still in transition from its centrally planned economy to a market-based system and has not yet established all the business and legal structures found in more developed economies. "The environment is often full of volatility and irrationality, so one of China's market rules is: The rules keep changing."

Formula 4: Be Flexible and Open to Local Needs and Practices

Adapting products, brands, and prices to the local market pleases consumers and the government, Lee asserted. Although he didn't come out and say it, this fourth formula seemed to deliver another pointed message to Microsoft, which throughout his tenure endured withering criticism in China for its lack of progress in lowering software prices. By maintaining prices that were outside the means of millions of Chinese, many experts believed, the company in essence encouraged piracy.

"Coca-Cola successfully avoided brand piracy by allowing its China subs [subsidiaries] to price products so affordably that it was no longer worth the effort to counterfeit them," Lee wrote. Taking the added step of creating or tailoring products specifically for China shows respect and value for local tastes, and does a better job of satisfying customer needs, he added.

(Of course, the software industry is different from soft drinks—and Microsoft may argue that its critics are "blaming the victim" to say the company's prices encourage piracy. But even relatively affluent Chinese professionals believe there is a lot of truth in the statement—and at least imply they would pay for software if they could only afford it.)

CHALLENGE 5: THE LOCAL ECONOMY GETS TOP PRIORITY

"China expects multinationals to help nurture [the] local economy in exchange for access to the China market, even if this means that the

MNCs are fostering future competitors," wrote Lee. One of China's top priorities is gaining economic independence from the West, he explained. Therefore, even as the nation entered the World Trade Organization in late 2001, the government made clear in law that it gives a preference to purchasing local products. Although it may seem counterintuitive, helping Chinese firms develop their processes, know-how, and training is one of the most valuable contributions a multinational corporation can make. While this makes lower-cost local competition inevitable, Lee advised, the trick for multinationals is to move up the value chain by creating more innovative products and services themselves.

"The MNCs ignoring this are considered self-serving," he warned.

Formula 5: Help Build the Local Business Ecosystem

China's prime goal is to develop a strong economy where domestic companies can thrive. That means going beyond providing cheap labor and low-cost manufacturing to developing high-tech exports in areas such as computing and services. "Offering to share business culture, management concepts, and technology skills is even more helpful to building trust and business collaborations," noted Lee.

Both Coca-Cola and KFC have long trained their local partners and suppliers in how to manage their businesses—moves Lee implied have paid dividends for the companies. IBM helped the local telecommunications firm Huawei redesign and improve its organization, incurring great favor for itself as Huawei rose to become Cisco's top competitor in China. For a world-class company like Microsoft to teach local firms about the software development process, he advised, would go a long way to establishing favor and ultimately winning business.

CHALLENGE 6: GOOD IMAGE CAN BE ELUSIVE

Lee once again raised a sore issue for Microsoft to make his point: the experience of former Microsoft China business manager Juliet Wu. The company touted Wu's appointment and promoted her heavily.

Then Wu wrote her tell-all book lambasting the company's arrogance and bullying marketing tactics—leaving the company reeling. "Juliet Wu was advertised by Microsoft China as a local heroine, and her departure sank Microsoft," Lee wrote.

But Microsoft wasn't the only foreign company struggling with its image in China. The delicate public relations situation is especially precarious for multinational firms, he noted, because press freedom is limited and the media is more easily manipulated than the Western press—leaving firms vulnerable to wide swings in public sentiment.

Formula 6: Build Trust from a Unified, Humble Organization

Take a low-key approach to public relations: always stay humble and focus attention on the partnership with China as opposed to touting personalities or boasting about the company, Lee advised. "To create a good image in China, other companies have worked hard to keep a consistent corporate message and a low PR profile. Rather than PR campaigns, they have concentrated on winning trust from government and local partners. Philips China has seventy times more revenue in China than Microsoft, but only one-tenth as much PR as Microsoft."

And remember, he cautioned, public relations is virtually meaningless unless it is built on a long-lasting framework of trust and strong relationships. The way to build trust and relationships, Lee advised: practice the formulas above.

Ultimately, success is all about fostering good *guanxi*. It's not altruism that drives Microsoft or any other company to follow these principles. However, firms trust that they will engender more support from academe and government—and eventually, concrete benefits—if they are sincere and generous in their relations. To the extent Microsoft nurtures the Chinese software ecosystem—training young engineers and computer scientists in R&D practices and management, entering into partnerships with local companies, and supporting universities—it will increase the number of stakeholders in the industry nationwide. That growth, in turn, will provide ever more incentive for China to strengthen its antipiracy efforts and bolster intellectual property protection—and for both the government and its citizenry to purchase Microsoft products.

Over the past eight years, the greatest successes that Microsoft has enjoyed in China—whether it be in attracting talent, generating research results, creating products, or improving its public image—have been achieved through its Beijing lab. By all accounts, including Kai-Fu Lee's, the lab has taken the company a long way toward meeting the China challenge—and is likely a core part of what Steve Ballmer meant in his videotaped deposition in the Lee case, when he said: "I feel like we have some secret sauce, so to speak, now in terms of how we do business in China, how we do R&D in China."

The lab has always been run by native Mandarin speakers, all except Lee born in mainland China. Long before the lab's founder had left for Google, the torch had been passed to other leading Chinese in the Microsoft organization—some who had been to school and worked in the United States, and a growing number trained entirely in China. All have done their part to build good *guanxi*.

Through the lab, Microsoft has donated millions of dollars in cash, software, and equipment to Chinese education, trained several thousand students, entered into hundreds of academic and industrial partnerships or collaborations—and become the only foreign-owned enterprise approved to grant postdoctoral degrees. When attempting new things, such as the creation of the Advanced Technology Center, it has carefully sought the counsel of Chinese officials. Events like the annual Computing in the 21st Century conference tour generate fantastic publicity in a way that lets Microsoft promote and even inspire a vision of changing the world through the power of computing without overly tooting its own horn. Legions of the best and brightest in Chinese computer science compete for every job Microsoft Research Asia offers.

The lab's reputation has impressed the highest levels of China's government. It was a topic of conversation for former president Jiang Zemin when he met with Bill Gates in early 2003. And largely through the enterprise, Microsoft's image in China is improving, adds director general of higher education Yaoxue Zhang. "Of course, getting better!" exclaims Zhang, whose Ministry of Education team was hosted by Microsoft at the Commune by the Great Wall in May 2005. "Because not just taking money from the people—now giving back."

Still, no matter how potent Steve Ballmer's "secret sauce," no one at Microsoft (or anywhere else) would say the company doesn't have far to go. It may be that Microsoft needs to unify its research and development efforts and present a more consistent face to China, as Lee has suggested, though there is good reason to believe this would cause as many problems within the company as it solves. And Microsoft needs to recover from its failed outsourcing promise. In China, as everywhere, the company battles its image as a bully that practices heavy-handed marketing. It could do far more to help close the digital divide by lowering the cost of its software and taking other steps to make its products more accessible to a wider swath of the population. "People can't afford to buy new Windows every two years!" relates Songde Ma, China's vice minister of science and technology. (Fortunately, perhaps, Vista has been delayed so long, that's not as big an issue as it could have been.)

Even when it comes to building a lab like MSRA and seemingly doing everything "right," a host of other issues loom. Some locals see such ventures as a form of brain drain, where companies like Microsoft pluck the best students from the best Chinese universities. "It's a shame the government and university authorities allow such a waste of talent," says Hongfei Wang, a professor at the Chinese Academy of Sciences' Institute of Chemistry. "It is good opportunity for these poor graduate students, since they actually don't have better choices. But by doing their dissertations on the Microsoft projects, their opportunity for their intellectual and academic growth is greatly diminished."

Wang is quick to say that he doesn't blame Microsoft for exploiting holes in China's system. But he notes that technology companies are hiring the cream of the crop—the men and women who are supposed to be China's future leaders. He wishes they would be put to work on matters of deeper importance than the next version of a proprietary software package, for example. "I care more about the social costs and human capital costs issues in this matter, and I care [about] the sustainable development and greater good for the whole civil society," he says.

In the end, while some problems may be particular to Microsoft, the challenges involved in developing *guanxi*—adapting products to the local market, investing in China's education and business infrastructure, training and mentoring local talent—confront any multinational firm wishing to do business in the country. There is no easy way to go about any of these matters. Every foreign company must forge a base of trust and grow its presence carefully. Progress can be slow; it comes in fits and starts and often involves setbacks. And no firm will ever satisfy everyone in a position of power and influence. While some of his contemporaries criticize the way foreign laboratories like Microsoft Research Asia lure top students who might otherwise join Chinese enterprises, Songde Ma sees the labs as part of a healthy cycle by which China is forced to improve its own system. "Some people are concerned about brain drain," Ma relates. "When MSR China opened, 200 meters from my lab [the Institute of Automation], there was competition for the best students and professors. But that turns out to be good—it caused the Chinese Academy of Sciences to raise salaries and funding. Otherwise, that wouldn't have happened."

Ultimately, what is most important isn't a lack of missteps but the consistency and sincerity of the efforts and purpose. This is perhaps the key point addressed in "Making It in China." Far more than any insights it provides into how Microsoft—and now, Google—intends to do business in China, the document should be seen as a metaphor for competition and innovation anywhere on the planet in the 21st century. It's a vivid reminder that the rules and conditions of doing business in emerging nations are changing, and that the stakes are only getting bigger. Emerging nations are not just emerging markets, they are the innovation wellspring of the future. The talent from these nations will not always go "west." Firms wishing to compete internationally must go to the source of the talent and lift up the nation, even if it makes things more challenging for the companies. And, increasingly, any such efforts must be made on the host country's terms, not the company's.

Viewed in this global light, the success or failure of individual companies—Microsoft, Google, IBM, Intel, or any other—is not that important, either. On his Web site, Lee noted in Mandarin that however his lawsuit turned out, "the ultimate winner will be Chinese young people—and China."

His old colleague and friend Hong Jiang Zhang agreed, but noted, too, that information technology will also get better, resulting in benefits that will spread across the world to individuals and companies alike—spurring economic growth and driving further innovations. "That's what competition is all about," he asserted.

The same scenario should play out in India, Russia, Singapore, or Brazil—in whatever nation and whichever field of endeavor the path of innovation leads.

Epilogue

"Congratulations, We Survived!"

October 28–November 5, 2005

The more great technology that comes from China, the better. Does that mean that business might be tough for somebody competing with them? Yeah, maybe—but that is the way that the whole entrepreneurial life cycle works.
—NATHAN MYHRVOLD

You're seeing a strong emphasis on Asia, including both Japan and China, that I think makes a lot of sense. The kind of innovation we have here . . . is really phenomenal.
—BILL GATES

There's a backbeat to China that's hard to identify amid the cacophony of a city like Beijing. The din of construction, the hum of traffic—millions of people speaking and writing a language few Westerners comprehend. But it gradually dawns on you: in some very real ways, China feels like America.

Throughout this vast country, deals are being forged, start-ups founded, contracts inked at a furious pace. Science and technology are revered. Tens of thousands of biologists, engineers, and computer scientists pour out of Chinese universities every year, while thousands more return to their native land after being educated and trained abroad. Their progress in everything from biology to nanotechnology to computing is stunning. Most importantly, when it comes to the coupling of this surging technological elite with academe and the business community, from the start-ups to venture cap-

275

italists to multinational corporations, the result is scores of competing centers of excellence that fuse to accelerate the pace of innovation—creating opportunities in places like Beijing and Shanghai that may only be rivaled by those around Boston or Silicon Valley.

Bill Gates is said to have called the Chinese one of the smartest peoples on earth. But it's not really that they are smarter than anyone else, it's that China is hungrier. With a surging middle class that is already 300 million strong and rapidly gaining access to education, capital, and opportunity, China's appetite will only grow—not just for consuming additional goods and services but also for creating them. So whether you're a seemingly invincible corporation like Microsoft, an economic heavyweight nation like the United States, or even an individual, the emergence of China as a center of innovation must be accepted—better yet, embraced.

The original architect of Microsoft's Beijing lab, Nathan Myhrvold, makes no bones about throwing his arms wide open. "The more great technology that comes from China, the better," the company's former chief technology officer asserts, brushing aside the outcry over outsourcing. "Does that mean that business might be tough for somebody competing with them? Yeah, maybe—but that is the way that the whole entrepreneurial life cycle works. People just get jealous and say we'll lose our number one position. But research is the kind of thing where technology one place almost inevitably helps technology every place. There's a Chinese seven-year-old somewhere in that big country that's going to get a Ph.D. in molecular biology. And then that seven-year-old is going to discover a drug that twenty years from now is going to save my life." He laughs. "How bad should I feel about this?"

"Whether it's drugs or another technology, the larger the community of people, the more engineers that work to solve the problem, the faster those problems are solved," Myhrvold continues. "So was it a bad thing for Massachusetts that Silicon Valley happened? No, I think it was a good thing. And was it bad for Massachusetts and Silicon Valley that Seattle developed? No, I don't think that was a problem either."

•   •   •

Like some medicines, the "goodness" of international competition can be tough to swallow. Microsoft was at the forefront of the information technology pack in starting a Beijing research lab; for nearly seven years it felt little competition from other Western corporations in attracting the best computer-science graduates China had to offer. Google's hiring of Kai-Fu Lee to open a Chinese research and development arm exposed a raw nerve and upped the ante in the battle for talent. The Beijing lab suffered a brief crisis of confidence when its founder left Microsoft on bitter terms. But Microsoft didn't wait long to respond, in a way proving Myhrvold's implied contention that if competition doesn't kill you, it will make you stronger.

On September 22, 2005, barely a week after the court ruled that Lee could begin to recruit for Google in China, Microsoft announced that Lee's old friend and colleague, Ya-Qin Zhang, would move back to Beijing as vice chairman of Microsoft China. In that capacity, Zhang would oversee Microsoft's research and development activities in China, working alongside Microsoft China chairman Tim Chen, who headed sales and marketing. The announcement of Zhang's return—his office would be on the sixth floor of the Sigma building—bolstered morale at the research lab and no doubt hastened its recovery from the shock of Lee's departure. Sending a second corporate vice president to China also signaled Microsoft's commitment to the region and its strategic importance in the company's long-term plans.

Initially, though, no one at Microsoft seemed exactly sure of Zhang's role. Clearly Microsoft's first concern was to get him on the ground to try and balance the effect of Lee's joining Google. On paper, his charge was to take control of *all* Microsoft's research and development activities in China, including the 200-odd staff members of Microsoft Research Asia and the 300-strong Advanced Technology Center, as well as some 300 staffers chiefly involved in software development, localization, and testing. (Many of these additional personnel worked in Beijing, including about 100 in the Sigma building. But Microsoft also maintained a Windows server group in Shanghai, and both a mobile messaging effort and a hardware development group in Shenzhen.)

That, at least, was his outward designation, facilitating *guanxi* by making it possible for Chinese officials to interact with one person who represented all of Microsoft's R&D activities in China. Internally, life at the Sigma Center would probably not change too dramatically. In late September and the first few days of October 2005, Microsoft's new ambassador of research and development made a whirlwind trip to his native country. At an all-hands meeting that included Microsoft Research Asia and Advanced Technology Center staffers, Zhang said that he would report to senior vice president of research Rick Rashid, at least for the time being. He also stressed that he did not want his presence to constrain ties to the Redmond product groups, though he left his exact role vague and asked staff members to give him time to devise a more specific agenda.

From what an outsider could tell, Zhang was handed something very close to the position Lee had advocated creating so that the company could present a more unified and coordinated image to Chinese officials, though it appeared to leave more wiggle room in the reporting lines than Lee had sought. Steve Ballmer almost certainly offered the job to Lee to keep him from joining Google. Lee had turned it down, apparently feeling he couldn't realistically succeed in the role given company turf wars and his own history at the firm. But his old friend and colleague saw things differently.

In Zhang, Microsoft got a leader for its China R&D operations who seemed just as media-savvy as Kai-Fu Lee. Zhang might not have been quite as revered by university students, but he was equally respected in academe, and arguably even more accomplished in his field of communication and multimedia than Lee was in speech and natural-language processing. What's more, Zhang was born in China, unlike Lee, and had spent much of his life there, including almost four years as head of Microsoft Research Asia—roughly double the time Lee had put in. He seemed very comfortable hobnobbing in business circles, and he was at least as well connected in government. Back in 2001, he had cut through the red tape surrounding *hukous*, or residency permits, to make it easier for the lab's new hires to move to Beijing: a city official had come to the lab to personally issue the permits. Zhang had also been the original architect of the Great Wall

Plan, under which Microsoft invested roughly $25 million in Chinese education between 2002 and 2005, mainly to support curriculum development and faculty and managerial training at the country's thirty-five software colleges.

Zhang's visit at the end of September was almost completely under the radar. There were no press announcements around the trip, and, uncharacteristically, Zhang didn't give any major university talks. He visited some potential new office sites and met with various Microsoft managers and product teams. He also conducted some hiring interviews and paid courtesy calls on several government officials. Zhang said he had a "good drink" with a high-ranking official from the Ministry of Education.

He came back to the States jazzed, planning to move to Beijing with his family early in 2006, by which time he expected Microsoft's R&D operations to have added another 200 staffers, reaching 1,000. He planned to double that figure the following year, most of it in product development arenas, making it all the more important to have a cohesive strategy and high-level, on-site management. "In the next few years, China will be a key base for us to grow in R&D. I'm passionate about the opportunity," he says.

As for competing with Kai-Fu Lee, he declined direct comment. But he did say this: "Microsoft, I'm still very confident, is a great company. It's not perfect, and there's lots of competition. But Microsoft is on the verge, at an inflection point, of moving to the next stage . . . Asia will be a key battleground in the next five, ten years. Competition helps you focus, innovate, move more efficiently."

Microsoft Research Asia was certainly moving efficiently a few weeks after Zhang's visit. Nearly a year had gone by since the whirlwind anniversary week of November 2004, when the lab had convened its Faculty Summit and technical advisory board meetings and launched the sixth Computing in the 21st Century tour. Now it was time to restage the festivities, more ambitiously than ever.

The fun began the evening of Thursday, October 27. Rick Rashid had just arrived from Redmond that day, and Harry Shum hosted a dinner for him that included former Princeton University computer scientist Andrew Yao,* a Turing Award winner who had returned to China, and Nobel Laureate Chen Ning Yang, who had spoken at the previous year's Computing in the 21st Century event. The next morning, Rashid, Shum, and university relations manager Lolan Song headed to the Ministry of Education in downtown Beijing to sign the agreement ushering in the Great Wall Plan's second phase, formalizing the accord celebrated at the luxurious Commune by the Great Wall the previous May.

The new deal renewed Microsoft's commitment to support China's software colleges for three more years. But it also contained a few added twists. The most important was an initiative that established Microsoft Research Asia as an official base or academy to train industrial researchers—an agreement that didn't involve any specific funding commitment, but did require Microsoft to create fellowships and other programs designed to help university students prepare for a career in R&D. Several large Chinese corporations already served as such training academies. As far as Microsoft officials could tell, however, it was the first time a non-Chinese entity had received such a designation. "It's a big deal," says Shum.

The signing ceremony was conducted, as planned, with Vice Minister Qin-Ping Zhao. But his boss, minister of education Ji Zhou, who was busy with another matter, asked the Microsoft representatives not to leave before he could also pay his respects, mentioning several times how much China could learn from Microsoft and how the country appreciated the Western firm's sharing its best practices through internships and other programs. The fact that he personally conveyed such remarks was good *guanxi*.

Homage from a Chinese minister was always worth the wait, but it put the Microsoft group behind schedule for the day's next order of

---

* In October 2005, Yao was the lead focus of a *New York Times* article detailing how China-born scientists living in the U.S. are being recruited back to their homeland.

---

business: unveiling a new weapon in the search war with Google. From the ministry, Shum, Rashid, and Song sped to the Olympic Village in north Beijing. There, early that afternoon, they were scheduled to announce a kind of sister organization to the Advanced Technology Center called the Search Technology Center. Dedicated to more speedily developing the Beijing research lab's search-related advances in information retrieval, data mining, machine learning, and other areas, the new organization would be housed in the Sigma building and headed by MSRA assistant director Hsiao-Wuen Hon. He planned to hire 50 people a year for the next three to five years.

Plans for the search center were under way long before Kai-Fu Lee's departure: this was the subject of the closed-door meetings the Beijing team had held with MSN executives just after TechFest the previous March. However, the escalating battle with Google raised the stakes, and Microsoft pulled out all the stops in announcing its creation. Sheila Shang rented a big room at the Crowne Plaza Hotel in the Olympic Village, also known as Five Continent Plaza. The space was divided by a partition emblazoned with the Microsoft logo. More than fifty reporters, from Beijing, Shanghai, Chengdu, and Guangzhou, were ushered into one portion of the room, with the barrier blocking what lay beyond. They had not been told what was afoot, only that Microsoft Research Asia would be making a significant announcement.

Soon, Shum took the stage and presented a quick overview of the lab's accomplishments of the past seven years. Now, he told them, Microsoft Research Asia had reached another milestone. With lights flashing, music blaring, the partition was drawn back. Rashid, Hon, search guru Wei-Ying Ma, and several others waited beyond, flanked by a dozen demos in clustering technology, mobile search, image search, video and news search, even a search-related shopping platform. Hon then explained the Search Technology Center in detail. After brief remarks from Rashid and an MSN program manager, who spoke about the collaboration between the center and Redmond, Shum came back onstage and invited the press members to experience the demos for themselves.

Microsoft was opening a major new front in the search war. Hon planned to draw much of his charter staff from the research lab or the Advanced Technology Center and felt their experience gave him at least eighteen months' head start on the new Google R&D center, which would be staffed primarily by fresh university graduates who would need a lot of on-the-job training. "This will be a huge advantage," Hon predicts.

That was not to say Microsoft didn't still have some catching up to do in terms of general search technology. "Today, people go to MSN search [and] they don't feel they get the same type of result back [as they do from Google]," Hon acknowledges. "As a company, we are late in terms of algorithmic search. And that's really a nonsecret. The most important thing for Microsoft to do today is not necessarily to make a lot of money in search. It's really how we can increase the rate of innovation, make our products truly innovative. The money will come later."

The day was capped off by an American-style pizza party and managers' meeting back at the lab. Then a group of twenty or so managers walked to the nearby Jade Palace Hotel for bowling in its basement alley. Rashid's mother and father had managed a bowling alley when he was a youth, allowing him a lot of practice time on unrented lanes. Bowling was still his favorite participant sport, and he consistently bowled in the 180s and 190s.

Shum had learned of his boss's prowess almost as an afterthought. The previous summer, Steve Ballmer had visited Beijing and he and Shum had played basketball with lab staffers and students at the Kerry Center. A bit later, Shum had gone golfing in the Redmond area with some MSN vice presidents. He got to talking with one Microsoft manager who told him, "Harry, you are doing so well. Now you are playing basketball with the CEO and golfing with VPs." At that point, Shum related, "I realized I haven't played anything with my boss!" He mentioned it to Rashid, and they decided on a bowling event.

At the Jade Palace, Shum good-naturedly implored his charges to uphold the lab's honor—but Rashid still won the night's high score, albeit with an uninspiring 164. "My team got the lowest score," relates Shum, "and we didn't deliberately do that."

Everyone went into overdrive after that. The lab's anniversary week officially opened on Monday, October 31—Halloween back in the States—with the annual Faculty Summit. The event took place in Hangzhou, capital of Zhejiang province and hometown of universal pen inventor Jian Wang, about one hundred miles southwest of Shanghai. It was the lab's first Faculty Summit held outside Beijing. Sheila Shang happily reported that 220 faculty members attended, including seven university presidents or vice presidents and about a hundred deans or chairs of computer-science-related departments. The guests represented eighty universities from fourteen nations. For the first time, a majority of summit attendees came from outside China.

Several faculty members hailed from Japan, home to a new arm of the Beijing research lab, the Microsoft Institute for Japanese Academic Research Collaboration, which had opened just a few months earlier. Directed by Katsushi Ikeuchi, a distinguished computer scientist who had been Harry Shum's mentor at Carnegie Mellon and later moved to the University of Tokyo, the institute was designed to serve as Microsoft's eyes and ears on Japanese computer science. Its job was to identify and fund research collaborations in robotics, wireless, graphics, and other areas that the company hopes will keep it atop the world of computing. "Technical results propagate through oral communications, not formal presentations," Ikeuchi says. "Unfortunately, Japanese researchers have few links with Western researchers in terms of personal contacts. If we can connect Japanese researchers with Microsoft Research Asia people tightly, from this [their work] will propagate worldwide."

The Faculty Summit attendees proved a wild and crazy bunch. After the day's sessions, Microsoft hosted a banquet for the group. A professor from Tsinghua University, perhaps inspired by the flowing wine, went onstage and sang part of the *Peking Opera*. He then called up a dean from Harbin Institute of Technology, who stunned everyone by belting out "Edelweiss" from *The Sound of Music*. Next came a professor from Peking University, who crooned a Russian ballad: he was the best singer of the night. This inspired a New Zealander, who wowed everyone with a Maori tribal dance routine. Finally, Lolan Song and her university relations team closed out the performances with a rendition of "Jingle Bells."

On November 1, the day after the Faculty Summit, the seventh Computing in the 21st Century tour kicked off in the People's Congress Hall, also in Hangzhou. Some 2,200 students, professors, and other dignitaries attended, mostly from the three or four top universities in the region. They packed the auditorium to capacity.

The event's theme was Data Centric Computing. MIT's Ronald Rivest, a Turing Award winner and the "R" in the computer security firm RSA Security, spoke on "Voting in the 21st Century."* Other keynoters included Jeannette M. Wing, head of Carnegie Mellon's computer-science department, UCLA mathematician Stanley Osher, and Bill Gates's hard-charging technical advisor, Alex "Go" Gounares. The event was timed to coincide with Hangzhou's famous West Lake festival, and Microsoft hosted a banquet that night that included the city's vice mayor, who teasingly reminded Rivest that Boston and Hangzhou were official sister cities. He asked the MIT professor to give his regards to Boston mayor Tom Menino.

The next day, Wednesday, the Microsoft contingent was invited to a spur-of-the-moment morning tea with Hangzhou's mayor. That afternoon, the main entourage piled into a large bus and took the three-hour ride to Shanghai, where the Technical Advisory Board was to convene the following morning in Microsoft's downtown business office. Simultaneously, Shum, Rashid, and Song jumped into a

---

* A researcher at Tsinghua University had recently cracked the RSA encryption code known as "SHA-1," but this did not come up at the event.

minibus and zipped to Shanghai Jiaotong University, where they formalized the creation of a new joint laboratory, the eighth such venture MSRA supported at universities around China.

After the Shanghai events, the core group hit the road again, heading this time to Hong Kong, where they closed out the week on Saturday, November 5, with the second and final leg of the Computing in the 21st Century event. Joining the headliner ranks was high-temperature-superconductivity pioneer Paul Chu, who had left the University of California at San Diego to become president of the Hong Kong University of Science and Technology. Chu hosted a dinner at his house that evening for Microsoft executives and keynoters.

When it was all over, some of the group went back to their hotel. But Shum and a few others took the famous tram ride to Victoria Peak. There, on the lab's seventh birthday, they met up with a group that included Hon and Shang and enjoyed the breathtaking view of the harbor and the shimmering lights of Kowloon. Glasses were raised to the toast "Congratulations, we survived!"

It had been quite a year, the most eventful ever for Microsoft Research Asia. The Beijing enterprise had almost doubled in size, to some 500 staff members (counting the Advanced Technology Center) and 300 students, almost taking over the Sigma building. It had opened a Japanese arm as well as the Search Technology Center, entered into a variety of new agreements with university collaborators around Asia, extended the Great Wall Plan, dominated international conferences in search and graphics with its papers, and seeded some twenty technologies or features into Microsoft products, including a dozen for the new Windows Vista operating system. Lab founder Kai-Fu Lee had left the company, but Ya-Qin Zhang was returning to China. Harry Shum had even secured the Microsoft box again for a forthcoming Yao Ming basketball game in Seattle. All told, the lab's *guanxi* seemed better than ever.

Looking ahead to 2006, Shum, who had suffered a fever for much of the anniversary week, worried about spreading his staff too thin.

"To sustain the growth of the lab we really should be very careful and don't kill ourselves," he says. Later in the month, the management team planned to sit down and develop a strategy for fulfilling their commitments and ambitions while pacing themselves a bit better. The lab had celebrated a great seventh birthday, Shum noted, but the best present "is to take care of ourselves."

For Microsoft Research, though, slowing down was not in the cards. The Beijing lab's success had provided an incentive—and a template—for opening a new research center in Bangalore, India, that was just starting to ramp up late in 2005. Reflecting on why Microsoft Research had made the move to another emerging market and developing economy, Rashid notes: "If you want to be able to grow to meet the needs that Microsoft has, you can't just grow in the United States. It [India] is different than China, but in some ways it has some of the characteristics of China. More people are interested in building their careers in India, not going somewhere else. We saw that in China as well."

A series of construction setbacks had delayed its opening, but finally the lab was up and running. Rashid planned to visit Bangalore for its first anniversary early in 2006, at which point he would likely find himself meeting with various technologists, academicians, and government officials on yet another whirlwind tour. This time, it might be samosas instead of dim sum, forks and fingers instead of chopsticks, and of course many of the social customs would be different. Still, as they discussed the future of rural computing and India's rise as an infotech world leader, some things would likely be very familiar.

The Hindi word for relationship is *sambandh*.

A Note on Sources

In chronicling this tale of an American-owned research lab in a foreign country, we sought to blaze trails in describing the future of innovation. Consequently, there was no large body of literature to consult. The greatest part of the book was researched through on-the-ground, firsthand reporting.

Between us, we made five extended trips to China in a little over a year, operating mainly in Beijing and the surrounding area, with one venture to Chengdu in the southwest. We spent weeks at the Microsoft lab, watched its operations, ate, drank, and even traveled and played basketball with Microsoft researchers—conducting scores of interviews and viewing dozens of demos in the process. We supplemented our time at the lab with visits to local universities and institutes, where we met with a variety of students, professors, and officials.

In addition, we made seven forays to the Seattle area, where Microsoft is headquartered, and conducted dozens of interviews there. We traveled to Tokyo to visit the director of Microsoft's new Japanese research institute and to ask Bill Gates a question or two, when the new effort was announced in June 2005. All told, we met or talked with well over 100 people, including the heads of five of Microsoft's research arms around the globe (its labs in Redmond, Washington, in China, England, and India, and at the research institute in Japan), and interviewed many of them multiple times. Most were Microsoft employees, but we spoke as well with former staff members, Chinese government officials, and faculty from universities in the United States, China, Japan, and a suite of other nations.

That is not to say we didn't read widely. Contemporary newspaper and magazine articles shed light on our story, as did the ability to reach back through time over the Internet and call up accounts of key events from past years—from Microsoft's antitrust case to its Venus debacle in China to the backgrounds of some of our key subjects. We consulted a wide variety of publications, including *The New York Times, The Wall Street Journal, BusinessWeek,* and *The Seattle Times,* but also *China Daily,* and the Chinese-language *People's Daily* and *Science Daily.*

We also drew on several books. Two stood out for helping us frame the context of China and its place in the world of innovation and economic growth: *China Inc.,* by Ted C. Fishman (Scribner 2005), and *The World Is Flat,* by Thomas L. Friedman (Farrar, Straus, and Giroux 2005). Two others were particularly important to understanding Microsoft and its views on research and talent: Bill Gates's *The Road Ahead* (Penguin Books, 1996 paperback edition) and *Microsoft Rebooted* (Penguin Books 2004), by Robert Slater. (For those specifically interested in industrial research, including the creation of Microsoft's labs, *Engines of Tomorrow,* by Robert Buderi [Simon and Schuster 2000], might also prove useful). Finally, one Chinese-language book, *In Search of Wisdom,* by Zhijun Ling (China Friendship Publishing House 2000), was immensely helpful in capturing the early days of Microsoft's Beijing lab. This book, whose author exhibits a keen eye for detail that we greatly admire, has not been translated into English, but we had much of it translated—and cited several quotations from it in our pages.

In the case of Kai-Fu Lee, in addition to several in-depth interviews and many e-mails, we are grateful to his own unpublished white paper, "Making It in China," which he kindly shared with us. When it came to the account of the legal battle with Microsoft over Lee's leaving to join Google, we read scores of articles from trade publications and national newspapers—as many as Google news bots brought to our inbox. We also benefited from the Internet in another way: within a day or two (sometimes within hours), almost all the court filings—briefs, declarations, judgments—were scanned and available online as PDFs.

Throughout our reporting, and with more urgency as it came time to go to press, we made every effort to check facts, verify accounts, and generally ensure the accuracy of everything we had written. For all reported events and conversations that we did not witness first-hand, we did our best to square the descriptions with the accounts of two or more people who were present. In the end, we caught many errors—most of them slight, but some significant. Any that remain are ours alone.

Acknowledgments

Guanxi grew out of our mutual interests in technology, innovation, and China. Over the course of several years, we had heard more and more (and from different sources) about a research lab in Beijing, run by Microsoft, that had soared from out of nowhere to a world-class level. This dramatic ascendance—both in research results and commercial impact—led to our June 2004 cover story in MIT's *Technology Review,* where we both worked at the time. That article, and the ideas and reporting surrounding it, inspired us to track down the larger story, one of global competition and innovation that we believe sheds light on where the world as a whole is heading, not just Microsoft or China.

In the process of planning and writing this book, a host of great people helped in ways that warrant special mention. First, many thanks to our agent, Rafe Sagalyn, and to Bridget Wagner at the Sagalyn Literary Agency; our editor, Alice Mayhew; and Roger Labrie and the whole team at Simon & Schuster. Rafe and Alice immediately grasped the importance of the subject and helped us shape and focus the book from inception to final printing.

Of course, we could not have written this book without the consent of Microsoft, and especially Microsoft Research, both of which were instrumental in providing open access to people and projects. In Redmond, special thanks go to Rick Rashid, Dan Ling, Ya-Qin Zhang, and X. D. Huang, as well as Kim Atkinson, Kim Davis, and the team at Waggener Edstrom public relations. Rashid and Ling, as the leaders of Microsoft Research, signed off on our project without putting restrictions on what we wrote. Special thanks go to Kai-Fu Lee as well, who found a professional way to continue helping us even under the cloud of a lawsuit that prevented him from speaking freely during the last few months of our project.

In Beijing, we thank everyone we met at Microsoft Research Asia and the Advanced Technology Center—students, researchers, managers—for their time and hospitality. Many, though, went above and beyond the call of duty. First and foremost, we owe a tremendous debt of thanks (and lunch with a view!) to Sheila Shang, for the huge amount of time and effort she spent setting up visits and interviews, and answering endless questions in person, by phone, and over e-mail on all things Microsoft and China. Quite simply, this book would not have been possible without her. Harry Shum and HongJiang Zhang, the leaders of MSRA and the ATC, also gave generously of their time—and shared meals, basketball, sightseeing, and humor. Jian Wang warmly and patiently answered all our questions, though he probably wishes we were digital. Hsiao-Wuen Hon, Kurt Akeley, Eric Chang, Bin Lin, Wei-Ying Ma, Baining Guo, Wenwu Zhu, Qian Zhang, Shipeng Li, C. B. "Crazy Bird" Hsu, Ming Zhou, Zheng Chen, Lei He, Steve Dahl, and Lolan Song were all gracious with their time and made us feel at home.

We drew on many people outside the Microsoft fold as well. Bows of gratitude to Nathan Myhrvold, the founder of Microsoft Research and original architect of the Beijing lab, and Shelby Barnes at Intellectual Ventures: this isn't the first time they have helped us out, either. Thanks also to Caroline Huang, Mike Phillips, Paul Debevec, and Raymond Pickholtz for their attention and help with technical topics.

We graciously thank Chinese officials (and professors) Songde Ma from the Ministry of Science and Technology and Yu Wei and Yaoxue Zhang from the Ministry of Education for their enlightening discussions. Professors Tieniu Tan, Yi Ma, and Nelson Kiang generously explained the workings of Chinese science.

For Chinese language and cultural issues, we also enlisted a lot of allies. On this front (and more broadly as well), we thank Thomas and Margaret Huang for helping pave the way in Chinese academia and aiding with translations; Yan Zhao for translation assistance and for providing source materials; Hujun Li and Hongfei Wang for discussions on Chinese culture and scientific issues; Stella Zhou, Jie Zhang, and Sean Gilbert for generous translation help; and Zhijun Ling for his insightful books and discussion.

Our colleagues and fellow journalists in the United States and the United Kingdom aided us in a variety of ways. Many thanks go to the editors at *Technology Review* and *New Scientist,* and to colleagues at MIT's Center for International Studies, for their support and feedback; to Herb Brody, Toby Lester, and Mike Lemonick for helpful discussions; Howard Anderson for good cheer, hoop talk, and, in the early days, office space; and Michael Schrage for his incisive comments on the manuscript, which made it better.

Most of our reporting was done far from home. In Beijing, hearty thanks go to Hongfei and Danhong Wang, Yan Zhao, Hujun Li, Lun Xin, and Guangyou Xu for sharing meals and conversation. Lee Burnside and Lisa Vig (and Ross Burnside) helped take care of us on trips to Seattle.

Last, and most important, thanks to our friends and families who sustained and supported us throughout the writing of this book. To Amy, and to Nancy, Kacey, and Robbie: we couldn't have done it without you, either.

Index

Adler, Dennis, 159
Advanced Technology Center (ATC), 14, 18, 150–67, 202, 230, 256, 262, 270, 277, 278, 281, 282, 285
  first anniversary of, 164–67
  funding of, 156–58, 238
  idea for, 150–52
  inception of, 152–58
  Lee as headquarters liaison to, 242
  recruiting for, 159–61, 165
  projects of, 155–56, 166–67, 170, 201
  Search Technology Center and, 281, 282
  TechFest and, 206
  wireless group, 227, 228
Advertising, online, 17–19, 155–56, 187–89, 195, 199–200, 206
  platforms for, 188, 200, 204, 207
  relevance verification for, 199–201
Aggregate computing, 185–86
Akeley, Kurt, 17, 145, 203–4
Allchin, Jim, 183
Allen, Paul, 104
Alta Vista, 207
Amazon, 194
Anandan, Padmanabhan, 206
Antitrust trial, 125, 131
Apple Computer, 37, 38, 40–44, 47, 52, 195, 235, 247
  iPod, 42, 230
  Macintosh OS X system, 36

Asian Pacific Economic Cooperation summit, 131–32
AT&T, 243
Audi, 216

Bach, Robbie, 213
Bai, Chunli, 57, 59
Baidu, 9
Ballmer, Steve, 106–7, 142, 169, 180, 210, 211, 236, 246–47, 271
  and annual review process, 144
  in China, 106, 137, 242, 282
  and inception of Advanced Technology Center, 156
  and Lee's defection to Google, 250, 251, 262, 278
  mobile e-mail service announced by, 231
Ban, Shigeru, 218
Barrett, Craig, 43
Barron's, 9
Be Your Personal Best (Lee), 235
Beida Founder, 61
Beihang University, 55, 161
Beijing Normal University, 172
Beijing Satellite Manufacturing Factory, 20
Bell, Gordon, 36
Bell Labs, 3, 35, 71, 124, 158n, 243
Bi, Juan-Shang, 115
Bian lian (face changing), 30–31
Bill & Melinda Gates Foundation, 4
BlackBerry, 225, 231
Block-based link analysis, 195–96, 204
Bluetooth, 180

Boxer Rebellion, 50
Brill, Eric, 191, 192
Brin, Sergey, 10, 247, 249
Buffett, Warren, 2
Bush, George W., 131
BusinessWeek, 58, 288

Cai, Deng, 195–96
California, University of
 Berkeley, 14, 22, 89
 Los Angeles (UCLA), 33, 284
 San Diego, 285
 Santa Barbara, 189
Cambridge University, 33, 34, 89
Carnegie Mellon University (CMU),
 36, 38, 40–41, 43, 52, 66, 89,
 90, 97, 101, 163, 210, 283, 284
Carnes, Jim, 11
Carrefour supermarket chain, 266
CDMA standard, 116
Cell phones, *see* Mobile devices
Chang, Eric, 120–21, 139, 140, 161,
 164, 227
Changhong, 216
Chao, Guoxing, 218
Chen, Eileen, 54, 109, 117
Chen, George, 51–52, 54, 63–65, 67,
 70, 91–92, 95, 124, 129, 136
Chen, Tim, 215, 243, 277
Chen, Zheng, 196–202, 204, 206,
 261
Chen, Zhili, 4–5
Chew, Chee, 227
CHIME (Chinese Microsoft Employ-
 ees association), 52
Chin, Roland, 22
China Daily, 129, 288
China Inc. (Fishman), 288
China Youth Daily, 244
China-Redmond Advisory Board
 (CRAB), 226, 242
Chinese Academy of Engineering,
 23, 141, 162
Chinese Academy of Sciences, 23, 46,
 53, 56, 57, 59, 89, 126, 158, 162

Institute of Automation, 272
Institute of Chemistry, 271
Chinese Communist Party, 4, 28, 146
Chinese Ministry of Education,
 23–24, 71, 135–36, 214,
 218–22, 279, 280
Chinese Ministry of Information
 Industry (MII), 53, 57–58
Chinese Ministry of Personnel, 128
Chinese Ministry of Science and
 Technology, 58, 59
Chinese National Natural Science
 Foundation, 10, 15, 82, 90, 133
Chinese National Reform and Devel-
 opment Commission, 136
Chinese University of Hong Kong, 22
Chu, Paul, 285
Cisco Systems, 268
Clinton, Bill, 66
Clustering, 197–98, 200, 206, 207,
 281
Clusty, 197
CNN, 196
Coca-Cola Corporation, 49, 265–68
Codex Leicest (Leonardo), 105
Columbia University, 40
Comdex (Consumer Electronics
 Show), 122, 154
Compression techniques, 101, 102,
 117
Computer Associates, 43
Computer games, *see* Games
Computer Life, 58
Computer vision, 52, 66, 122, 123,
 142, 198, 206, 213
Computing in the 21st Century
 conferences, 10, 15, 24–27, 29,
 89–92, 130–34, 144, 164, 215,
 217, 270, 279, 280, 284, 285
Concentric mosaics, 100–102, 123
Contel Corporation, 116
Cosmo, 42, 43
"CRAB"(China-Redmond Advisory
 Board) committee, 226
Cultural Revolution, 115, 125, 162

Dalian University of Technology, 223

Data-driven software, 185

Data mining, 188, 189, 192, 194, 199, 206

Deep Blue chess computer, 145

Dell, 171

Deng Xiaoping, 28, 73, 81, 85, 100, 141, 147

Denmark, Technical University of, 163

Digital Equipment Corporation, 36, 207

Digital ink, 139, 169–70, 175, 176

Dot-com bubble, 74

Draper Prize, 14, 36

Duh, Jia-Bin, 1

E-commerce, 76–77

"863" program, 171

Einstein, Albert, 119

Electronic Science and Technology, University of, 29

Engines of Tomorrow (Buderi), 288

Ericsson, 61, 265

Ethernet, 36, 159

Eustace, Alan, 248

Excel, 175

Faculty Summit, 15, 21–23, 164, 283–84

Fishman, Ted C., 288

Flying Against the Wind (Wu), 91

Fortran computer language, 40

Friedman, Thomas L., 288

Fudan University, 65

Fuji, 49, 265

Fujitsu, 61

Games, 15–16, 76, 100, 122–23, 169, 202

  see also Xbox

Gao, Jack, 91, 243*n*

Gates, Bill, 9–11, 21, 31, 45, 106, 167, 169, 224, 225, 236, 239, 241–43, 275, 276, 284, 287, 288

  admiration in China for, 4, 57, 62

  in China, 1–5, 9, 48–49, 64, 130–34, 154, 228–29, 270

  and creation of Microsoft Research, 33, 159

  at DevCon 2005, 230

  Lake Washington home of, 52, 104–5

  and Lee's defection to Google, 250, 251, 254, 262

  multimedia company owned by, 52

  Myhrvold's China pitch to, 36

  and opening of Beijing lab, 55–58

  Rashid and, 14, 144, 156, 158*n*

  reviews of research projects by, 77–85, 87–89, 99–105, 107, 120, 121, 127, 138, 139, 172, 176–80, 185, 237

  search war declared by, 187–90, 201

  Song's visit to, 142–43

  Think Week retreats of, 180–83

  and Xbox, 122, 213

Ge, Daokai, 218

Ge, Honglin, 29, 217

General Electric, 74

George Washington University, 116

Gonzalez, Steven, 253, 255

Good Morning America, 41–42

Google, 8, 15, 17–18, 156, 163, 187–88, 191, 207, 272, 273, 281, 282

  annual revenue of, 188

  Desktop Search, 239

  Lee hired by, 10, 247–63, 270, 277, 278, 288

  PageRank technique of, 195

  recruitment by, 198, 213

  relevance verification by, 201–2

Gore, Al, 225

Gounares, Alex, 180, 182–83, 185, 227, 284

GPS Continuum, 52
Graphics, 15–17, 52, 66, 76, 142,
    156, 167, 203, 213
  concentric mosaics, 100–102, 123
  demos of, 133–34
  Internet, 176
  products using, 139 (*see also*
    Games, video and computer)
  3-D, 42, 71, 100–102, 122–23
  for wireless devices, 224
Gray, Jim, 37, 91
Great Wall Plan, 135–39, 141,
    218–20, 279, 280, 285
GTE Laboratories, 116
Gu, Binglin, 24
Gu, Lie, 101
Guo, Baining, 28, 87, 122–23

Han, Cherry, 129
Handwriting interfaces, 139, 167,
    169–70, 172–79, 183–84
Hangzhou University, 71
Harbin Institute of Technology, 23,
    91, 284
Harvard University, 25, 165
Hawking, Stephen, 33
HDTV, 117, 121
He, Lei, 210, 212
Heisenberg's Uncertainty Principle,
    119
Help features, 237–40
Hewlett-Packard (HP), 34, 48, 62, 72,
    164, 189, 231, 265
Hoisington, Mary, 54
Hon, Hsiao-Wuen, 17, 26, 30, 145,
    203–4, 237, 261, 285
  at Great Wall Plan meeting, 218,
    219
  interviews of prospective
    researchers by, 60, 63
  and recruitment of Lee, 43, 54
  Search Technology Center headed
    by, 281–82
  at Seattle Supersonics basketball
    game, 210, 212

Hong Kong, University of, 66
Hong Kong University of Science and
    Technology, 22, 23, 135, 193,
    214, 285
Houston Rockets, 8, 209–11
Hsu, Feng-Hsiung "C.B.," 145
HTC, 231
Hu Jintao, 141
Huang, Changning "Tom," 72, 76,
    95, 98
Huang, Xuedong "X. D.," 43–44, 54,
    64, 78, 79, 90, 108–9, 138,
    237
Huawei Technologies, 149, 228, 268
Huazhong University of Science and
    Technology, 136
Hukous (residency permits), 82,
    127–28, 278

IBM, 33, 74, 157, 250, 268, 273
  China Research Lab of, 34, 61, 62,
    71
  recruitment from, 37, 145
  ViaVoice diction software, 79
Ikeuchi, Katsushi, 66, 283
In Search of Wisdom (Ling), 299
Inktomi, 188
Institute for Japanese Academic
    Research Collaboration, 283
Institute of Electrical and Electronics
    Engineers (IEEE), 66, 121, 163
International Conference on
    Computer Vision, 214
Intel, 43, 61, 62, 87, 122, 273
Intelligent Decision Support System
    (iDSS), 199
Interactive systems, 75, 99
  demo of, 79
Interfaces, *see* User interfaces
Internet, 9, 15, 42, 71, 74, 176, 187,
    238–40, 243*n*, 255
  browsers, 181, 188
  censorship of, 20, 57
  graphics, 176
  mining, 18

multimedia, 76, 121
routers, 219
search, *see* Search technology
Internet Explorer, 160, 204

Jackson, Thomas Penfield, 125
Java, 247
Jiang, Kun, 86
Jiang Zemin, 1–3, 5, 7, 9, 130, 141,
    154, 241–42, 270
Jobs, Steve, 41, 42, 47
Johns Hopkins University, 191
Johnson, Kevin, 226
Justice Department, U.S., 125, 131

Kai, Cui, 218
Kasparov, Garry, 145
KFC, 268
Knook, Pieter, 223, 231
Kodak, 49, 265
Koizumi, Junichiro, 131
Korea Advanced Institute of Science
    and Technology, 135
Kuomintang (Nationalist Party),
    38–39, 146

Lampson, Butler, 37, 89
Lee, Kai-Fu, 37–110, 112, 118,
    125–26, 202, 222, 233–47, 270,
    271, 281, 285, 288
  and Advanced Technology Center,
    165, 167
  background of, 38–43, 162
  at Bill G. reviews, 77–84, 89, 90,
    99–104, 127
  at Beijing lab's first anniversary
    party, 85–88
  Computing in the 21st Century
    conferences organized by, 89–92
  at Dragon Villa retreat, 94–99, 235
  family of, 48, 135, 234
  farewell parties for, 109–10
  founding of Beijing lab by, 3, 10,
    47–59, 120, 144
  with Gates in China, 3–4, 154
  hired by Google, 10, 247–63, 273,
    277, 278, 279, 288
  honors received by, 163
  interviewing and hiring of
    research staff by, 60–64, 67–71,
    92, 128
  Jian Song and, 142, 146
  Jian Wang and, 168, 172, 173,
    176, 179
  Making It in China report of,
    262–69, 272
  promoted to corporate vice presi-
    dent, 105–9, 145, 213, 226
  proposal to unify R&D in China,
    246–47
  research agenda of, 73–77,
    99–100, 138, 152
  recruitment of, 37, 38, 43–47
  recruitment of top researchers by,
    65–67, 71–73, 82, 117, 121,
    124–25, 168, 172
  university education in China
    criticized by, 92–93, 114, 234
Lee, Kai-Lin, 39–40
Lee, Shen-Ling, 46–48, 198, 234, 256
Legend, 48, 61
Lei, Chaozi, 218
Lenovo, 48, 61
Leonardo da Vinci, 105
Li, Jin, 73, 79, 81, 100, 104
Li, Shipeng, 100, 124, 227
Li, Tien-Min, 38–39, 45
Li, Yah-Ching, 39
Li, Ying, 199, 200
Libra, 207
Lin, Bin, 153, 158–61, 164
Ling, Dan, 37, 44, 81, 100, 101, 104,
    108–9, 117, 179, 191, 261
  in China, 14, 16, 19, 24–26, 50,
    54, 56, 64, 90, 144, 227
  at TechFest, 206
Ling, Xiaoning, 51–52, 54–55, 80, 88,
    104
Ling, Zhijun, 48, 51, 53–55, 57, 126,
    288

Linux, 6
Liu, Qi, 127
Liu, Zhanshan, 218
Liu, Zhihua, 127
Liu, Zicheng, 54, 64–65
Loeb, Alex, 176–77
London, Joan, 42
Longhorn, *see* Windows: Vista
Lu, Xuzhong, 218
Lucent Technologies, 61, 124

Ma, Songde, 214, 271, 272
Ma, Wei-Ying, 17–19, 167, 188–90,
        192–96, 198–200, 202, 206–7,
        281
Mach operating system project, 36
Magneto, *see* Windows: Mobile
Malik, Jitendra, 14, 22
Mao Zedong, 28, 38, 39, 114, 125
Martin, Hugh, 41
Massachusetts Institute of Technol-
        ogy (MIT), 22, 89, 90, 116, 120,
        121, 163, 214, 248, 284
    Distinguished Lecture series, 42
    Computer Science and Artificial
        Intelligence Laboratory, 14–16
Media Center software, 156, 160
Mehdi, Yusuf, 204, 208
Meng, Helen, 22
Menino, Tom, 284
Microsoft Japan, 131
Microsoft Rebooted (Slater), 288
Microsoft Research (MSR), 8, 32–34,
        56, 107, 145, 156–59, 237
    Cambridge lab of, 34, 44, 90, 174,
        198, 206, 250
    San Francisco lab of, 91, 206
Microsoft Research India, 206, 250,
        286
MindSwap, 227–28
Ming Dynasty, 217
Mitsubishi, 48
Mobile devices, 16, 20
    multimedia for, 67, 121

platforms for, 26
    see also Wireless technology
Mobile and Embedded Developers
        Conference (DevCon 2005),
        229
Mobile and Embedded Devices divi-
        sion, 223, 145
Motorola, 231, 243, 264, 265
MPEG data compression standards,
        79, 117
MSN, 18–19, 188, 208, 239, 281
    adCenter, 204, 207
    Sandbox, 207
    Search, 8, 155–56, 167, 191,
        194–96, 198–200, 204, 207,
        210, 237*n*
    Shopping, 196
    Underdog, 207
MSR Search Summer Camp, 191–93
Muglia, Bob, 107
Multimedia, 17, 42, 52, 65–67, 71,
        73, 75, 99, 100, 122, 199, 203
    coding and communication, 117,
        121
    conference sessions on, 83
    demos of, 133–34
    Internet, 76
    products using, 139
    scalable wavelet coding, 101, 102
    search, 189, 190, 192
    video compression technique for,
        101–3
    for wireless devices, 224, 230
Mundie, Craig, 81, 101, 132, 215–16,
        226
Myhrvold, Nathan, 7, 44, 45, 49, 56,
        62, 77, 81, 261
    founding of Beijing lab, 32–38
    on global competition, 275–77

Nagel, David, 41
*Nan Zheng Bei Zhan (South Conquest,
        North Battle)* (movie), 146, 169
Nanjing Institute of Technology, 66

Index

Nanjing University, 64
Nanofluids, 41
National Academy of Engineering, U.S., 203
National Basketball Association (NBA), 209, 210
National Chengchi University, 39
National Defense University, 64
National Taiwan University, 135
Natural Interactive Services Division (NISD), 236–37
Natural-language processing, 67, 72, 75, 76, 99, 120, 236–37
    demo of, 78–80, 83–84, 172
    relevance verification and, 201
NEC, 61, 198
Needham, Roger, 90
.NET initiative, 101, 103, 107, 244
Netscape, 181, 188, 204
Networking, 91
    wireless, 123–24
New York Times, The, 230, 280n, 288
NGWS, *see* .NET initiative
Nokia, 8, 16, 27, 166, 213, 225, 231
Nortel, 34, 61
North Carolina, University of, 205n
Nuance Communications, 121

Oak Ridge National Laboratory, 38, 39
Office, 139, 160, 179, 185, 246
    2003, 84
    XP, 138
OneNote, 178
Oracle, 250
Oregon State, 52
Osher, Stanley, 284
Outlook, 160
Outsourcing, 242
Overture, 188, 200, 204

Page, Larry, 10, 247, 249
PageRank, 195, 196
Palm, 16, 166, 225, 231
PalmSource, 41

Panda Breeding and Research Center, 215
Pascal, Blaise, 54
Pascal computer language, 40
Payne, Christopher, 193–94, 208
Peking University, 19, 46, 50, 63, 89–90, 101, 137, 193, 197, 215, 284
Pen interfaces, 171, 173
    see also Digital ink; Universal pen
People's Daily, 78, 109, 131, 288
PepsiCo, 41, 49, 265
Personal computers (PCs), 9, 20, 26, 62, 74, 75, 185, 186
    interfaces with, *see* User interfaces
    Pocket PC, 224, 230
    Tablet PC, 139, 167, 170, 171, 176–77, 180–81
Personal digital assistants (PDAs), 16, 41, 212, 223–25
Philips, 269
Pickholtz, Raymond, 116, 118, 124
Pinyin, 38, 78, 83
Piracy, 61, 119
Pixar, 37
Planck's constant, 119
Platinum Software, 43
PlayStation, 16, 213
Pocket PC, 224, 230
Porsche, 216
PowerPoint, 98–99, 109–10, 175, 185, 228, 230
Princeton University, 33, 89, 116, 280
Putin, Vladimir, 131

Qin Shi Huangdi, 221
Qing Dynasty, 31, 49
Query log analysis, 192
QuickTime, 42, 247

Raikes, Jeff, 180
Rashid, Rick, 8, 36, 68, 74, 117, 134, 142, 170, 205n, 211, 236, 247, 278, 286

Rashid, Rick *(continued)*
  and Advanced Technology Center, 154–59, 164
  at Bill G. reviews, 80–82, 84, 101, 104, 179
  in China, 14, 16, 19, 24–27, 29–31, 54–57, 64, 90, 132, 144, 279–83, 285
  Lee recruited by, 38, 44, 261
  and Lee's defection to Google, 250–51
  and Lee's promotion to corporate vice president, 106–9
  and search war, 191
  and staffing of Beijing lab, 62, 70
  at TechFest, 206
  at Technical Advisory Board meeting, 143
Rawding, Michael, 131
RCA Laboratories, *see* Sarnoff Laboratories
Real Space, 66
Red Guards, 114
Reddy, Raj, 40, 41, 52, 66, 89–90, 97
Reform of 100 Days, 53
Relevance ranking and verification, 17, 192, 195, 200–202
Research in Motion (RIM), 225, 231
Rivest, Ronald, 284
Road Ahead, The (Gates), 9, 169, 288
Robotics, 66
Rosenberg, Jonathan, 249
RSA Security, 284
Rudder, Eric, 101, 108, 237, 249–52

Samsung, 231
Sang, Seung H., 218
Sarnoff Laboratories, 65, 72, 116–17, 225
SARS epidemic, 126, 140, 190, 192, 193, 264
Scalable wavelet coding, 101, 102
ScanSoft, 121
Schmidt, Eric, 247–49, 262, 263

Schofield, Kevin, 206
Science Daily, 1, 2, 288
Science and Technology, University of, 65, 91, 92, 115, 132, 137, 141
Science Times, 88
Sculley, John, 38, 41–42
Search technology, 11, 15, 17–18, 75, 155–56, 167, 187–208, 210–11, 281–82
  block-based link analysis, 195–96, 204
  clustering, 197–98, 200, 206, 207, 281
  desktop, 238–39
  and Lee's defection to Google, 257–58
  multimedia, 121
  query log analysis, 192
  relevance ranking and verification, 17, 192, 195, 200–202
  at TechFest 2005, 206–7
  structured data format, 100
  see also Advertising, online
Search Technology Center, 281–82
Seattle Supersonics, 9, 209–12, 234
Seattle Times, The, 288
September 11 terrorist attacks, 132
Servers and Tools group, 101, 107–8, 237
Shanda Interactive Entertainment, 9, 243*n*
Shang, Sheila, 25–26, 93, 113, 125, 128, 151, 285
  at Dragon Villa retreat, 95
  at Great Wall Plan meeting, 218, 219
  at Hangzhou Faculty Summit, 283
  parties organized by, 86–88, 109
  at Search Technology Center announcement, 281
Shanghai Jiaotong University, 65, 67, 131–34, 137, 193, 214, 285
Shui Hu Zhuan (Outlaws of the Marsh) (novel), 111

Shum, Heung-Yeung "Harry," 26, 31, 65–67, 72, 85, 94, 109, 118, 135, 144–46, 162, 182, 209–23, 261
background of, 66
as Beijing lab managing director, 4, 13–17, 202–5, 212–13, 278, 285–86
at Bill G. reviews, 80, 84, 176, 178–79
at Computing in the 21st Century conference, 30
at Dragon Villa, 95
with Gates in China, 4, 5, 133–34
guest professorships of, 89
and Guo's graphics group, 122–23
honors received by, 214
and inception of Advanced Technology Center, 155, 156
at international Faculty Summit, 21–22
and Jian Song's visit to Beijing lab, 142
and Lee's defection to Google, 256, 257
on lecture circuit, 214, 223
at MindSwap, 227
and Ministry of Education officials, 218–22, 280
multimedia research of, 76, 99–101, 104
Mundie and, 215–17
recruitment of, 52, 54, 56, 60, 87
promoted to assistant managing director, 108, 114
publishing research results advocated by, 214–15
Rashid and, 282–83
and search war, 187, 281
at Seattle Supersonics basketball game, 209–12
at TechFest, 154, 206
university PR visits by, 62–64
Wang and, 173, 184

Zheng Chen and, 197
at Zhuhai retreat, 148, 149, 151
SIGGRAPH, 17, 123, 214–15
SIGIR, 17, 194, 196, 198, 199, 204
Silicon Graphics (SGI), 17, 38, 42–44, 145, 235
Simonyi, Charles, 37
Sina.com, 248
Singapore, National University of, 135
Institute of Systems Science, 163
Sinofsky, Steven, 185, 246–47, 251
Slater, Robert, 288
Smith, Alvy Ray, 37
Song, Jian, 141–43, 146, 162, 169
Song, Lolan, 218, 219, 280, 281, 284, 285
Sony, 8, 15, 157, 213, 265
Southeast University, 66
Southern California, University of, 73
Speech interfaces, 17, 38, 40–43, 67, 75–76, 78, 90, 99, 120, 121, 173, 236–38, 241
conference sessions on, 91
demos of, 41–42, 79, 84, 87
products using, 138
quality control software for, 121
see also Text-to-speech
Speech Platforms product group, 138
Spread-spectrum radio, 116
Stanford University, 17, 37
Starkweather, Gary, 37, 91
Statistical machine learning techniques, 198
Stone, Linda, 37, 101
Summarization technology, 239
Sun, Ming-Ting, 210
Sun Microsystems, 247
Sydney, University of, 135
Symbian, 225, 231

Tablet PC, 139, 167, 170, 171, 176–77, 180–81
Tan, Sitong, 53–54
Tang, Jun, 243n

TechFest, 154, 180, 199, 205–8, 209, 210, 281

Technical Advisory Board, 143–44, 164–67, 284

Technology transfers, 140, 149–54, 159, 160, 164

Television
high-definition, 117, 121
interactive, 75, 79
Web surfing via, 90–91
for wireless devices, 224

Text-to-speech technology, 139–40, 156, 167, 176, 237–38, 240

Thacker, Chuck, 14, 24, 25, 29, 30, 36

Thermodynamics, Second Law of, 119

"Think Week," 181

Thought Explorer, 181–83

Time magazine, 125

Tohoku University, 219

Tokyo, University of, 89, 135, 283

Toshiba, 265

Toy Story (movie), 37

Toyota, 49, 265

Treo digital organizer, 225, 231

Tsinghua Tongfang, 61

Tsinghua University, 9, 19, 23–24, 29, 46, 50, 64, 69, 138, 161, 195, 193, 196–97, 202, 219, 259, 284
Computing in the 21st Century conferences at, 24–27, 164
Department of Computer Science and Technology, 126
Gates at, 48–49
and Great Wall Plan, 137
guest professorships at, 214
research papers from, 214

Turing Award, 37, 89, 91, 280, 284

Universal pen, 167, 170, 174–80, 183–84, 216

User Interface Technology Division, 237n

User interfaces, 15, 17, 75, 77, 107, 168–71, 181–83, 203
aggregate computing, 185–86
camera, 184
demos of, 78–80, 83–84, 139
for entertainment files, 156
handwriting, 139, 167, 169–70, 172–79, 183–84
Help, 240
multimodal, 171–72
for search, 192, 197–98
speech, *see* Speech interfaces

Venus set-top box, 90, 241, 288

Video games, *see* Games

Virtual reality, 71

Vision technology, *see* Computer vision

Vista, *see* Windows: Vista

Visual Studio, 244

Volkswagen, 49, 265

Wall Street Journal, The, 288

Wal-Mart, 266

Wang, Hongfei, 271–72

Wang, Jian, 71–72, 80, 82, 83, 95, 139, 140, 167–86, 210, 261, 283

Wang, Shuo, 125

Washington, University of, 210

Wei, Yu, 56–57, 59, 219, 261

Wen, Ji-Rong, 195–96

Wen Jiabao, 4

Wi-Fi, 224

Williams, Lyndsay, 174

Windows, 1, 6, 19, 26, 62, 83, 131, 182, 183, 186, 188, 203, 223, 277
CE, 90, 166, 224, 225
Mobile, 16, 166, 212, 224–31
Movie Maker, 139, 166
Server Division, 107
Vista, 8, 29, 140, 156, 167, 238, 240, 271, 285
XP, 133, 166

Index

Winfrey, Oprah, 225
Wing, Jeannette M., 284
Wireless technology, 17, 20, 27, 144,
    166, 203, 212, 224–31
    China market for, 226–27
    networking, 123–24, 166
    products using, 139
    for universal pen, 180
Word, 49, 175, 239
World Economic Forum, 188
World Health Organization (WHO),
    140, 192
World Is Flat, The (Friedman), 288
World Trade Organization (WTO), 268
World Wide Web, 20, 121
    see also Internet
Wu, Jichuan, 57, 59
Wu, Juliet Shihong, 48, 91, 241,
    243*n*, 268–69
Wuhan University, 65, 70
Wuhua (five-stroke) inputting
    method, 83
WYSIWYG word-processing
    program, 37

Xbox, 8, 16, 122–23, 133, 139, 182,
    203, 213
Xerox Palo Alto Research Center
    (PARC), 36, 89, 91, 159
Xi'an Jiaotong University, 89
Xie, Shengwu, 133
Xu, Ming, 218
Xu, Songtao, 129
Xu, YingQing, 98

Yahoo, 18, 188, 191, 201
Yang, Chen Ning, 25–26, 30, 215,
    280
Yang, Frank, 80
Yang, Shiqiang, 126
Yao, Andrew, 280
Yao, Baogang, 18, 167, 204
Yao Ming, 8, 9, 209–11, 214, 223,
    228, 285
Yim, Rocco, 218

Yin-yang, 88–89
Yu, Albert, 43

Zellweger, Renée, 218
Zeng, Feng-Ping, 193
Zhang, Brandon, 101, 105, 135
Zhang, Dongmei, 16
Zhang, HongJiang, 13–14, 124, 133,
    144, 161–63, 205*n*, 228, 261,
    262, 273
    Advanced Technology Center
        headed by, 14, 163–67, 201,
        202, 256–57
    at Bill G. review, 80
    at Dragon Villa retreat, 95
    guest professorships of, 89
    at Hewlett-Packard Labs, 72
    and inception of Advanced Tech-
        nology Center, 152–56, 158
    in meetings with product groups,
        140
    multimedia research of, 76,
        99–101, 104, 121
    papers published by, 121–22
    promoted to assistant managing
        director, 108, 114
    recruitment of, 72–73, 87
    and search technology research,
        187–90, 204
    at TechFest, 154
    at Zhuhai retreat, 148, 149,
        151–52
Zhang, Jenny, 105, 135, 210, 256
Zhang, Qian, 65, 70–71, 124, 210,
    227
Zhang, Sophie, 105, 135
Zhang, Xin, 217
Zhang, Xuezhong, 215–16
Zhang, Ya-Qin, 11, 65–66, 72, 105–6,
    108–38, 178, 198, 209, 218,
    233–34, 256, 261
    and Advanced Technology Cen-
        ter, 150–52, 154, 155, 158–59,
        162–65
    background of, 65–66, 115–16

Zhang, Ya-Qin (*continued*)
    as Beijing lab managing director,
       106, 108–15, 118–29, 144, 176,
       213, 278
    at Bill G. review, 80
    on Computing in the 21st Century
       tour, 25–27, 29, 30, 130–34
    at Dragon Villa, 95, 96, 99
    family of, 105, 135, 234
    farewell party for, 145–46, 169
    Great Wall Plan of, 135–38, 141,
       279
    guest professorships of, 89
    honors received by, 66, 117, 163,
       214
    interviews of prospective
       researchers by, 71
    as Microsoft China vice president,
       277–79, 285
    as Mobile and Embedded Devices
       vice president, 144–45, 166,
       202, 223–32
    multimedia research of, 76,
       99–104
    and name change to Microsoft
       Research Asia, 134–35
    promoted to corporate vice presi-
       dent, 144
    recruitment of, 65–67, 87,
       117–18
    at Sarnoff Laboratory, 65, 116–17
    during SARS quarantine, 140–41
    at Seattle Supersonics basketball
       game, 210–12
    and Song's visit to Beijing lab,
       141–42
    University of Science and Tech-
       nology visited by, 91
    at Zhuhai retreat, 148–52
Zhang, Yaoxue, 22, 137, 218–22,
    271
Zhao, Qin-Ping, 137, 280
Zhao, Xinshui, 110
Zhejiang University, 23, 71, 89, 132,
    137, 168, 171, 172
Zhenghou University, 162
Zhongshan University, 148
Zhou, Ji, 130, 135–37, 280
Zhou, Ming, 146
Zhu, Lilan, 59
Zhu, Wenwu, 124–25
Zue, Victor, 14, 16, 90

About the Authors

ROBERT BUDERI is the author of two acclaimed books, *Engines of Tomorrow,* about corporate innovation, and *The Invention That Changed the World,* about a secret lab at MIT in World War II. He lives in Cambridge, Massachusetts.

GREGORY T. HUANG is a features editor at *New Scientist* and holds a Ph.D. in electrical engineering and computer science from MIT. His work has appeared in *Nature, Wired,* and *Technology Review.* He lives in Cambridge, Massachusetts.